MOSES

GOD PREPARES AND STRENGTHENS HIS MAN

Vol. I

by Theodore H. Epp
Founder
Back to the Bible

Back to the Bible

Lincoln, Nebraska 68501

110,000 printed to date—1986
(5-4631—2M—56)
ISBN 0-8474-1200-8

Printed in the United States of America

Foreword

Few studies affected Theodore H. Epp's life and ministry more than the study of the life of Moses. In Moses, Mr. Epp saw a man mightily used of God, and he saw the lessons a person must learn before he can be used in such a way. Moses had to be brought to the end of self and taught to trust God completely.

Moses, Vol. I, is a study of Moses' life from his birth to his leadership in delivering the Israelites from the Egyptians. It is a moving account of how he was humanly prepared as a leader in the court of Egypt and of how he first had to be divinely prepared in the backside of the desert for the gigantic task of leading the Israelites from Egypt to Canaan.

Moses, Vol. II, is a study of Moses' life from the victory at the Red Sea to his death on top of a mountain after he was allowed to view the promised land. Moses was great in his works, in his meekness and in his farewell—and even in his death.

But the life of Moses was not left on the pages of Old Testament history; Mr. Epp made many applications to believers of the present age who desire to be used of God. You will find this a rewarding study not only because of what you will learn about Moses but also because of what you will learn about yourself.

—The Publishers

Contents

Michelangelo's *Moses*

Chapter 1

Moses: The Man of God

The Bible records many details concerning the remarkable man, Moses. Information is given about his birth, his long life, and his death. Perhaps his entire life and relationship to the Lord is best summed up in the words "Moses the man of God." This description of Moses is recorded in Deuteronomy 33:1 and Ezra 3:2.

A description of Moses that also reveals his relationship with the Lord is found in Deuteronomy 34:5: "Moses the servant of the Lord." These phrases are doubtlessly related—only when Moses was a choice servant of the Lord could he also be a man of God.

Deuteronomy 34:7 records the length of Moses' life and his physical condition at the time of his death: "And Moses was an hundred and twenty years old when he died: his eye was not dim, nor his natural force abated." This same book concludes by saying, "And there arose not a prophet since in Israel like unto Moses, whom the Lord knew face to face, in all the signs and wonders, which the Lord sent him to do in the land of Egypt to Pharaoh, and to all his servants, and to all his land, and in all that mighty hand, and in all the great terror which Moses showed in the sight of all Israel" (vv. 10-12).

What a man! From Adam to Christ none was greater. Yet, Moses was just like any other man. Although he had great qualities that needed to be developed and improved, he had many flaws and deficiencies that would have made him powerless except for the all-sufficient grace that he eventually learned to appropriate.

It is interesting to note that the life of Moses is sketched from his infancy to his death. The Lord has not given this much information about every great Bible character. For instance, Elijah is introduced with only a short descriptive phrase: "Elijah the Tishbite, who was of the inhabitants of Gilead" (I Kings 17:1). Nothing else is known about the background of Elijah; but God has graciously provided many, many details about Moses.

Moses was a man on such intimate terms with God that the Bible says, "The Lord spake unto Moses face to face, as a man speaketh unto his friend" (Ex. 33:11). This intimate relationship resulted from a long process of growth and maturing. The Book of Hebrews addresses those who were in need of maturing, and says, "For when for the time ye ought to be teachers, ye have need that one teach you again which be the first principles of the oracles of God; and are become such as are in need of milk, and not of strong meat. But strong meat belongeth to them that are of full age, even those who by reason of use have their senses exercised to discern both good and evil. Therefore . . . let us go on unto perfection [maturity]" (Heb. 5:12,14; 6:1). Moses was the type of man who went on to maturity.

Thus, the story of Moses was one of failure and weakness on one hand, but of victory and strength on the other hand. He experienced failure and weakness when he relied on himself, but he experienced victory and strength when he relied on God.

The Key to Moses' Life

The key to Moses' life was the simplicity of his faith, his constant communion with God, and his willingness to become a channel through which God's purpose was achieved. Hebrews 11 provides a divine commentary on Moses' life, and "by faith" is a key phrase in this commentary. "By faith Moses, when he was come to years, refused to be called the son of Pharaoh's daughter. By faith he forsook Egypt, not fearing the wrath of the king. Through faith he kept the passover, and the sprinkling of blood. By faith they passed through the Red sea as by dry land" (vv. 24,27,28,29). "By faith"—this was the secret of Moses' life.

We make a serious mistake when we think that men like Moses had extraordinary qualities of courage and strength.

To do so is to miss the point of the repeated teachings of the Scriptures which reveal the key to be faith in God.

This fact was evident in the case of the disciples also. After Peter and John had been instrumental in the healing of a lame man, the people flocked around them, but Peter said, "Ye men of Israel, why marvel ye at this? or why look ye so earnestly on us, as though by our own power or holiness we had made this man to walk?" (Acts 3:12). The disciples were no different from ordinary men—except in their faith. In ordinary life, the disciples were inferior to many people. But they possessed explicit faith in God which supplied them with greater powers, and thus they were mightily used by Him.

The Object of Faith

It is important to realize that more than faith is required; faith must be placed in the right object. Many have faith in themselves or in a particular church or denomination, but the right object of faith is God. Because Moses had faith in God, his faith was cited as the secret of all that he did with and for his people.

God's incessant demand is for faith, even though it may be as small "as a grain of mustard seed" (Luke 17:6). The greatness of one's faith is not important; what matters is the object of faith. On one occasion the Lord told His disciples: "Have faith in God" (Mark 11:22), or actually "Have the faith of God." Christ went on to explain: "For verily I say unto you, That whosoever shall say unto this mountain, Be thou removed, and be thou cast into the sea; and shall not doubt in his heart, but shall believe that those things which he saith shall come to pass; he shall have whatsoever he saith" (v. 23). No wonder Jesus said, "All things are possible to him that believeth" (Mark 9:23).

Faith is not a special quality of only certain men which enables them to accomplish special results that others may not realize. It is available to everyone. It is that attitude of heart, which, after it has ascertained the will of God, and believed God, is willing to be used of God to fulfill His will. True faith commits itself to God in complete obedience, expecting that God will work out His purpose through the individual.

Consider what is involved in faith. It is appropriating God to the utmost limit so one becomes a channel through which God works. It is appropriating God Himself, not just some promise. It is good to understand and rely on the promises, but the believer is always to remember who made the promise. Our faith should not be in the promise alone but in the One who made the promise.

The believer who pleases God is the Spirit-filled, or Spirit-controlled, person who allows God to perform His will through him. Such a believer performs God's will and does it willingly, recognizing that all that has been accomplished has been done by God through him.

The Elements of Faith

At least five elements are included in true faith. First, there must be a sense of helplessness and of nothingness. The Lord Jesus said, "Abide in me, and I in you. As the branch cannot bear fruit of itself, except it abide in the vine; no more can ye, except ye abide in me" (John 15:4). But the one who abides in Christ can say with the Apostle Paul: "I can do all things through Christ which strengtheneth me" (Phil. 4:13).

Second, true faith involves an absolute assurance of being in God's will. A person cannot believe God and have true faith if he is not sure of being in His will. Someone once said, "To know the will of God is the greatest knowledge; to find the will of God is the greatest discovery; to do the will of God is the greatest achievement."

Third, there must be a total commitment and surrender, or consecration, so God may work out His will and purpose through the believer's life.

Fourth, true faith must be nourished by daily studying His Word and basking in His absolute faithfulness. Note, it is *His* absolute faithfulness. "Faith cometh by hearing, and the hearing by the word of God" (Rom. 10:17).

Fifth, there must be a daring to act in dependence on faith alone, not feeling. Believers are to act on the basis of a faith which relies absolutely and only on God's faithfulness.

The Bible says, "God is not a man, that he should lie; neither the son of man, that he should repent: hath he said, and shall he not do it? or hath he spoken, and shall he not make it good?" (Num. 23:19). "Faithful is he that calleth you, who also will do it" (I Thess. 5:24). "If we believe not, yet he abideth faithful: he cannot deny himself" (II Tim. 2:13). "Let us hold fast the profession of our faith without wavering; (for he is faithful that promised)" (Heb. 10:23). God is absolutely faithful. We can depend on this fact. So believe Him and proceed to do His will by the grace He provides. "God is able to make all grace abound toward you; that ye, always having all sufficiency in all things, may abound to every good work" (II Cor. 9:8).

Active Faith

Throughout the remarkable life of Moses it is evident that, as James said, "faith wrought with his works" (James 2:22). That is, faith was active with his works. It is apparent from the second chapter of James that the faith which does not produce works is not a saving faith. James wrote: "What doth it profit, my brethren, though a man say he hath faith, and have not works? can faith save him?" (v. 14). In other words, can that kind of faith save him? The answer is no. Genuine faith is evidenced by the works it produces. If a person has true faith, he will act on it; he will go forward regardless of what is ahead.

Although Moses doubtlessly had a great mind because of his extensive learning, his success was not due to these factors but to the faith that knit his soul to God. As someone said, "His faith sufficed to do what all other qualities, without faith, would have failed to do."

Moses' walk of faith was not learned in a day but over a long time. During a period of 40 years in the desert, after his first great failure in Egypt, he learned to believe and trust God. He was allowed to make that first great effort toward the emancipation of his people in the energy of his own strength (in the energy of the flesh), and he was allowed to fail absolutely and completely. God permitted this, and Moses had to flee to Midian; this was God's way of dealing with Moses. While there, Moses abandoned all hope of ever delivering the people of Israel from the land. Until then, Moses had felt he was God's man and he believed that Israel would realize he was God's man—but to his amazement they did not. In exile and solitude, Moses was reduced in his own eyes to nothing. As we study Moses' life in detail, we will see that he was so convinced of his inability that later it was difficult for God to persuade him to do what He wanted. This was the process of applying death—death to self. Believers in the 20th century need to look back to the cross and apply the fact that they have died to self with the Lord Jesus Christ, but they are also to realize that they now are to live unto God by His life (Rom. 6).

A Man Needed

God had an eternal purpose in creating, emancipating, and building the great nation of Israel. All of this was done not merely for the sake of having a special chosen nation but to create a testimony through this nation for the sake of others. God did not select Israel for a pet but for a pattern.

God chose the nation of Israel so He could give a progressive revelation of Himself. Later revelation did not contradict earlier revelation; it simply added more details about the Person and work of God. It was to Israel that God gave the Scriptures which revealed His person, and it was of this nation that Jesus Christ was born, according to the flesh.

It is difficult to find any place in the Bible where God displayed His magnificent power more than He did with the people of Israel. For this, God needed a man—a common man—who would dare to believe God, a man who would dare to commit himself totally to God. So through simple faith and absolute obedience, Moses became the most commanding figure of the ancient world—in character, in faith, and in the unique position which was assigned to him. He became the mediator of the old covenant, and because of his achievements he stands among the best known of all the heroes of the Old Testament. "Faith" and "obedience"—those two words will appear over and over again in the study of Moses' life.

Moses became a prophet; that is, one who proclaimed God's message. He was also a priest in that he interceded for his people—and what a great intercessor he was! Moses also became like a king, leading and administrating his people. He became as thoroughly yielded to the purpose of God as the staff which he held in his hand was yielded to his will. Just as Moses could do what he wanted with his staff, so God could do what He wanted with Moses. That's the secret we need to learn. If you have trusted Jesus Christ as Saviour, God can use you if you yield yourself to Him. It doesn't matter who you are, God is able to use you.

Moses was called "the servant of God" (Deut. 34:5) which really means "the slave of God." Moses asked no questions; what God said, he did. A phrase that repeatedly occurs in the account of Moses' life is, "As the Lord commanded Moses."

Moses feasted daily on the promises of God and claimed them in his every prayer. When God told Moses to go, he went. Moses stepped out in faith where there was nothing to stand on. In launching the wilderness journey, Moses cast himself and 3 million people completely on the care of God, assured that God's faithfulness could always be counted on.

Thus, his faith in God made Moses all that he was. It took considerable time to bring Moses to this place; in fact, two-thirds of his life. We can have this same kind of faith if we are willing to endure God's disciplining. There is no limit to what God can do with such a man—one who dares to believe Him and then acts on his faith.

A believer must ask himself, Am I willing to be counted dead to my own will and strength and to rely completely on Him in total obedience? Am I willing to go where God wants me to go and to do what God wants me to do—even if it seems humanly impossible?

Moses was such a person and it is easy to see what God accomplished through Moses once He had him in His complete control.

The life of Moses easily divides itself into three periods of 40 years each. The first 40 years were spent in Egypt—the first few in his home and the rest in the court as a prince; the second 40 were spend in the desert of Midian as a shepherd; the third 40 were spent in Egypt and the wilderness as a leader and legislator.

Each of these three periods began with a crisis which was met by faith, and which in turn resulted in a strategic choice.

Concerning Moses, I. M. Haldeman has written with insight: "The life of Moses presents a series of striking antitheses. He was the child of a slave, and the son of a queen. He was born in a hut, and lived in a palace. He inherited poverty, and enjoyed unlimited wealth. He was the leader of armies, and the keeper of flocks. He was the mightiest of warriors, and the meekest of men. He was educated in the court, and dwelt in the desert. He had the wisdom of Egypt, and the faith of a child. He was fitted for the city, and wandered in the wilderness. He was tempted with the pleasures of sin, and endured the hardships of virtue. He was backward in speech, and talked with God. He had the rod of a shepherd, and the power of the Infinite. He was a fugitive from Pharaoh, and an ambassador from heaven. He was the giver of the Law, and the forerunner of grace. He died alone on Mount Moab, and appeared with Christ in Judea. No man assisted at his funeral, yet God buried him" (cited in *Gleanings in Exodus*, by A. W. Pink, p. 16).

Chapter 2

The Birth of Moses

Although there is the tendency to assume that Moses was a special kind of person, it is evident from a study of his birth and life that he was like anyone else. That which was distinctively different about him was the extent to which he took God at His word. Although it was difficult at first, Moses finally came to the place where he did not rely on his own abilities but on God and His word.

The birth of Moses is recorded in Exodus 2:1-10. We are not given the specific names of his mother and father in this passage; we are only told that both of them were descendants of Levi (v. 1). When Moses was born, his mother observed that he was "a goodly child" (v. 2). The word translated "goodly" here refers to form and has the sense of "beautiful." Hebrews 11:23 refers to Moses at birth as a "proper child." The word translated "proper" means "beautiful" or "well formed." This same word is used in Acts 7:20 where it is translated "exceeding fair." In its entirety, Acts 7:20 says: "In which time Moses was born, and was exceeding fair, and nourished up in his father's house three months."

The Condition of Israel

When Moses was born, his mother "hid him three months" (Ex. 2:2). The nation of Israel was in an extremely sad condition at the time of Moses' birth. The nation was in Egypt, and was actually a nation of slaves to Pharaoh and the Egyptians. However, the Egyptians feared that the Israelites might become so numerous they would eventually be able to

15

overthrow the Egyptian government. Thus, Pharaoh instructed the midwives attending the births of Hebrew children to kill all the male babies (1:16). This is why it was necessary for Moses to be hid by his mother for three months after his birth.

Apparently the pressure brought to bear by Pharaoh and the Egyptians had great effect on many Israelites. The indication is that the once strong religious beliefs of the Israelite nation were beginning to fade and that some of the Israelites were participating in the idolatrous rites of the Egyptians. Such a conclusion is drawn from Joshua 24:14, which records Joshua's words to the Israelites: "Put away the gods which your fathers served . . . in Egypt." Joshua was aware that some of the Israelites were guilty of serving pagan gods while in Egypt.

This weakness of the Israelites toward idolatrous practices was evident even after the nation was later delivered from Egypt. The nation gathered around Mt. Sinai while Moses was on the mountaintop receiving instructions from God. When they feared that something had happened to Moses, the people used their jewelry to make a golden calf as an object of their worship (Ex. 32:1-6).

The Book of Ezekiel also refers to the idolatry of the Israelites while in Egypt. Ezekiel 20:6-8 records the words of the Lord: "In the day that I lifted up mine hand unto them, to bring them forth of the land of Egypt into a land that I had espied for them, flowing with milk and honey, which is the glory of all lands: then said I unto them, Cast ye away every man the abominations of his eyes, and defile not yourselves with the idols of Egypt: I am the Lord your God. But they rebelled against me, and would not hearken unto me: they did not every man cast away the abominations of their eyes, neither did they forsake the idols of Egypt: then I said, I will pour out my fury upon them, to accomplish my anger against them in the midst of the land of Egypt."

The Faith of Moses' Parents

So from these references it is clear that many Israelites were attracted to the licentious heathen festivals in Egypt, and even later when they were delivered from Egypt, idolatrous practices kept cropping up. But some Israelite families remained faithful in Egypt, even in the midst of idolatrous corruption. God always seems to have His remnant, and Moses' parents were a bright illustration of this. Exodus 6:20 records the names of Moses' parents—Amram and Jochebed. They believed God and had confidence that He would deliver the nation from Egypt. As Hebrews, they would have been well versed in God's instructions to Abraham, as recorded in Genesis 15: "And he [God] said unto Abram [Abraham], Know of a surety that thy seed shall be a stranger in a land that is not their's, and shall serve them; and they shall afflict them four hundred years" (v. 13).

And Moses' parents would no doubt have been aware of God's promise that followed these instructions to Abraham: "And also that nation, whom they shall serve, will I judge: and afterward shall they come out with great substance. And thou shalt go to thy fathers in peace; thou shalt be buried in a good old age. But in the fourth generation they shall come hither again: for the iniquity of the Amorites is not yet full" (vv. 14-16). God told Abraham that in the fourth generation after Abraham's death the Israelites would be delivered from Egypt.

As Amram and Jochebed became the parents of Moses, the 400 years were drawing to an end, for Moses was one of the fourth generation. Amram and Jochebed had good reasons to believe that Moses would have an important part in Israel's destiny. The historian Josephus says that a dream announced to Amram that Moses would become the deliverer of his people Israel. Of course, Josephus' account is only tradition, not Scripture.

Moses was God's sovereign choice to lead the Israelites out of Egypt, but Moses' parents did not know this for sure at the time of his birth. However, they could not forget the promise given earlier to Abraham that the Israelites would be delivered from Egypt in the fourth generation.

The question might be asked, Why didn't God choose Aaron for this task? Aaron was the older brother of Moses, and it seems logical that God would have chosen him if he were choosing someone in this family. But God does not always do what seems logical to us. God had a sovereign purpose for Moses that no one else could fill. Aaron would be a part of what God wanted to do through Moses, but Moses was the specific individual that God was using.

Moses' birth was a time of crisis, but it was met by faith which resulted in a crucial choice. It is a timeless principle that "without faith it is impossible to please him [God]" (Heb. 11:6). Also, Romans 14:23 says, "Whatsoever is not of faith is sin." But Amram and Jochebed had faith. Hebrews 11:23 refers to their faith: "By faith Moses, when he was born, was hid three months of his parents." The faith of Moses' parents caused them to make a clear-cut choice that affected them, their families, and eventually the entire nation.

It is important that Christian parents realize their children are loaned to them by God to be spiritually trained and prepared for His use. It's not enough to provide only materially and physically for the children. It is a sobering responsibility as Christian parents realize that—by training their children for God's use—many lives may eventually be affected by those children. But from the life of Moses we see that God expects that faith to begin with the parents.

The spiritual responsibility of parents to their children is seen in Acts 16. When the Philippian jailer asked Paul and Silas, "What must I do to be saved?" (v. 30), they said, "Believe on the Lord Jesus Christ, and thou shalt be saved, and thy house" (v. 31). The jailer's household was referred to, but the members of his household did not become believers just because he did. Notice that the following verse says, "They spake unto him the word of the Lord, and to all that were in his house." From these verses we see the principle that parents have the responsibility of showing their children the way to Christ. This is part of giving proper training which God desires. A parent's responsibility for his children is also evident in the words of Joshua 24:15: "Choose you this day whom ye will serve; . . . but as for me and my house, we will serve the Lord." Joshua exercised his responsibility of leadership in his family.

It is sobering for parents to realize that, in a sense, they live again in their children. That is, the attitudes and habits of the parents, and the quality of training they give, are usually reflected later in their children. This can be either bad or good. The Bible says, "Be not deceived; God is not mocked:

for whatsoever a man soweth, that shall he also reap" (Gal. 6:7).

Although there are many examples of children who walk in the evil ways of their parents, an important lesson concerning Moses is that his parents set a good example for him to follow. They walked by faith. They demonstrated their faith at Moses' birth by recognizing God's sovereign purpose for him and hiding him for three months (Heb. 11:23). Later, Moses reflected this same kind of faith for the Bible says, "By faith Moses, when he was come to years, refused to be called the son of Pharaoh's daughter" (v. 24), and "by faith he forsook Egypt, not fearing the wrath of the king" (v. 27). Thus, in a sense, the parents lived again in the child.

Characteristics of Genuine Faith

Moses' parents were virtually unknown members of a nation in slavery, yet they ranked in the gallery of the faithful ones, as recorded in Hebrews 11. In considering the faith exercised by Moses' parents, we receive valuable insights concerning the characteristics of true faith.

First, faith sees. Hebrews 11:23 says that Moses' parents "saw he was a proper child." Because of their faith, they saw more than a new baby when Moses was born. They saw matters that ordinary eyes would not see. They realized that God had a sovereign purpose for this baby; thus, they hid him three months. Those who have faith see what others do not. This was the case when Jehoshaphat was surrounded by the enemy, for he prayed: "O our God, wilt thou not judge them? for we have no might against this great company that cometh against us; neither know we what to do: but our eyes are upon thee" (II Chron. 20:12). Ephesians 1:18 also speaks of the ability to see things spiritually. Paul prayed for believers that "the eyes of [their] understanding" would be enlightened.

Second, faith acts. Moses' parents acted to save the life of Moses because they were convinced that God had a special purpose for him. But just having faith that God had a purpose for him was not enough; it was necessary for them to act on the basis of their faith. They hid Moses for three months, and the Bible says "they were not afraid of the king's commandment" (Heb. 11:23). Faith produces courage; it swallows up fear. Because they believed God, they courageously acted to preserve Moses' life.

Parents have a serious responsibility toward those they bring into this life. Think of it! God has given a father and mother the ability to bring into existence one who has an immortal soul. This act has more far-reaching consequences than any other act man can accomplish. Once brought into existence, that one will live someplace forever, either in heaven or in hell. So it is tremendously important that parents train their children and do all they can to see that they have every opportunity to trust Christ as Saviour and to live a life that pleases God.

Children must overcome all kinds of obstacles today if they are going to lead a life that pleases God. They are bombarded from every side by the world's system and its low values. In fact, the average child living today will spend at least nine years of his entire life viewing television. What examples of faith are children seeing that will lead them into a life of faith?

The method of rearing children is also one of concern today. Often, the training is left to a baby-sitter. Sometimes this is truly a necessity, but often it is done only because father and mother must both work to maintain the level of living they desire.

One of the primary responsibilities of parents is to keep their child from evil. Some say that protecting children in this way makes "house plants" of them. However, every farmer realizes if he is to produce a good crop he cannot let weeds run wild; he has to protect the plant while it is growing

Third, faith risks. At the time of Moses' birth, Pharaoh had instructed that all boy babies be killed, so it was necessary for Moses' father and mother to take risks if they were to preserve his life. They could not keep him in their own home, so Moses' mother made an "ark of bulrushes, and daubed it with slime and with pitch, and put the child therein; and she laid it in the flags by the river's brink" (Ex. 2:3). It involved great risk to entrust this baby to that little crib. It involved committing him entirely to the Lord if he were to live. The parents had to face the fact that he was as good as dead, for the chances were that if he were discovered he would be put to death in obedience to Pharaoh's command.

Acts 7:21 refers to Moses' being "cast out" when he was placed in this little crib. But at this point God began to work. When Moses' parents faced the fact that Moses was as good as dead, God began to work mightily. This reminds us of the principle stated in John 12:24: "Except a corn of wheat fall into the ground and die, it abideth alone: but if it die, it bringeth forth much fruit."

By their faith, Moses' parents laid hold of God's sovereignty. They trusted God to keep him. This reveals how Moses' parents had committed themselves to God.

The Bible encourages believers: "Commit thy way unto the Lord; trust also in him; and he shall bring it to pass" (Ps. 37:5). We should be able to say with the Apostle Paul: "I know whom I have believed, and am persuaded that he is able to keep that which I have committed unto him against that day" (II Tim. 1:12). We are assured of God's keeping power by such verses as I Peter 1:5 which says that believers "are kept by the power of God through faith unto salvation ready to be revealed in the last time."

God honored the faith of Moses' parents and provided for his needs. It is possible that his mother knew the bathing spot of the king's daughter and placed Moses there, hoping that Pharaoh's daughter might take pity on him. It is also possible that when Pharaoh's daughter discovered Moses, she guessed what was being plotted. She was in need of an heir to the throne, so she would have been especially sympathetic to adopting a son as her own. And she may have suspected a plot behind it all, for she would realize that it was not natural for a mother to forsake her baby like that. But she would also have remembered her father's stern edict that all boy babies were to be killed.

Then Miriam, Moses' sister, suddenly came and offered to find a Hebrew nurse to care for the child (Ex. 2:7). Pharaoh's daughter saw her opportunity to have an heir to the throne so she instructed Miriam to do as she suggested. Miriam left and brought her mother back to meet Pharaoh's daughter. Pharaoh's daughter said to Moses' mother: "Take this child away, and nurse it for me, and I will give thee thy wages. And the woman took the child, and nursed it" (v. 9). Imagine it! Moses' parents had not only saved his life but God had arranged it so they still had the privilege of training him during those crucial, early years. And in addition to that, Moses' mother was even paid for nursing him!

A mother has a tremendous influence on her child. Have you ever noticed in reading about the kings of the Old Testament that their mothers are often mentioned? A mother has a great part in her child's life—either for good or for bad. Moses' mother realized she would not have him in her home long, so it was important to make wise use of the time while she had him. Moses' situation was an unusual one, but even under normal circumstances there comes that time when a child leaves home, so it is important for the parents to give effective training early in life. Research indicates that 50 percent of a child's basic attitudes are learned during the first three years of his life. This poses an awesome responsibility for parents, and they should not turn this responsibility over to someone else unless forced to do so under extreme circumstances. If you have young children at home, consider what you would do if you knew you could have them for only eight to twelve years. It's worth thinking about, because this may be as long as you have to give them the training God wants you to give them.

The Wisdom of God

When God answered the prayers of Moses' parents beyond all that they could ask or think, He revealed how much higher His ways are than man's ways. God made foolishness out of man's wisdom. When the Egyptians began to fear the increasing of the Israelites, Pharaoh said, "Come on, let us deal wisely with them; lest they multiply" (Ex. 1:10). The wisest plan Pharaoh could come up with was to put the boy babies to death, but God worked in Moses' case in such a way as to reveal the foolishness of Pharaoh's wisest plans. In the end, God worked in such a way that Pharaoh was compelled to give room and board, as well as proper training, to the person who accomplished the exact thing that Pharaoh was trying to prevent! Thus, Pharaoh's wisdom was turned to foolishness, and Satan and his devices were defeated. Job 5:13 says of God: "He taketh the wise in their own craftiness: and the counsel of the froward is carried headlong."

God often works through those the world considers foolish in order to bring to foolishness what the world considers wise. Paul reminded believers of God's method of working when he said, "For ye see your calling, brethren, how that not many wise men after the flesh, not many mighty, not many noble, are called: but God hath chosen the foolish things of the world to confound the wise; and God hath chosen the weak things of the world to confound the things which are mighty; and base things of the world, and things which are despised, hath God chosen, yea, and things which are not, to bring to naught things that are" (I Cor. 1:26-28). And why does God work in this way? The following verse gives the answer: "That no flesh should glory in his presence."

Chapter 3

Moses' Early Training

Although Moses belonged officially to Pharaoh's daughter, God allowed his own mother to have the privilege of giving him his early training. The exact number of years Moses was in the care of his own mother is unknown, but it was long enough for her to give him the basic training that would last throughout his lifetime. It was doubtlessly under his mother's care that Moses trusted God for his salvation. Also, it would have been only normal for his mother to have impressed on him the need for the Israelites to be delivered from Egypt. Perhaps his mother reminded him often that God promised to deliver the Israelites in the fourth generation and that he was a member of that generation.

The Influence of Moses' Parents

In a sense, Moses' parents influenced the course of history, although they were slaves to the Egyptians at the time. Think of what they personally accomplished by properly rearing Moses. One never knows how one person or group may affect large numbers of people—even the world.

Isaiah 1:9 reveals how much influence a small group can have. "Except the Lord of hosts had left unto us a very small remnant, we should have been as Sodom, and we should have been like unto Gomorrah." This remnant influenced the course of Israel's history.

The faith of Moses' parents caused them to risk the wrath of the king. Their love for God and for their child caused them to devise an ingenious way to evade the king's ruthless edict. God honored their faith and rewarded their love. As a

24

result, Moses had the benefit of a godly home and the heritage of his Hebrew parents, which proved to be more than enough to counteract the later adverse education received from the Egyptians.

From the example of his parents, Moses learned what it is to have faith in God and fearless courage. Those early years made indelible impressions on Moses, as was evidenced in later life. Just as his parents exercised faith, not fearing the wrath of the king, Moses later "forsook Egypt, not fearing the wrath of the king" (Heb. 11:27). Faith and fear do not go together. Hebrews 11:6 tells us: "Without faith it is impossible to please him [God]." Romans 8:31 reminds us: "If God be for us, who can be against us?"

Later, when Moses received Egypt's culture and wealth, with all of the advantages and prestige Egypt had to offer, he could not be changed from what his basic education had made him. He never forgot his God and His promise for his people.

Perhaps Moses sensed that he was going to be used of God to deliver Israel; at least he was committed to the fact that God would deliver Israel someday. In Moses, we see the fulfillment of the promise: "Train up a child in the way he should go: and when he is old, he will not depart from it" (Prov. 22:6).

As Moses considered God's plan for Israel, the bones of Joseph would have been a vivid reminder. Before Joseph died, he told the nation, "God will surely visit you, and ye shall carry up my bones from hence" (Gen. 50:25). Joseph made the Israelites promise that they would obey his command to take his bones with them when they left Egypt. Moses would have been aware of this through the instruction of his parents, and this would have served as a reminder that God was going to deliver Israel someday. Moses would also have been told about the history of his own people and how God had brought them to Egypt to preserve them during the time of famine. Perhaps he even realized that God was right then preparing him for a future role in His plan for the emancipating of his people.

All of this shows us how important it is that parents be faithful to the responsibility of preparing their children for what God may want to do with them. Many Scripture passages deal with the responsibility of parents to their children. Deuteronomy 11:18,19 says, "Therefore shall ye lay up these my words in your heart and in your soul, and bind them for a sign upon your hand, that they may be as frontlets between your eyes. And ye shall teach them your children, speaking of them when thou sittest in thine house, and when thou walkest by the way, when thou liest down, and when thou risest up." Every aspect of life in the Christian home is to be permeated with the Word of God. Paul told Timothy: "But continue thou in the things which thou hast learned and hast been assured of, knowing of whom thou hast learned them; and that from a child thou hast known the holy scriptures, which are able to make thee wise unto salvation through faith which is in Christ Jesus" (II Tim. 3:14,15).

The Importance of Early Training

Consider the admonition "train up a child" (Prov. 22:6). The word "child" indicates that an age limit is involved; it involves training the person before he reaches adulthood. The early years are the formative, impressionable years of life in contrast to the later years when the character and habits are more rigidly established.

"Child" involves that time of life which is the age of memory. Scripture verses taught children in the early years stay with them throughout the rest of their lives. So also, this is the time of memorizing gospel songs and hymns that lift their hearts to God.

"Child" includes the habit-forming years. Research indicates that 90 percent of a person's habits are formed before age 20. In particular, statistics indicate that the drinking habit is begun before the age of 21 in over 90 percent of all cases of drunkenness. Also, records indicate that 75 percent of the young people who leave church do so during the junior high age.

However, "child" is also the age of faith. Indications are that 85 percent of those who trust Jesus Christ as Saviour do so before the age of 18. These early years are tremendously important for the fixing of beliefs. What a person believes after he is through college depends largely on what he has been taught in the formative years. Therefore, the wrecking of the faith of a Christian youth does not depend so much on what he is taught in college but on what he was *not* taught when he was younger.

It is what one does not do that often impresses his child the most. A parent who does nothing for his child contributes to that child's becoming a delinquent. Those who think there should be no restrictions on anyone should remember that such thinking began in the Garden of Eden—and Satan originated it. Essentially, he said to Eve, "God is protecting you. He's not letting you do certain things. If God really loved you, He would let you do anything you wanted to do." However, God has given responsibility to parents to train their children—which involves restrictions—to prepare them for the future.

In the command "train up a child" (Prov. 22:6) it is important to note all that is involved in training. So often, training of children is considered by parents to be only scolding or spanking for wrongdoing, but proper training involves much more. Training involves at least three elements—education, example and discipline. Education is the process of transmitting to a child the knowledge and experiences of humanity. We must also communicate to them spiritual principles; we must teach them that God blesses those who obey and He withholds His blessings from those who disobey.

We also train by example, as we have previously discussed. Children learn from others and this is especially true in the home. It is normal for children to imitate their parents, so it is tremendously important that parents live in a way that is pleasing to the Lord.

Training also includes discipline, which may be defined as that method of training whereby we seek to make doing right pleasant and doing wrong unpleasant. This involves correction as well as reward.

Causes for Decline in Proper Training

There are many reasons for the decline of proper training today—such as a low view of family life—but one of the main reasons is the decreasing value that has been placed on spiritual training. Families are not spending as much time together nor as much time studying God's Word. Personal standards of living have become so high that frequently mother and father must both work for an income. This keeps them so busy that it is difficult for them to spend time at home with the children, and the children suffer in the process.

If we want our children to have spiritually effective lives in the future, we must train them now. By training a generation of born-again children, we can greatly affect the future of other families, the church, society, and even the nation. The path of least resistance will not produce what our children will need in the future. We must invest in the lives of our children, and we can be sure that our investment will bring eternal dividends. However, if we are negligent in our responsibility to properly train our children, we can also be sure that society will be in even greater disruption in the future. As Edmund Burke, a British statesman, wrote: "The only thing necessary for the triumph of evil is for good men to do nothing."

Note that the Bible says we are to train a child "in the way he should go" (Prov. 22:6). Consider what we are doing with our children. We send them to school five days a week for five or six hours a day to prepare them for this life, but we send them to church only one day a week for one or two hours to train and prepare them for eternal life. We need to be giving far more to our family than what they are getting from the brief time in church if we are to counter the philosophies of this age that so many of them are receiving in the public school system. Some areas are more fortunate than others in that Christian schools, which educate children academically *and* spiritually, have been established. Of course, true education for the believer is integrating Christ in every subject.

Chapter 4

Moses' Training in the Egyptian Court

Eventually the time came when Moses had to be given up by his mother to the daughter of Pharaoh. The Bible says, "The child grew, and she brought him unto Pharaoh's daughter, and he became her son. And she called his name Moses: and she said, Because I drew him out of the water" (Ex. 2:10).

In his sermon, recorded in Acts 7, Stephen referred to Moses and said, "And when he was cast out, Pharaoh's daughter took him up, and nourished him for her own son. And Moses was learned in all the wisdom of the Egyptians, and was mighty in words and in deeds" (vv. 21,22).

Josephus, a first-century historian, wrote that Moses grew to be so handsome that passersby would stop to look at him. No doubt the heart of Moses' mother was heavy as she brought him to the gate of the great palace to give him to Pharaoh's daughter. But even as she had faith as she placed her baby in a little basket in the Nile, she now had faith that God would keep him in the midst of the evils he would face. And there would be many evils, such as the godless Egyptian teaching and idol worship. Although Proverbs 22:6 had not been written yet for encouragement to her, Moses' mother practiced the principle of doing what she could while she had Moses and then entrusting him to God when he had to leave home.

The Historical Background of Moses' Time

An understanding of the historical setting of Moses' time helps us to better understand the significance of the events

that followed. At that time, the queen was the rightful heir
to the throne; thus, the king held power only by right of
marriage to her. The king then on the throne had no son, but
he had a daughter of outstanding ability, and she was in line
for the throne. However, she would not be allowed to reign
because, according to Egyptian custom and law, the reigning
monarch was to be a man. But because of her connection to
the throne, she could determine who the next king would be.
That dynasty had been in power for only about 40 years.
Under the previous dynasty the nation of Israel had been well
accepted by the Egyptians, and one of the
Israelites—Joseph—had even been the prime minister. But this
was all changed, for "there arose up a new king over Egypt,
which knew not Joseph" (Ex. 1:8). The new dynasty was not
sympathetic to the Jews.

At this time, there were rumblings of war: Invasions were
threatened from the north, and since the Israelites lived north
of the Egyptian capital, they were in danger of being invaded
first of all. The Egyptians were concerned because the
Israelites made up over half of the total population, and if
the Israelites would join the enemy they could easily
overthrow Egypt. No wonder the unfriendly Egyptian
pharaoh decided that something had to be done to keep the
Israelite population from increasing. His decision was that all
male Israelite babies should be killed (v. 16).

Totally unknown to the pharaoh was the prophecy given
to Abraham of Israel's eventual emancipation from Egypt
(Gen. 15:13-16). Not only did he not know about this
prophecy, but he also had no way to even suspect that the
actual person who was to be used to deliver the Israelites was
being trained right in his own court! What a marvelous way
God has of working, and thus He reveals that the wisdom of
the world is foolishness!

As it became evident that the pharaoh would not live
long, it was the responsibility of the king's daughter to
determine who the rightful heir would be. In this we see that
God not only rules but also overrules, for each event
happened with the perfect timing of His own plan. It was
then that Moses was born, and God gave guidance to his
mother as to what she should do to preserve his life.

Although Pharaoh's daughter could not rule on the throne herself, she could adopt a son who could rule on the throne. Of course, it would be important for such a son to have proper training in the king's court, and this was what Moses was given.

During the possibly 10 or 12 years that Moses was cared for and taught by his own mother, there were probably occasional visits to the palace. But eventually the day came for a final parting from his mother as Moses left his humble, godly environment and entered the royal court to receive his education as a prince. This training would obviously include total indoctrination in the mysteries of the Egyptian cults, the highest literary culture of the time, and intensive military training. Such training was why Stephen could say that "Moses was learned in all the wisdom of the Egyptians" (Acts 7:22).

Since Egypt was the greatest nation on earth at this time, it would have possessed the best in technical, scientific and military knowledge that the world had to offer.

God had evidenced his sovereign control of all the circumstances of Moses' life by selecting the court of Pharaoh as the training ground for Israel's future deliverer. On the surface, it does not seem that such a luxurious, even sensuous, court with its soft living and rich foods would be an ideal training ground for the future nomadic life in the desert. But more was to be included in God's training program for Moses than the training in Pharaoh's court. Later, there would also be further training for Moses in the backside of the desert.

The loose morals and intrigue of the palace do not seem to be the most conducive atmosphere for further developing the godly character that Moses acquired in his early home training. But God's ways are not always man's ways. Man usually reasons that isolation and seclusion are needed to avoid contamination. However, God's method is *insulation* rather than *isolation.* Moses' early training was of the quality that kept him pure for God throughout his Egyptian training. Thus, his earlier, godly training had insulated him against the effect of Egyptian licentiousness. Moses had been formed in his early home training as a basic instrument for God's use, but the palace became the testing fires to temper God's instrument.

When the basic training given a child is in line with God's principles, that child will be able to stand against the temptations of the Enemy.

Moses in the Egyptian Court

In the Egyptian court, Moses had everything any young man could wish for. He was treated as Pharaoh's grandson, which meant that he probably rode in his own horse-drawn carriage with its attendant servants and that he floated down the Nile River in a golden barge amid the strains of luxurious music giving sensual gratification. Anything Moses wished for was within his reach.

Because Moses was being trained to be the next ruler in Egypt, it was necessary for him to be versed in the wisdom and science of Egypt. Acts 7:22 says that he was "mighty in words," which probably refers to his training to be a statesman; and it also says that he was "mighty . . . in deeds," which probably refers to his military training.

Historian Josephus stated that Moses was mighty in his military achievements—the armies under his leadership won great victories. Tradition indicates that Moses was well trained in organization and was made the head of the Egyptian armies. This position took him into various parts of the world over which Egypt had influence. One account indicates that when the Ethiopians invaded the land of Egypt, Moses was put at the head of the army. He routed the enemy, which raised him to high esteem in the Egyptians' eyes.

His military training and experience equipped Moses to be a skilled organizer with the ability to handle large crowds and great armies of men. His was a superb training in discipline, patience and decision making. Moses also received valuable training in such important areas as administration and communications. Although Moses did not have mass media as we know them today, his position would have required his competence in using the communication systems of his day to their best advantage.

He was also trained in the matter of authority. This included not only how to use authority but also how to properly delegate it to others. He learned to know men and to know which ones he could depend on. From all of this training, Moses emerged with a mind gifted in many areas of knowledge.

But it should be remembered that God is often pleased to use men who have been denied such opportunities of training. One does not have to be brilliant or trained in the best methods of the world to be used of God. The important matter is that a believer place himself completely at God's disposal, willing to do whatever He desires. True, many types of Christian service require specialized training, and one needs to acquire training if he is to be competent in these areas. However, one's confidence must not be in his training but in God's ability to use him with his training.

The training Moses received greatly benefited him because he was dedicated to using all of his abilities for God. As a result, the world—both Jew and Gentile—owes an incalculable debt to him. He was used of God as the instrument of giving the Law and as the writer of the first five books of the Old Testament.

The Apostle Paul was comparable to Moses in that he also received the best training this world had to offer. And because of his love for Jesus Christ, all of his knowledge was dedicated to the glory of God.

Moses' Decisions

Historical sources indicate that while Moses was still in his 20s his foster grandfather—the Pharaoh of Egypt—died. Since Pharaoh's daughter was not able to reign, Moses' opportunity came to ascend the throne and rule over all Egypt. But Moses refused. Seeing his own people suffer, and knowing God's plans of deliverance for Israel as recorded in Exodus 15, Moses chose not to ascend the throne of Egypt. Perhaps he was even convinced at this time that God would use him to deliver the Israelites.

Since Moses did not assume the throne, his foster mother—Pharaoh's daughter—married a half brother, thus acquiring someone for the throne. But after reigning a short time, he died. This meant that Moses, at the age of 25, had to make another choice, for there was another opportunity for him to assume the throne of Egypt. Again he refused.

Pharaoh's daughter married again—another half brother, who became an ambitious and ruthless ruler. He was a jealous king who wanted no rivals.

When Pharaoh's daughter died, this left Moses in great jeopardy. Understandably, Moses was a threat to the present pharaoh. While she was alive, Pharaoh's daughter was able to protect Moses, but now his life was in danger because of a pharaoh who wanted no rivals.

Although Moses was unpopular with the present pharaoh, he was popular with the army, with the Egyptian court, and with the Egyptian slaves; that is, his own people. With this kind of a following, Pharaoh counted him as a potential, powerful enemy.

History suggests that Pharaoh had detectives assigned to cover Moses' every movement and report any incident that might justify getting rid of Moses. The biblical record bears this out, for later, when Moses killed an Egyptian, the news reached Pharaoh immediately.

Moses could not forget that his real parents were slaves to the Egyptians and that they—like all Israelites—were groaning under the lash of the Egyptian taskmasters. Nor could Moses forget God's promise to liberate his people from bondage.

Thus, at the age of 40, Moses made his final decision to reject the Egyptian throne and all it had to offer. His decision was firm and permanent. Hebrews 11:24-26 refers to this final decision: "By faith Moses, when he was come to years, refused to be called the son of Pharaoh's daughter; choosing rather to suffer affliction with the people of God, than to enjoy the pleasures of sin for a season; esteeming the reproach of Christ greater riches than the treasures in Egypt: for he had respect unto the recompence of the reward."

Chapter 5

Another Crisis; Another Choice

When Moses was 40 years old, he faced a crisis which demanded a choice. As mentioned previously, his foster mother (Pharaoh's daughter) was dead, and as a rightful heir to the throne, Moses still had the possibility of ruling over all Egypt. As he thought of the plight of his people in slavery and wanting to return to the land of their fathers, he would have done much thinking about the best way to accomplish this goal. Perhaps he even thought of Joseph, who many years earlier became Prime Minister of Egypt and was used of God in this capacity in preserving Israel.

Moses may have thought that if he ascended to the throne he could deliver the people just as Joseph had preserved them. On the other hand, Moses obviously did not have peace that this was what he should do. He had rejected the throne previously, and now he was faced with a momentous decision: Would he personally ascend the throne and endeavor to help his people in this manner, or would he personally have a part in leading them out of Egypt? There is no indication that he ever considered the alternative of coexistence—he realized that God had before told Abraham that the people of Israel would separate from the Egyptians and return to the land of Canaan after 400 years. His early parental teaching would have impressed on him God's promise that the Israelites would be delivered from bondage in the fourth generation after Abraham's death.

Moses knew how to pray to God. He knew God's purpose and plan for his people. And Moses could not shake the conviction that his own destiny was to lead his people out of Egypt, even though he may have been able to benefit them

35

somewhat by ruling on the throne. For some time, the conviction that he should personally lead the people out had been locked in the depths of his own heart, but now he was faced with circumstances that demanded a decision. What would he choose? Which way would he go?

Consider the way God had sovereignly worked up to this time to accomplish His purposes and plans for Israel. He had provided training for Moses in his own home which laid a foundation for his spiritual uprightness in days to come. Then God had arranged for Moses' training as a prince in Pharaoh's court, and this was now completed. But there was some training that Moses still needed—some extremely important training—and this could be accomplished only by God Himself in the loneliness of a desert.

But before Moses could be ready for this next stage of important training, he had to experience total failure in his own methods. Although Moses was honest in his relationship with God at this point, he still looked to himself and his own ability and training to accomplish what needed to be done. Moses may have been relying on his previous military training and thinking that he could lead an insurrection and thus free his people. But as valuable as Moses' training was, God did not want him relying on his training to accomplish the task at hand; God wanted Moses to rely on Him alone. Moses had to die to his own ideas and background and be totally open to God. There had to be first this negative—dying to self—before there could be the positive—living to God.

This was the second crisis in Moses' life. The first crisis was at his birth when his parents had to make the decision of what to do, and as they relied on God by faith, He rewarded them. But in this second crisis, Moses stood alone; only he could make the decision concerning what he should do. God had already chosen Moses, but now Moses had to choose what he would do concerning the future.

Keys to Moses' Decision

The key elements determining what Moses would choose were his parents' faithful, early training; his explicit faith based on God's plan and promise; and his weighing of the future against the present. We have noted the training he received from his mother and also the explicit faith Moses had in God's word. As to his weighing the future against the present, the Bible says, "Choosing rather to suffer affliction with the people of God, than to enjoy the pleasures of sin for a season; esteeming the reproach of Christ greater riches than the treasures in Egypt: for he had respect unto the recompence of the reward" (Heb. 11:25,26).

Such a decision was the fruit of the training he had received from his mother. Mothers should never underestimate how influential the early training of their children is in determining future choices. Moses' decision at age 40 was the greatest payment his mother could ever receive for what she had done for him.

Key words that appear in Hebrews 11 concerning Moses are "refused" (v. 24), "choosing" (v. 25), "esteeming" (v. 26) and "forsook" (v. 27).

Notice what Moses refused—he "refused to be called the son of Pharaoh's daughter" (v. 24). In other words, he denied his rights to the throne. His saying no to the throne was one of the most epoch-making nos in all of world history. First, it changed everything in Moses' own life. Second, it marked a beginning of the history of Israel as a nation. Third, it meant the eventual doom of Egypt as a world power in the ancient world. What a no in its proper place can do! May God give believers in this age the courage they need to say no at the right time.

Moses' decision was not made on an impulse of the moment, as youth often make decisions; rather, his decision was the result of a man who had experienced much in life and knew the value of proper choices. His decision was made "when he was come to years" (Heb. 11:24), "when he was full forty years old" (Acts 7:23). Twice before he had said no to the throne, but this was his final no. With nothing to gain and all to lose, and after a thoughtful examination, Moses descended from the footsteps leading to the loftiest throne in the world to share his life with his slave people and with his God.

Moses' decision to refuse, with finality, the throne of Egypt was a result of the faith which was instilled in him in his youth. He refused because he balanced the future against

the present. He esteemed, or considered, "the reproach of
Christ greater riches than the treasures in Egypt" (Heb.
11:26). Moses saw beyond this present life—as verse 27 says,
"Seeing him who is invisible."

Negative and Positive Choices

A refusal is actually a negative. The positive side is the
choice made after refusing. But both are necessary—there
must be a negative as well as a positive.

At the time of salvation, a person is set apart, or
sanctified. In a way, that is a negative action because it
involves being set apart *from* something. But it is also
positive, for it is a setting apart *to* something. Many Christians never get beyond the negative stage—they concentrate
only on that from which they have been set apart. Their lives
are characterized by what they do not do. However, God
wants us to emphasize the positive, recognizing that we have
been set apart to Him to please Him in the way we live. Such
a life emphasizes what a person does. We are "created in
Christ Jesus unto good works" (Eph. 2:10).

A person has no choice about his heredity. He cannot
choose who his parents are to be nor the color of his hair or
eyes. And, after being born into this world, a child at home
has little choice about his environment. But the individual
does choose what he will do with his life—not only his
vocation but also his relationship with God. At some point in
life, each person must choose one of two roads—his own way
or God's way. The Apostle Paul made known his choice when
he said, "None of these things move me, neither count I my
life dear unto myself, so that I might finish my course with
joy" (Acts 20:21).

Your life can either be what God wants it to be or it can
be shallow and full of misery. It is the decision you make
that determines which it will be.

Moses' decision was based on his attitude toward the will
of God. It was a positive attitude, for he chose, by faith,
God's plan for him. Through the eyes of faith, Moses saw
God's plan to deliver Israel from its prolonged misery in
Egypt. If Moses was to save his people, he could not save
himself. He must sacrifice himself, his future, his comfort, his

royal prestige—everything. Moses' choice meant giving up name, honor, riches, glory and position.

Moses rejected the allurement of an easy life and chose instead to endure hardship with his people. His choice reflected what is embodied in the words of Christ: "If any man will come after me, let him deny himself, and take up his cross daily, and follow me. For whosoever will save his life shall lose it: but whosoever will lose his life for my sake, the same shall save it" (Luke 9:23,24). If one is to be Christ's disciple, he must deny himself and take the position of death against all these things. In these verses, the Lord Jesus is not referring to eternal life but to a life of usefulness here and now. Of course, the believer who serves God well in this life will be rewarded in the life to come.

A believer can be certain that Satan will use all of his wiles to deter him from choosing a path that pleases God. Satan even attempted this with the Lord Jesus Christ. Matthew 4 records Satan's temptations of the Lord Jesus, but in every case, the Lord answered Satan with scripture. But Satan did not give up. When Christ was on the cross dying for the sin of the world, Satan caused others to jeer and say, "He saved others; himself he cannot save. If he be the King of Israel, let him now come down from the cross, and we will believe him" (Matt. 27:42). But Christ endured the shame of the cross for us. How wonderful are the words of II Corinthians 8:9: "For ye know the grace of our Lord Jesus Christ, that, though he was rich, yet for your sakes he became poor, that ye through his poverty might be rich."

Although Satan would have attempted to keep Moses from making such a significant decision, Moses "refused to be called the son of Pharaoh's daughter" (Heb. 11:24). Moses had already refused the throne twice, but now he refused to be called the son of the daughter of Pharaoh. Why? He rejected all possibilities of any relationship to the throne so no one would consider him for that position again. He completely renounced his relationship with the one who gave him the rights to the throne. This decision was firm and final. Never again did he have to face this decision.

Moses could have ascended the throne and brought about a reform in favor of the Israelites, but he was convinced that Israel could not remain in Egypt. God's promise to Abraham was clear, and Joseph's unburied bones were a constant reminder of the need for Israel to leave Egypt and return to the land of Canaan. There could be no coexistence of Israel and Egypt if the Israelites were to do God's will.

Application to the Believer's Life

Think of this in relation to the believer's personal life. The believer is told: "Love not the world, neither the things that are in the world. If any man love the world, the love of the Father is not in him. For all that is in the world, the lust of the flesh, and the lust of the eyes, and the pride of life, is not of the Father, but is of the world. And the world passeth away, and the lust thereof: but he that doeth the will of God abideth forever" (I John 2:15-17). What could be plainer than this?

Ephesians 5:11 says, "Have no fellowship with the unfruitful works of darkness, but rather reprove them." Verses 15 and 17 in this same passage say, "See then that ye walk circumspectly, not as fools, but as wise. Wherefore be ye not unwise, but understanding what the will of the Lord is." And we may be sure that the will of the Lord will not be made known to us until we present ourselves totally to Him.

Believers are also told: "Be ye not unequally yoked together with unbelievers: for what fellowship hath righteousness with unrighteousness? and what communion hath light with darkness? Wherefore come out from among them, and be ye separate, saith the Lord, and touch not the unclean thing; and I will receive you" (II Cor. 6:14,17). For those who consider taking the middle of the road rather than choosing one path or the other, Christ's words are especially sobering: "I know your deeds, that you are neither cold nor hot; I would that you were cold or hot. So because you are lukewarm, and neither hot nor cold, I will spit you out of My mouth" (Rev. 3:15,16, NASB). Never were more emphatic words spoken to a generation! These words need to be taken seriously today.

Moses had to refuse before he could make a proper choice. He refused his physical relationships and the benefits they could give him, and chose to rely on God alone. One of the most difficult things to do is to put God above even one's own family. The Lord Jesus Christ said, "If any man come to me, and hate not his father, and mother, and wife, and children, and brethren, and sisters, yea, and his own life also, he cannot be my disciple. And whosoever doth not bear his cross, and come after me, cannot be my disciple" (Luke 14:26,27). The word "hate" as used here does not mean a person should despise his family. It was a term of comparison, showing that one's love for God was to be so much greater than his love for his own relatives that it would be as if one compared love with hate. To properly please God, one must deny himself and any fleshly desires as well as one's family—he must put God first. Colossians 3:1-3 tells believers: "If then you have been raised up with Christ, keep seeking the things above, where Christ is, seated at the right hand of God. Set your mind on the things above, not on the things that are on earth. For you have died and your life is hidden with Christ in God" (NASB).

The believer must also reject worldliness if he is to be pleasing to God. Worldliness is an attitude toward the world system with the things and prestige that it has to offer. The believer needs to reject sin, especially the sin of the lack of faith; for that which is not of faith is sin (Rom. 14:23). Hebrews 12:1 reminds us that we are to "lay aside every weight, and the sin which doth so easily beset us, and let us run with patience the race that is set before us."

We also need to refuse men's applause, or honors. The most important matter to us should be the approval of God rather than the approval of men. Many temptations can hinder a Christian from being effective for the Lord, and the best advice to follow is what the Apostle Paul told Timothy to do concerning various temptations: "Flee these things" (I Tim. 6:11).

In addition to fleeing temptations, it is tremendously important that we reckon ourselves to have died to sin, as we are told in Romans 6:11,12. We are not to let sin reign as king in our lives. This is the negative—it is what we must refuse to permit. Positively, we are to yield ourselves to the Lord to do whatever He desires. There are many wonderful illustrations of those who tried to please the Lord by relying totally on Him, and there are many sad illustrations of those who have tried to serve the Lord in their own strength and wisdom.

Choosing

The choices a person makes are tremendously important. As a young man, Daniel chose not to contaminate himself with the king's food. When Daniel was taken captive by Nebuchadnezzar's army, the Bible says, "But Daniel purposed in his heart that he would not defile himself with the portion of the king's meat, nor with the wine which he drank" (Dan. 1:8).

As an older man, Joshua made the choice for himself and his family to serve the Lord regardless of what others did. Joshua told the Israelites: "If it seem evil unto you to serve the Lord, choose you this day whom ye will serve; whether the gods which your fathers served that were on the other side of the flood [Euphrates], or the gods of the Amorites, in whose land ye dwell: but as for me and my house, we will serve the Lord" (Josh. 24:15).

Even the Lord Jesus Christ Himself had a significant choice to make. He had to choose whether to cling to the glories He had as God or to give up the external manifestation of His attributes in order to come to earth to die on the cross for our sin. The Bible says, "Although He existed in the form of God, did not regard equality with God a thing to be grasped, but emptied Himself, taking the form of a bond-servant, and being made in the likeness of men. And being found in appearance as a man, He humbled Himself by becoming obedient unto the point of death, even death on a cross" (Phil. 2:6-8, NASB).

The Apostle Paul made a choice that changed the entire direction of his life. Writing about this choice, he said, "What things were gain to me, those I counted loss for Christ. Yea doubtless, and I count all things but loss for the excellency of the knowledge of Christ Jesus my Lord: for whom I have suffered the loss of all things, and do count them but dung, that I may win Christ" (Phil. 3:7,8). So determined was the Apostle Paul that even when he faced persecution and imprisonment, and possible death, he said, "None of these things move me, neither count I my life dear unto myself, so that I might finish my course with joy" (Acts 20:24).

Moses' refusal was essential before he could make a choice. By faith he refused and by faith he chose. He had to refuse more than just the throne; he had to refuse to be the son of Pharaoh's daughter. He chose to be a son of God in the fullest sense instead of a son of Pharaoh's daughter. He chose to be a member of the despised Hebrews rather than a member of the royal family. He refused to be a leader in a progressive nation so he could be a leader in an apparently lost cause. He refused the glitter of Egypt and chose the gloom of Israel.

Even though Moses' refusals had great significance, those refusals in themselves were not enough. It is not sufficient just to turn one's back on the past—essential as that is—one must also turn to God. These are not necessarily two separate acts, for turning to God involves turning from the things of the world. But even though they may not be separated by time, both are tremendously important—to turn from the past and to turn to God.

Romans 6:11 emphasizes both of these aspects as they relate to the believer. We are to recognize that we have died to sin (past), but we are to be "alive unto God through Jesus Christ our Lord" (present). Dying to sin is the negative aspect; living to God is the positive aspect.

Too many people do not go all the way in this matter. No amount of negativeness will make us either good or great. No one ever became a Christian by virtue of what he did not do, or what he refused. That's only one side of it. No personal holiness was ever attained solely by saying no to evil. We have to turn our back to the things of the world, but we must also turn to God. This is what sanctification is all about, for the word itself means "to be set apart." We are to be set apart from the world to God. In the believer's life this means saying no to sin and yes to righteousness. The power to turn from one's sin comes as he turns to God in faith. As a person turns to God in faith, God enables him to turn from everything that does not please Him.

Note what James says in chapter 4 of his New Testament book. Verse 7 says, "Submit yourselves therefore to God. Resist the devil, and he will flee from you." There is first a submitting to God which, of course, is a turning away from everything that is evil. This submission puts into practice saying no to the old life and yes to the new righteousness. Ephesians 4:22-24 also emphasizes both the negative and positive: "That ye put off concerning the former conversation the old man, which is corrupt according to the deceitful lusts; and be renewed in the spirit of your mind; and that ye put on the new man, which after God is created in righteousness and true holiness." The negative is summed up in the words "put off" and the positive is summed up in the words "put on." The Greek tense indicates the putting off and putting on to be past acts. It involves one's standing with God. Paul was admonishing believers to practice what had already been accomplished for them positionally.

A similar emphasis is found in Colossians 3:9,10: "Lie not one to another seeing that ye have put off the old man with his deeds; and have put on the new man, which is renewed in knowledge after the image of him that created him." If you are born again, you have said no to these other things and have said yes to Christ. You have experienced what II Corinthians 5:17 says: "Therefore if any man be in Christ, he is a new creature: old things are passed away; behold, all things are become new." This is God's way of doing things.

Suffering Affliction and Reproach

"Moses . . . refused to be called the son of Pharaoh's daughter; choosing rather to suffer affliction with the people of God" (Heb. 11:24,25). Instead of choosing to remain in his relationship as the son of Pharaoh's daughter and all that went with it, Moses chose affliction and reproach with his own, despised people. You can undoubtedly see parallels in your own life with what Moses chose. If affliction is your lot, remember the words of the Lord Jesus Christ: "In the world ye shall have tribulation: but be of good cheer; I have overcome the world" (John 16:33) A tremendous promise is is also found in I Peter 4:13: "But rejoice, inasmuch as ye are partakers of Christ's sufferings; that, when his glory shall be revealed, ye may be glad also with exceeding joy." How can you be glad with "exceeding joy" when you are going through tribulation, or trials? Because of the glory that is to follow.

If you are experiencing reproach, remember what the Lord said to His disciples: "If the world hate you, ye know that it hated me before it hated you. If ye were of the world, the world would love his own: but because ye are not of the world, but I have chosen you out of the world, therefore the world hateth you. Remember the word that I said unto you, The servant is not greater than his lord. If they have persecuted me, they will also persecute you; if they have kept my saying, they will keep your's also" (John 15:18-20).

When experiencing reproach we also need to remember Hebrews 13:12-14: "Wherefore Jesus also, that he might sanctify the people with his own blood, suffered without the gate. Let us go forth therefore unto him without the camp, bearing his reproach. For here we have no continuing city, but we seek one to come."

Moses chose to identify himself with his own, despised people rather than claim the throne of the greatest world power of that time. Because of his faith, he looked beyond the present and chose what counted for eternity. He realized that the pleasures of Egypt would be shortlived.

By faith, Moses saw the future and chose that which had eternal reward. The Bible says about Moses' choice: "Esteeming the reproach of Christ greater riches than treasures in Egypt, for he had respect unto the recompence of the reward" (Heb. 11:26). Many of us do not seriously look at the future; we think only of the present. Sadly, many of God's children determine their course of action by the values of time rather than by the values of eternity.

Abraham, like Moses, chose on the basis of eternal values. The Bible says of Abraham: "By faith he sojourned in the land of promise, as in a strange country, dwelling in tabernacles with Isaac and Jacob, the heirs with him of the same promise: for he looked for a city which hath foundations, whose builder and maker is God" (Heb. 11:9,10).

Concerning these heroes of faith, the Bible says, "These all died in the faith, not having received the promises, but having seen them afar off, and were persuaded of them, and embraced them, and confessed that they were strangers and pilgrims on the earth. For they that say such things declare plainly that they seek a country" (vv. 13,14). So we see that faith shows the true value of the things of this life, considers affliction worth more than pleasure and considers reproach more than treasure. This kind of faith gave Moses strength to endure. This kind of faith enabled him to look ahead and see "him who is invisible" (v. 27).

Each of us needs to ask himself, Where do I have my eyes fixed today? Are they on the things of this life, or are they on the things of eternity? It is extremely important that we do the proper refusing and choosing if we are to honor God in the way we live.

Have you considered how you will enjoy heaven? As we think about the future, let's not just think of the next 10 years or 20 years or 50 years; let's think about the hundreds and thousands and millions of years we will spend with the Lord. What kind of capacity for enjoying heaven do you think you will have?

We know that the interests of a person change as he matures. For instance, a baby in a crib is content with rattles or things that move. He is able to have the time of his life with such things, but that stage soon passes. Before too long he is old enough to want a tricycle and he'll consider rattles very childish. But then there soon comes a time when he wants a bicycle and his tricycle will be considered a childish thing. And then there's a car, and so on. You see, as he matures his capacity for enjoyment changes.

So also, our capacity for spiritual enjoyment changes. What does it take to make you content spiritually? This is an indication of your spiritual maturity. Is it the things of this world? If so, you are in the immature stage of spiritual life, for as you progress on to spiritual maturity, only the things of eternity and the Lord Jesus Christ Himself will offer contentment.

Some people, as they think of heaven, think only of its physical descriptions—mansions, streets of gold and so on—but the most important matter about heaven is being personally with the Lord Jesus Christ Himself. The real pleasures of heaven will be the fellowship we will have with the Eternal God, who gave His Son that we might live with Him forever. What a shame it would be if when we get to heaven we are more concerned about the things in heaven than we are about the Person of Christ Himself.

Balancing the Present Against the Future

Because Moses had his spiritual eyes fixed on the eternal future, his faith gave him the strength to endure the adverse things of time. He balanced the present against the future; he weighed the pros and the cons of the choice that lay before him. He did not make a hasty decision when he chose to refuse to be called the son of Pharaoh's daughter, thereby completely relinquishing any future opportunity to ascend the throne. It wasn't a snap judgment to throw everything overboard and join his people. His first refusal of the throne was made when he was about 20 years old, and the second refusal when he was about 25. Then at the age of 40 he totally renounced his relationship with Pharaoh's daughter.

Because of the time involved, it is evident that Moses' decision was a calm, deliberate choice. He put the radiant future of his position on one balance of the scales, and the bleakness which might result from renouncing that position on the other side of the scale. Weighing the present against the future, he came to the conclusion that he could experience joy in the future only by suffering afflictions with God's people in the present. Although he recognized there was pleasure in sin for a season, he knew it was only for a season. His faith in God as the object of his worship empowered him to go through with his choice. He not only endured but actually prized the affliction because he saw in it something for the future. He saw the greater joy in the future.

As Jesus faced the cross, He also looked beyond the present to the future. He saw the joy that awaited Him if He suffered the affliction of the cross. Concerning Jesus, Hebrews 12:2 says, "Who for the joy that was set before him endured the cross, despising the shame, and is set down at the right hand of the throne of God." Why? What did He see? He saw the day when those of us who know Him as personal Saviour would join Him for all eternity. What a tragedy it would have been for us if the Lord Jesus Christ had let the suffering and shame of the present outweigh the joys of the future.

Think of it! Christ considered fellowship with us so important that He was willing to experience shame on the cross to bring it about. As God, He could have enjoyed eternity without us, but having us with Him obviously adds a great deal to His enjoyment or He never would have gone to the cross. Just as we can enjoy the beauty of nature by ourselves but find it much more enjoyable when our loved ones enjoy it with us, the Lord Jesus Christ wanted us with Him forever. To see us enjoying heaven because of the redemption He provided—somehow this brings far more enjoyment to the Lord Jesus Christ than He could otherwise experience.

Because Christ was aware of the reward, He was willing to suffer shame on the cross. As the Bible says, Christ "made himself of no reputation, and took upon him the form of a servant, and was made in the likeness of men: and being found in fashion as a man, he humbled himself, and became obedient unto death, even the death of the cross" (Phil. 2:7,8). The reward that followed is stated in the next verse: "Wherefore God also hath highly exalted him, and given him a name which is above every name."

It is important that we, too, look at the future if we are to have the right attitude about the present. I remember so well the words of my former personal assistant, who is now in heaven with the Lord. His responsibility was to rewrite my messages and adapt them for printed form, and he did an excellent job of it. Of course, because they were my messages, people would compliment me for what was said in the books, and I realized I was getting glory for his hard work of making my sentences flow easily so people could benefit even more from them. One day I asked him, "John, how can you take it? I get all the glory and honor for what's been written, but you are the one working behind the scenes to make it possible." With a glowing face, he pointed toward heaven and said, "I know who is keeping the books!" He was looking at the future, not at the present.

Rewards for the Faithful

Let us not forget that God rewards, or recompenses, those who serve Him faithfully. Moses had "respect unto the recompence of the reward" (Heb. 11:26). Those who trust Christ as Saviour during the Church Age will receive their rewards at the Judgment Seat of Christ. It is sobering to realize that someday every Christian will give account of himself to the Lord. Referring to this judgment of believers, II Corinthians 5:10 says, "For we must all appear before the judgment seat of Christ; that every one may receive the things done in his body, according to that he hath done, whether it be good or bad."

The believer will not be condemned at this judgment, because he has been delivered from condemnation by receiving Christ as Saviour (John 5:24). Rather, the Judgment Seat of Christ will be a time of evaluating what the believer has on earth to glorify the Lord. The Lord will abundantly reward those who have served Him well. Knowing there will be a future reward should encourage all of us, especially when we are experiencing trials.

Paul told Timothy: "All that will live godly in Christ Jesus shall suffer persecution" (II Tim. 3:12). But note the encouraging word that Paul also gave Timothy and all believers: "If we suffer, we shall also reign with him" (2:12). From this statement it is obvious that we will not be able to reign with Christ in all of His glory unless we suffer for Him in this life. The time of reigning referred to is doubtlessly the Millennium. The suffering Paul mentioned does not refer to physical suffering but to enduring reproach as a result of being a child of God.

One who has suffered reproach can look forward to the rewards to follow. The Apostle Paul had suffered much reproach, and at the end of his life he was able to say, "I have fought a good fight, I have finished my course, I have kept the faith: henceforth there is laid up for me a crown of righteousness, which the Lord, the righteous judge, shall give me at that day: and not to me only, but unto all them also that love his appearing" (II Tim. 4:7,8). What a wonderful fulfillment of the desire Paul had previously expressed: "None of these things move me, neither count I my life dear unto myself, so that I might finish my course with joy" (Acts 20:24). Second Timothy is the last letter written by the Apostle Paul, and it is evident that he finished his course with joy.

From these examples we see the importance of weighing the future against the present. This is what Moses did—he did not look at the things which are seen, but he looked to "him who is invisible" (Heb. 11:27). The pleasures of sin, Moses recognized, would be of brief duration, so he chose that which would have lasting value. Even the reproach he would suffer would be brief in comparison with eternity. So he purposely chose to suffer in the present that he might rejoice in the future. This is also what we need to do, and Romans 8:17,18 tells us: "If children, then heirs; heirs of God, and joint-heirs with Christ; if so be that we suffer with him, that we may be also glorified together. For I reckon that the sufferings of this present time are not worthy to be compared with the glory which shall be revealed in us." What wonderful encouragement!

Because of this bright future, Christ said, "Blessed are they which are persecuted for righteousness' sake: for their's is the kingdom of heaven. Blessed are ye, when men shall revile you, and persecute you, and shall say all manner of evil against you falsely, for my sake. Rejoice, and be exceeding glad: for great is your reward in heaven: for so persecuted they the prophets which were before you" (Matt. 5:10-12).

Moses' choice was correct, noble, thorough, honorable, God-ward—and he followed his choice with a surrender; he gave up everything to follow God. Yet, something was still lacking. For some reason, God did not accept him for His special purpose, nor did Moses' people accept him. Acts 7:25 says Moses' people "understood not." What was wrong?

The Sin of Indecision

Before we go further, let's consider the seriousness of indecision—we might even refer to it as the sin of indecision. God has harsh words to say about indecision.

God's words that pointedly touch on this subject are recorded in Revelation 3. The Lord Jesus Christ told the Church of Laodicea. "I know thy works, that thou art neither cold nor hot: I would thou wert cold or hot. So then because thou art lukewarm, and neither cold nor hot, I will spue thee out of my mouth" (vv. 15,16).

This does not necessarily refer only to the liberal church. These words were addressed to a self-sufficient Laodicean people who saw no need to completely rely on the Lord. This is evident from the following words: "Because thou sayest, I am rich, and increased with goods, and have need of nothing; and knowest not that thou art wretched, and miserable, and poor, and blind, and naked" (v. 17). These self-sufficient people were in a despicable condition, as far as the Lord was concerned. Therefore, He said, "I counsel thee to buy of me gold tried in the fire, that thou mayest be rich; and white raiment, that thou mayest be clothed, and that the shame of thy nakedness do not appear; and annoint thine eyes with eyesalve, that thou mayest see" (v. 18).

This was the Lord's way of saying, "Wake up!" Their senses were spiritually dull, and the Lord despised this middle-of-the-road decision. To this lukewarm church, the Lord said, "Behold, I stand at the door, and knock: if any man hear my voice, and open the door, I will come in to him, and will sup with him, and he with me" (v. 20). This verse is commonly used in dealing with the unsaved, but the context indicates it should be used in dealing with those who are spiritually lukewarm. In effect, the Lord was saying, "You are busy with many things, but you are not considering Me; if you open the door, I'll come in and have fellowship with you."

The Lord also said, "To him that overcometh will I grant to sit with me in my throne, even as I also overcame, and am set down with my Father in his throne" (v. 21). The Lord was apparently addressing those who had trusted Him as Saviour but were not serious about going on with Him in the Christian life. As a result, there was no joy of fellowship with Him, but the Lord promised that when these lukewarm Christians opened the doors of their hearts He was ready to fellowship with them.

The passage concludes with the words: "He that hath an ear, let him hear what the Spirit saith unto the churches" (v. 22). What does this mean? It is one thing to have physical ears, but it is quite another to have ears that really hear and obey. Are we really listening to what God is saying? God wants to speak to us, but He cannot do so if we are indecisive and refuse to go on with Him. The sin of indecision is perhaps one of the greatest, and most common, sins of Christians today.

We should not stand still, even when we come to a fork in the road in our lives. We should go one direction or the other. I've come to those places in my life when I wasn't sure which way I should go. At those times, I have taken the attitude of total dependency on the Lord and have said to Him, in effect, "Now Lord, I don't know which way You want me to go, but this way seems best so I'm going to start down this road. But I'm depending on You to stop me if I'm on the wrong road." And there have been times when God has clearly indicated that I was on the wrong road; He blocked the way, and I had to backtrack and take the other road. We can depend on God to guide us if we are willing to step out and give Him the opportunity. I encourage you to study Psalm 25 in regard to God's guiding us.

The Old Testament account of Abraham and Lot illustrates what it is to make a right choice, as well as what it is to make a wrong choice. Lot was Abraham's nephew, and both of them had many possessions. However, their servants had a difficult time getting along, and Abraham and Lot needed more pasture to graze their herds. For these reasons, Abraham said to Lot: "Let there be no strife, I pray thee, between me and thee, and between my herdmen and thy herdmen; for we be brethren. Is not the whole land before thee? Separate thyself, I pray thee, from me: if thou wilt take the left hand, then I will go to the right; or if thou depart to the right hand, then I will go to the left" (Gen. 13:8,9).

Abraham gave the first choice to Lot, which in itself involved a choice on Abraham's part—he had to choose to put Lot first. This gave Lot opportunity to have the best land. By this decision, Abraham indicated he would let God give him whatever He wanted him to have.

The Bible records Lot's choice: "Lot lifted up his eyes, and behold all the plain of Jordan, that it was well watered every where, before the Lord destroyed Sodom and Gomorrah, even as the garden of the Lord, like the land of Egypt, as thou comest unto Zoar. Then Lot chose him all the plain of Jordan; and Lot journeyed east: and they separated themselves the one from the other" (vv. 10,11). Lot saw the well-watered land, but he did not see as God sees or he would have seen the wicked cities and would have considered their effect.

After Lot made his choice and went away, God appeared to Abraham and said, "Lift up now thine eyes, and look from the place where thou art northward, and southward, and eastward, and westward: for all the land which thou seest, to thee will I give it, and to thy seed for ever" (vv. 14,15). Abraham's confidence in God was so great that he was not afraid to let Lot have first choice of the land. God rewarded Abraham's faith by promising to give an eternal deed to him and his descendants for the entire land. God's covenant with Abraham is still in effect today, but Lot died a pauper. This shows us the result a single choice can have.

There comes a time when God refuses to work with the individual who rebels against going forward with Him. The Bible says, "He, that being often reproved hardeneth his neck, shall suddenly be destroyed, and that without remedy" (Prov. 29:1). Why is this the case? Because such a person does not give God any chance to work in his life—there is no choice to let God have His way. What a horrible sin it is to refuse to let God work in one's life.

Chapter 6

Moses Joins His People

In making the choice not to be called the son of Pharaoh's daughter, Moses literally disinherited himself of all the riches of Egypt and of the throne that could have given him power over all of Egypt. He made a firm choice that called for action.

Moses' Action

The kind of action that Moses pursued is indicated in Exodus 2: "It came to pass in those days, when Moses was grown, that he went out unto his brethren, and looked on their burdens: and he spied an Egyptian smiting an Hebrew, one of his brethren. And he looked this way and that way, and when he saw that there was no man, he slew the Egyptian, and hid him in the sand" (vv. 11,12). This was drastic action for Moses to take, and we see that it brought repercussions.

The biblical account continues: "And when he went out the second day, behold, two men of the Hebrews strove together: and he said to him that did the wrong, Wherefore smitest thou thy fellow? and he said, Who made thee a prince and a judge over us? Intendest thou to kill me, as thou killedst the Egyptian? And Moses feared, and said, Surely this thing is known" (vv. 13,14).

When Pharaoh heard what Moses had done, he tried to kill him. The Bible says, "Now when Pharaoh heard this thing, he sought to slay Moses. But Moses fled from the face of Pharaoh, and dwelt in the land of Midian" (v. 15).

The New Testament commentary on Moses' actions is recorded in Acts 7:23-29: "And when he was full forty years old, it came into his heart to visit his brethren the children of Israel. And seeing one of them suffer wrong, he defended him, and avenged him that was oppressed, and smote the Egyptian: for he supposed his brethren would have understood how that God by his hand would deliver them: but they understood not. And the next day he shewed himself unto them as they strove, and would have set them at one again, saying, Sirs, ye are brethren; why do ye wrong one to another? But he that did his neighbour wrong thrust him away, saying, Who made thee a ruler and a judge over us? Wilt thou kill me, as thou didst the Egyptian yesterday? Then fled Moses at this saying, and was a stranger in the land of Madian, where he begat two sons."

So having made the choice not to be called the son of Pharaoh's daugher—a choice which literally disinherited himself—Moses tried to identify with his own people who were slaves, not citizens of Egypt. But to Moses' surprise, his fellow Israelites did not accept him. When he killed the Egyptian struggling with the Israelite, Moses was hoping to make it known to his countrymen that he was their deliverer. As Acts 7:25 says, "He supposed his brethren would have understood how that God by his hand would deliver them: but they understood not." Imagine what a sad moment this was for him. He had renounced his rights to the Egyptian throne because he was so convinced that his own people needed a deliverer, yet he was not recognized or received as their deliverer.

Moses had all the education necessary—he had been given the best diplomatic and military education and training available. He might have thought that his own people would surely welcome him as their leader, but they did not. In his bewilderment and confusion—as well as in fear of his life—Moses fled to the desert. No doubt he was greatly discouraged.

In the desert, Moses joined himself to the family of a priest and served as a lonely shepherd. Exodus 2:21 says, "Moses was content to dwell with the man: and he [the priest] gave Moses Zipporah his daughter." The name of the priest occurs in 3:1: "Now Moses kept the flock of Jethro his father in law, the priest of Midian."

Genesis 46:34 tells us what Egyptians thought of shepherds: "Every shepherd is an abomination unto the Egyptians." What could have been worse? Moses stepped from the possibility of ruling on the most powerful throne in the world to that of becoming a despised shepherd in the desert. What went wrong?

Moses was so sure that God intended to deliver Israel, and he was so sure that he was to be the deliverer. Was Moses mistaken in either or both of these matters? No, he was not mistaken in either case, but he still had a great deal to learn. God's promise to Israel and His call to Moses were sure, but Moses was far from ready for the task which God had called him to perform. There was no question as to his knowledge of God in redemption, and his early training by his mother was outstanding. His further training in the courts of Pharaoh was also excellent preparation for the job ahead. But he still lacked something; he lacked knowledge of the way God moves to perform His will and accomplish His purpose.

Another Important Lesson

The lordship of Almighty God had not yet been firmly established in the mind and heart of Moses. Since he did not know how God was going to perform this deliverance, Moses thought it was his responsibility. His faith was good, as far as it went, but his actions revealed that he had a zeal without knowledge. He had not learned the meaning of true union with the Lord. He had to learn one of the most important lessons any child of God has to learn.

Moses had to learn what it was to be dead to self and truly alive to God. Jesus stated this principle in these words: "Except a corn of wheat fall into the ground and die, it abideth alone, but if it die, it bringeth forth much fruit" (John 12:24). The Lord Jesus further stated the need to be dead to self: "If any man will come after me, let him deny himself, and take up his cross daily, and follow me" (Luke 9:23).

The great secret of Moses' life of usefulness had not yet been realized. The experience of death to self and of the new resurrected life was yet to be his. He eventually learned this lesson, but it took him 40 years.

The killing of the Egyptian was far from an act of faith. Rather, it sprang from an uncontrolled, selfish zeal. He wanted to do what God wanted him to do; he wanted to emancipate the people. But he took it upon himself to perform this task instead of inquiring about, and waiting on, God's orders and God's methods. Moses still had to learn that spiritual ends are never achieved by carnal means, and that the emancipation of God's people had to be completely God's undertaking. Moses was to be the instrument, but the deliverance itself had to be God's work entirely.

Also, Moses' intervention at this time was premature. God's people were not yet ready, and God had said that they would be in Egypt 400 years (Gen. 15:13). Although Moses was of the promised fourth generation, the 400 years were not yet up. Since Moses had several important lessons yet to learn, God took him alone to the desert where He could train him. Moses still had plenty of courses to master in God's private school, for he was much too strong for God to use.

The Source of True Strength

Can people be too strong for God? Yes, especially when their strength originates with self rather than with God. Moses had yet to learn that true strength could result only when he recognized his own weakness.

The Apostle Paul also had to learn this lesson. Paul had a "thorn in the flesh"; he had asked God three different times to remove it from him, but God did not choose to do so. As a result Paul learned a valuable lesson, which he recorded in II Corinthians 12:9,10: "And he [God] said unto me, My grace is sufficient for thee: for my strength is made perfect in weakness. Most gladly therefore will I rather glory in my infirmities, that the power of Christ may rest upon me. Therefore I take pleasure in infirmities, in reproaches, in necessities, in persecutions, in distresses for Christ's sake: for when I am weak, then am I strong."

That true strength originates in recognizing one's weakness is also seen in Hebrews 11:34, which records the

acts of the heroes of the faith who "quenched the violence of
fire, escaped the edge of the sword, out of weakness were
made strong, waxed valiant in fight, turned to flight the
armies of the aliens." Notice the phrase "out of weakness
were made strong." This is what every believer needs to learn
if he is to please God and to accomplish anything for Him in
his daily walk.

Moses had not yet learned this lesson, and his impulsive,
premature act of endeavoring to deliver the Israelites ushered
him into the second 40-year period of his life. This involved
private tutoring in the school of God. Very little is recorded
in the Scriptures about what took place during those 40 years
in the desert. But we can surmise what took place by viewing
the incidents in Moses' life before and after those 40 years.
Before the 40 years began, his independence was
demonstrated in the killing of an Egyptian. But 40 years
later, it was evident that Moses realized what it meant to be
dead to self, for he stood before Pharaoh with confidence
only in God, not in himself. Moses, in true union with God,
destroyed all the power of Egypt after he had been schooled
by God for 40 years.

Moses had externally surrendered himself to God, but he
had not completely abdicated the throne of his life in
total servitude to God. Self was still much too strong in his
life. He was far from ready to stand firm under the
complaints and criticism of his fellow men, which God knew
would come. Later, Moses not only suffered ridicule from the
Egyptians, but his own people murmured against his
leadership. He would never have been able to stand against
these criticisms had he not had the schooling in the desert
alone with God. He had to realize that when the Israelites
murmured against him, they were really murmuring against
God. He realized then that the whole work of emancipating
his people was God's work, not his. He was only the
instrument in God's hands.

This reminds me of an incident that took place when I
was a young preacher. A member of the church I was
pastoring became extremely angry with me and spoke very
harsh words to me. As he talked to me, he must have
wondered why I wasn't getting mad, but somehow what he
said did not bother me personally. When he was through, I

said, "You know, the Lord Jesus must have stood between you and me, because everything you said hit Him, not me." In his anger this man turned white and left. Later, he and I had a wonderful reunion in the Lord, but at the time of his attack I learned a valuable lesson.

This is the same kind of lesson that Moses had to learn—that attacks on him were not personal but were against the One he was representing. When one is relying on self, he takes everything personally, and such a person cannot be an effective servant for the Lord. Even consecrated self is still only helpless self and can bring only shipwreck rather than victory or power.

Romans 12:1 states what every believer needs to do: "I beseech you therefore, brethren, by the mercies of God, that ye present your bodies a living sacrifice, holy, acceptable unto God, which is your reasonable service." Note that we are told "present your bodies." But how are we to present them? We are to present them as "a living sacrifice." These are the key elements in this verse. It is not enough just to present our bodies to the Lord; we must present them as living sacrifices. In a way, "a living sacrifice" is a paradox. Normally a sacrifice is dead. God doesn't want us to physically die; instead, He wants us to die to self and in this way be "a living sacrifice" for Him. Moses had presented his body, but he did not yet recognize what it was to be "a living sacrifice." Neither have many well-meaning Christian workers today learned this lesson, and that is why their work is so often ineffective.

Dead to Self; Alive to God

Just as Moses needed to learn to be dead to self and alive to God, so every believer today needs to recognize the truth of Romans 6, which emphasizes these two elements. Verse 6 says, "Knowing this, that our old man is crucified with him, that the body of sin might be destroyed, that henceforth we should not serve sin." Having died to sin with the death of Christ, we then need to live to God. This element is emphasized in verse 11: "Likewise reckon ye also yourselves to be dead indeed unto sin, but alive unto God through Jesus Christ our Lord."

The two elements of being dead to sin and self and alive to God are also stressed in Galatians 2:20: "I am crucified with Christ: nevertheless I live; yet not I, but Christ liveth in me: and the life which I now live in the flesh I live by the faith of the Son of God, who loved me, and gave himself for me." In the original language these verses—Romans 6:6,11; and Galatians 2:20—refer to the believer's death with Christ as a past, completed act.

So often Christians say that they want to die to this or that. If you have had similar thoughts, then you need to realize that you have already died to these things in Jesus Christ. Therefore, claim this fact and recognize yourself alive to God. Although death normally follows life, in the spiritual realm living follows dying. When we trust Jesus Christ as personal Saviour, we participate in His death and die to the old man, but we also participate in His resurrection and are made alive to God. Only as we recognize that we have died with Christ are we able to live the resurrected life as God wants us to live it. If we are constantly thinking about dying to what we have already died to, then we cannot focus our attention on living for God. We need to count the dying as a past fact and then move forward in glorifying God in our daily lives. (Read again Romans 6:11-13.)

After Paul received Jesus Christ as personal Saviour, he considered himself to be dead to the things of the past life and to be living for the single purpose of glorifying God. We read Paul's testimony in Philippians 3:7,8: "But what things were gain to me, those I counted loss for Christ. Yea doubtless, and I count all things but loss for the excellency of the knowledge of Christ Jesus my Lord: for whom I have suffered the loss of all things, and so count them but dung, that I may win Christ." As Paul considered his past with his prestigious qualifications, he considered them all mere refuse. His burning desire as a Christian was to know Jesus Christ as his life and his Lord. Paul had no confidence in the flesh whatsoever; his confidence was only in Jesus Christ, who indwelt him (Col. 1:27,29).

In Moses we have a clear illustration of the helplessness of a consecrated life which does not know vital union with God. It is in reality only the consecrated self-life, so it is still self. God will not—and cannot—use any of a person's self-life.

Although God uses the individual's personality, God refuses to use the person who relies on self instead of Him. When a person is under the control of the indwelling Holy Spirit, God will effectively use that person.

In Romans 7 Paul recorded the struggle that he experienced with the old man. He said, "For I know that nothing good dwells in me, that is, in my flesh; for the wishing is present in me, but the doing of the good is not. For the good that I wish, I do not do; but I practice the very evil that I do not wish. But if I'm doing the very thing I do not wish, I am no longer the one doing it, but sin which dwells in me. I find then the principle that evil is present in me, the one who wishes to do good. For I joyfully concur with the law of God in the inner man, but I see a different law in the members of my body, waging war against the law of my mind, and making me a prisoner of the law of sin which is in my members" (vv. 18-23, NASB).

After recording this frustrating struggle at this time of his life, Paul added: "Wretched man that I am! Who will set me free from the body of this death?" (v. 24, NASB). Paul answered his own question in the next verse: "Thanks be to God through Jesus Christ our Lord!" (NASB). This provided the basis for Paul's being able to say, "For the law of the Spirit of life in Christ Jesus has set you free from the law of sin and of death" (8:2, NASB).

Reasons for Disappointment

At the time that Moses surrendered himself to God and to the deliverance of his people, he must have wondered where God was in his crisis. He had left all to follow God and to deliver the Israelites, but the Israelites refused to accept him as the deliverer. God was apparently absent when this test came, but He only *seemed* to be absent. Perhaps Moses even wondered if the hope he had for delivering the people was all a mere illusion. Quite possibly, he also questioned his own call by God. All Moses could do at that moment was to give up and flee for his life. And God allowed this to happen, for He still had a greater purpose to accomplish with Moses. It was Moses' disappointment, but it became God's appointment. God allowed Moses to become so disappointed

and disillusioned that he had to flee. Then God could give
him private schooling in the desert.

This is the way God sometimes has to work with us.
Occasionally He has to allow great disappointments and even
permit us to go backward for a time so we can get our eyes
fixed on Him to go forward as we should. God allows this
because He wants to train us in a better school.

In Moses' case, he was on the backside of the desert for
the next 40 years being molded into what God wanted him
to be. He learned there what he could not learn anywhere
else, and he learned by being alone with God. In this process
he learned that God alone was going to accomplish His own
purposes concerning Israel. Moses learned that it was to be
entirely God's undertaking to emancipate His people. Moses
eventually realized that God was the God of the universe and
that He alone could, and would, deliver Israel and bring
judgment upon the Egyptians.

Someone once said, "If it were Moses versus Egypt, then
poor Moses; but if it were God in Moses versus Egypt, then
poor Egypt!"

As the Bible records the life of Moses, it does it in a way
that is not common in biographies written by man. The Scriptures record the weaknesses as well as the strengths. So often
human biographies reveal only that which is glamorous or a
strength to the person involved; they seldom focus attention
on the failures and faults. But the Scriptures, inspired by the
Holy Spirit, are faithful in recording both aspects of Moses.

Moses was truly a wonderful character and later
expressed extraordinary faith, yet the Holy Spirit did not
conceal his defects. Moses displayed true heroism when he
stepped down from Pharaoh's throne to join his own people,
who were slaves of Egypt. However, he had much to learn
before he could fulfill the task to which God had called him.
Later, Moses knew the ways of God, for God had made them
known to him. Psalm 103:7 says concerning God. "He made
known his ways unto Moses." As a result Moses was
empowered and used as very few have been used.

Psalm 77:20 reveals something beautiful concerning
Moses, for the psalmist expresses to God: "Thou leddest thy
people like a flock by the hand of Moses." Think of it! Moses
was like the hand of God in leading the people of Israel.

Moses eventually became like God's hand—he did whatever God wanted him to do, even as our hands do what we want them to do.

But Moses could not be compared to God's hand when he fled into the desert after killing the Egyptian. At that time he was full of his own ways and ideas, and he acted in his own strength. He was such a man of God later, but at that point he was full of self—rash, impetuous and headstrong. God is faithful in showing us this side of Moses as well as his strong side. When Moses was through his private school of training in the desert, he was the meekest man who ever lived (Num. 12:3). He would not thrust himself forward or intrude where he was not commanded to go. He was completely changed, and he became a tremendous man of God. We must remember that when the Bible refers to Moses as the meekest man who ever lived, it is not referring to him at the age of 40 but at the age of 80—after God had finished training him.

Moses became conscious of his own weaknesses, and then in every step he looked to God for guidance and power. Moses had already received excellent training, first in his own home and then in the courts of Egypt. But he was relying on his training rather than on God and had not yet learned to ask for God's counsel in every step he was to take.

Each of us must carefully consider the instructions in Proverbs 3:5-7: "Trust in the Lord with all thine heart; and lean not unto thine own understanding. In all thy ways acknowledge him, and he shall direct thy paths. Be not wise in thine own eyes: fear the Lord, and depart from evil." These are truths that Moses had to learn, and they are truths we desperately need to learn.

Notice other verses in Proverbs that give us counsel in this regard: "The fear of the Lord is the beginning of knowledge" (1:7); "The Lord giveth wisdom: out of his mouth cometh knowledge and understanding" (2:6); "Happy is the man that findeth wisdom, and the man that getteth understanding" (3:13).

The Lord has promised to guide those who serve Him, and we must have His guidance if we are to succeed in His work. God tells us: "I will instruct thee and teach thee in the way which thou shalt go: I will guide thee with mine eye" (Ps. 32:8). What a wonderful truth! God sees beyond today, and He will guide us in what we should do as we are sensitive to His will. We can see only what is happening today, but He sees tomorrow and the days to follow. What a comfort this is as we rest in Him for the future.

Psalm 25 has been of much help to me, and I have turned to it dozens of times when in need of leadership from the Lord. Verse 9 says, "The meek will he guide in judgment: and the meek will he teach his way." Verse 12 says, "What man is he that feareth the Lord? him shall he teach in the way that he shall choose." The fear referred to in this verse is a reverential trust in the Lord. The psalmist goes on to say: "His soul shall dwell at ease; and his seed shall inherit the earth. The secret of the Lord is with them that fear him; and he will show them his covenant" (vv. 13,14).

Moses had potential to be the man of God, as he is later referred to, but he needed special training at this time. Because Moses was pliable, teachable and moldable, he learned his lessons well and became the man of God the Scriptures say he was. How sad it is when a person is not teachable; there is no hope for that kind of person. But Moses was open to what God wanted to do with his life, even though it took many long, lonely years of waiting and trials before his strong and self-reliant nature could be broken and he could be shaped into a vessel appropriate for his Master's use. But by a process God prepared Moses for the great work He had for him to do.

God also has work for us to do, and He supplies all our needs to perform it. Second Corinthians 9:8 tells us: "God is able to make all grace abound toward you; that ye, always having all sufficiency in all things, may abound to every good work." We must remember that all of God's work on earth can be done only by chosen and prepared instruments. What a wonderful privilege it is to serve God in this way. God could have used other means, but He chooses to use people to accomplish His purpose, and we benefit from the privilege.

We learn much concerning the ways of God with His own as we evaluate the basic causes for Moses' failure. These provide valuable lessons for us and reveal pitfalls we need to avoid. There are at least four which we need to consider at this time.

Human Sympathy

First, Moses' desire to deliver his people sprang from human sympathy. As he visited his people, he saw how they were mistreated by the Egyptians, and he was filled with pity for them. But that pity soon turned to indignation against the oppressor as he retaliated in behalf of his fellow Israelites. He meant well by his act of defending an oppressed Israelite, but when he killed the Egyptian it revealed the emotion bottled up within him. At the time of this incident he did what he was in the habit of doing—he exercised his authority. But impulsive action stemming from pity could never be strong enough to sustain him through the grueling years in the desert that he would later experience as Israel's leader. God, looking ahead, knew all that would happen, and He could not use a man who had only pity.

Pity, in itself, is not wrong. But if Moses had only the impulse of pity, he would have given up under the pressure of constant provocation by his people after they were delivered from Egypt. Nor could Moses have asked God to blot him out of His book for the sake of his people if he had only pity (Ex. 32:30-35). No man, apart from Christ, ever interceded for another man as Moses did for his people.

Moses had much to learn about distinguishing between pity for a people and God's determined purpose for a people. God was not moving Israel to their land out of pity for them because of the Egyptian oppression; in fact, God allowed this condition to come upon the Israelites because He had a purpose in it. He was preparing His people for the great exodus out of Egypt. God was accomplishing a special purpose with His people, and there could not be any failure. So the person chosen to lead them out had to be one who was prepared for everything that would arise. And just the quality of pity would not qualify Moses to be what God wanted him to be.

Even from our experience at Back to the Bible we have seen that pity is not enough. For instance, in the early years of the ministry we endeavored to carry on a missionary program by having various missionaries speak on the program. As they appealed for help they told some interesting stories of the conditions on the mission fields, but this aroused mostly pity from the listeners. Although there was some response because of the pity involved, it soon died out because the people were acting on the basis of feeling rather than on the basis of what God wanted them to do. They lacked true biblical conviction. It wasn't until we saw the need of consistent, solid missions teaching that we were able to establish a sound missions program. All of us need to respond not just out of pity but out of true conviction and commitment to God, because we have seen what He wants to accomplish in the world. Our giving to the Lord's work should not be based on a momentary feeling of pity but on solid conviction and commitment to do what God's Word says we should do.

We must learn to sacrifice the mere natural impulse and saturate our minds and souls with a strong sense of what is right, in spite of the circumstances of the moment. This is the key to doing God's will. If we know we are in the direct will of God, no treatment of man—whether good or bad—will make any difference. We will be determined to accomplish God's will regardless of the circumstances.

David exemplified this principle. Although he had many kinds of opposition from others, he was determined to do God's will. Notice his words in Psalm 56: "When I am afraid, I will put my trust in Thee. In God, whose word I praise, in God I have put my trust; I shall not be afraid. What can mere man do to me? All day long they distort my words; all their thoughts are against me for evil. They attack, they lurk, they watch my steps, as they have waited to take my life. . . . Thy vows are binding upon me, O God; I will render thank offerings to Thee. For Thou hast delivered my soul from death, Indeed my feet from stumbling, so that I may walk before God in the light of the living" (vv. 3 6,12,13, NASB). David's confidence was in God and in His purpose and plan.

When Moses learned that the deliverance of Israel was really God's undertaking, not his, he was able to stand up under all the provocation of the people during the many years in the desert. One of the purposes of the 40 years alone in the desert with God was to show Moses that pity was not enough.

Premature Action

A second reason for Moses' failure in the 40th year of his life was that his action was premature. He had zeal for his own people, but it was not based on knowledge. He was in too big a hurry—he was running ahead of God. According to the schedule God gave Abraham in Genesis 15, it was not yet time for Israel to be delivered from Egypt. At least 40 more years had to pass, and the iniquity of the Amorites was not yet full (v. 16). Even in this reference to the Amorites we see the grace and longsuffering of God. He wanted to give these people time to repent of their evil deeds and turn to Him.

Moses was also ahead of schedule as far as his own education was concerned. It would take at least 40 more years to take away his self-will and self-reliance and to be taught to rely only on the Lord. Moses had the best education the world had to offer, for he "was learned in all the wisdom of the Egyptians" (Acts 7:22). But he still needed personalized training by God Himself for this great task of delivering the Israelites from Egypt.

Moses' action was also premature in that the Israelites were not ready to leave Egypt. Although they complained about their Egyptian oppressors, they were not really ready to leave Egypt and begin all over again in a new country. So it was necessary for God to work with the Israelites as well as with Moses before they were ready to leave Egypt.

How hard it is to wait for God's time. Moses thought he was ready to deliver the Israelites from Egypt, and he saw no need for waiting. But he was not sensitive to God's timing.

We also experience the difficulty of waiting on God's timing as we pray for the salvation of loved ones. Perhaps we've prayed for years that they might come to know Jesus Christ as Saviour, and we can't understand why there does not seem to be any progress. All we can do is wait on God's timing. Our responsibility is to see that they know the message of salvation and that we are living in a manner that is consistent with God's Word.

Jesus Christ Himself was the perfect example of waiting on the timing of His Heavenly Father. More than once He responded: "My time is not yet come." The disciples were overanxious about wanting Christ to accomplish His mission immediately, but Christ was content to wait on the Father's timing. Before the Lord Jesus ascended to heaven, the disciples asked: "Wilt thou at this time restore again the kingdom to Israel?" (Acts 1:6). The Lord answered them, "It is not for you to know the times or the seasons, which the Father hath put in his own power" (v. 7). Even as far as establishing the kingdom of God on earth, the Lord Jesus was willing to wait for the perfect timing of the Father.

Since it was not yet God's time to deliver Israel from Egypt, Moses acted prematurely in killing the Egyptian who was fighting with the Israelite. But when it was God's time to deliver Israel, God used Moses to destroy all of Egypt. When Moses acted in his own strength, it was one man against one man, but when Moses acted in the Lord's strength, it was God through Moses against all of Egypt.

Human Strength

A third reason for Moses' failure to deliver Israel in his 40th year was that his action was executed in human strength. Moses did not yet know what was necessary for him to know about strength and power originating from God. As potential king of Egypt, Moses was accustomed to acting in his own strength because he had the power to do so. He held various high positions in government—the head of Egypt's military forces, for one. He was accustomed to simply saying "Do this" and seeing it done. With his leadership ability and the power to carry out his will, he just assumed that the Israelites would recognize him as their leader to deliver them from the Egyptians. He seemed sure that his fellow Israelites would understand that, under his leadership, they would make the nation of oppressors reel and fall before his blows. He would thus be hailed as their God sent deliverer.

It is apparent that Moses planned a deliverance by force. However, his method was not God's method. It was not going to be an insurrection on the part of Israel, nor was it going to be a system of assassination which Moses had already begun. Having killed one Egyptian, Moses expected the Israelites to turn to him for leadership, but the following day he was rebuffed by a fellow Israelite for what he had done.

Moses needed to learn the truth of Zechariah 4:6: "Not by might, nor by power, but by my spirit, saith the Lord of hosts." God's method of operation is not human might but His Holy Spirit.

We must not think that Moses' later success in leading Israel was due to his natural abilities and training. Although God used these as they were properly surrendered to Him, Moses' success resulted from relying on God, not on himself.

We see this truth illustrated in the Bible in the life of Gideon, as recorded in Judges 7. When Gideon went to war against the Midianites, he had an army of 32,000 men. With an army like that, God knew that the Israelites would glory in their own strength when they won the battle. So He instructed Gideon to eliminate soldiers by various means until there were only 300 left. Such a small army realized the need to rely on God and that any victory would have to be of God. It obviously wasn't the strength of the army or Gideon's military brilliance but God alone who brought victory to the small band.

This reveals the principle that God cannot use some people because they are too big for Him; that is, they have too much confidence in themselves. God does not share His glory with another. He does not give or entrust His power to others until they are humbled and emptied of any consciousness of their own self-reliance. As they are conscious of their own helplessness and turn to God, He then becomes the needed strength. This is why Ephesians 6:10 says, "Be strong in the Lord, and in the power of his might."

Jesus Himself was a perfect example of One who emptied Himself and relied totally on the Heavenly Father. The Bible says concerning Christ: "Who, although He existed in the form of God, did not regard equality with God a thing to be grasped, but emptied Himself, taking the form of a bondservant, and being made in the likeness of men. And being found in appearance as a man, He humbled Himself by becoming obedient to the point of death, even death on a cross" (Phil. 2:6-8, NASB).

Because the Lord Jesus willingly emptied Himself, He was later able to say, "All power is given unto me in heaven and in earth" (Matt. 28:18). The word translated "power" means "authority." So Christ was really saying, "All authority is given to Me in heaven and in earth." Christ is the final word. Here he tells us to go, but He promises to be with us in this authority. After He had humbled Himself, it is said of Him: "Therefore also God highly exalted Him, and bestowed on Him the name which is above every name, that at the name of Jesus every knee should bow, of those who are in heaven, and on earth, and under the earth" (Phil. 2:9,10, NASB).

God's way is not always man's way, as is indicated in I Corinthians 1:18: "For the preaching of the cross is to them that perish foolishness; but unto us which are saved it is the power of God." The "preaching of the cross" not only refers to the preaching of Jesus Christ, who was crucified for our sins, but it also refers to the fact that we were crucified with Him. Teaching both aspects of the cross, which involves death to self and life to God, is not always popular. In fact, the people who reject it consider it to be foolishness. But those who have trusted Jesus Christ as Saviour and Lord recognize it as the power of God. First Corinthians 1 goes on to say: "For it is written, I will destroy the wisdom of the wise, and will bring to nothing the understanding of the prudent. Where is the wise? Where is the scribe? Where is the disputer of this world? Hath not God made foolish the wisdom of this world?" (vv. 19,20).

That God operates in different ways than man in order to show His glory is also indicated in I Corinthians 1:27,28: "For consider your call, brethren, that there were not many wise according to the flesh, not many mighty, not many noble; but God has chosen the foolish things of the world to shame the wise, and God has chosen the weak things of the world to shame the things which are strong, and the base things of the world and the despised, God has chosen, the things that are not, that He might nullify the things that are" (NASB).

The reason that God works in such a way is clear from the following verse: "That no flesh should glory in his presence" (NASB).

The Apostle Paul also realized the need for relying completely on the Lord. Although he was bothered by weaknesses, Paul finally came to realize: "When I am weak, then am I strong" (II Cor. 12:10). Paul recognized that the key to his strength lay in his weaknesses. God is unable to use a person as a channel for His work when that person relies on his own sufficiency. We are not sufficient by ourselves, and God cannot use us as He desires until we recognize this fact. Ephesians 1:19 alludes to this truth when it says: "What is the exceeding greatness of his power to us-ward who believe, according to the working of his mighty power." Notice that it is "his power" and "according to the working of his mighty power."

So to be used of God, we must come to the end of ourselves. This involves an act of the will and faith. We must determine—not just feel—that we are nothing but that in God we can be something. This is not necessarily a gift but a process of learning. That's why it took Moses 40 years to really learn this great lesson. So much was at stake in emancipating the people of Israel that it was extremely important that God not use Moses until he had learned his lesson well.

Apprehensive of Others' Judgment

The fourth reason God was not able to use Moses at this time was that Moses was too apprehensive of what others thought. The Bible says, "He looked this way and that way, and when he saw that there was no man, he slew the Egyptian, and hid him in the sand" (Ex. 2:12). This verse indicates that Moses' conscience was not clear; he was obviously not sure that he was in the will of God. He simply took matters into his own hands and did what he thought he should do.

Moses had no direct orders from God to kill the Egyptian. When a person is unsure of God's will he is usually apprehensive concerning what others say or think about his actions. If Moses had known with certainty that he was within the will of God, he would not have been concerned about what others thought. Moses' eye was not on God but on man, and "the fear of man bringeth a snare" (Prov. 29:25).

After killing the Egyptian and hiding him in the sand, the Bible says, "When he [Moses] went out the second day, behold, two men of the Hebrews strove together: and he said to him that did the wrong, Wherefore smitest thou thy fellow? And he said, Who made thee a prince and judge over us? intendest thou to kill me, as thou killedst the Egyptian? And Moses feared, and said, Surely this thing is known" (Ex. 2:13,14). Even Pharaoh knew what Moses had done and tried to have Moses killed because of it.

Consider the words "Moses feared" (v. 14). This fear was the result of not following the Lord's will. When one does not follow the Lord's will, he becomes concerned about what men think, and this brings fear.

This is why God told Joshua: "Have not I commanded thee? Be strong and of a good courage; be not afraid, neither be thou dismayed: for the Lord thy God is with thee whithersoever thou goest" (Josh. 1:9). There is no reason to fear when one has his eyes fixed on the Lord. The Lord also told Jeremiah: "Thou therefore gird up thy loins, and arise, and speak unto them all that I command thee: be not dismayed at their faces, lest I confound thee before them. For behold, I have made thee this day a defenced city, and an iron pillar, and brasen walls against the whole land, against the kings of Judah, against the princes thereof, against the priests thereof, and against the people of the land. And they shall fight against thee; but they shall not prevail against thee; for I am with thee, saith the Lord, to deliver thee" (Jer. 1:17-19).

We also have the example of the Lord Jesus Christ. He never looked "this way" or "that way," nor did He hide what He was doing. He received His orders from the Heavenly Father, so He was able to say, "I do nothing of myself; but as my Father hath taught me, I speak these things. And he that sent me is with me: the Father hath not left me alone; for I do always those things that please him" (John 8:28,29).

Notice also the encouraging words of Proverbs 4:25-27: "Let thine eyes look right on, and let thine eyelids look straight before thee. Ponder the path of thy feet, and let all thy ways be established. Turn not to the right hand nor to the left: remove thy foot from evil."

Thus we see that believers need to keep their eyes on God, and then they will have no need to look in other directions to see what others are thinking. May we follow Christ's example and not do our own will "but the will of the Father" (John 5:30; 6:38).

The Bible speaks of this as keeping one's eye single. Matthew 6:22 says, "The light of the body is the eye: if therefore thine eye be single, thy whole body shall be full of light." Having singleness of eye means to have one's eye fixed on only one object; and for the Christian that object should be Jesus Christ.

Moses had to learn to keep his eyes fixed only on God rather than trusting in his own training and abilities. Moses became worried that Pharaoh might take vengeance on him for killing the Egyptian. Moses would have remembered well that the present pharaoh was on the throne only because Moses had declined it and that the present pharaoh was anxious to eliminate him. Pharaoh probably had his spies out, waiting for an opportunity to trap Moses in some act that would incriminate him. There was no doubt about it— Pharaoh knew that Moses had killed the Egyptian and had given orders to have Moses killed in return. The Bible says, "When Pharaoh heard this thing, he sought to slay Moses" (Ex. 2:15).

Being afraid of what would happen, there was nothing else Moses could do except flee. But even in this we notice the wonderful providence of God, for He had already prepared a place for His servant. Exodus 2:15 says, "Moses fled from the face of Pharaoh, and dwelt in the land of Midian: and he sat down by a well."

As the biblical narrative continues, we see how God's sovereign purpose was being accomplished: "Now the priest of Midian had seven daughters: and they came and drew water, and filled the troughs to water their father's flock. And the shepherds came and drove them away: but Moses stood up and helped them, and watered their flock. And when they came to Reuel their father, he said, How is it that ye are come so soon to day? And they said, An Egyptian delivered us out of the hand of the shepherds, and also drew water enough for us, and watered the flock. And he said to his daughters, And where is he? why is it that ye have left the man? call him, that he may eat bread" (vv. 16-20).

God allowed all of this to happen to bring Moses into the exact place He wanted him. God arranged circumstances so

Moses could find a place to stay while God trained him on the backside of the desert. From Genesis 46:34 we know that a shepherd was an abomination to the Egyptians, but this is precisely what God was preparing Moses to become. But at this time Moses did not know what would happen; his only concern was to get away from the Egyptian pharaoh who was trying to kill him. As a shepherd he was an outcast to the Egyptians, so they would not likely harm Moses even if they found him. Moses had fallen as far as he could on the social ladder of Egypt—from a potential king to a despised shepherd.

Moses' First Lesson

God did not falter because Moses had run ahead of him. In fact, God had permitted Moses to do so in order to teach him the first of the many lessons he had to learn. Of course, all of this was in God's master plan to train Moses to be what He wanted him to be.

Moses' first lesson concerned the matter of dependence rather than independence. He needed to learn to rely on his union with God rather than on himself. At this time Moses didn't fully realize that God was Captain of the host of the Lord.

This was a lesson that other great men of the Bible had to learn. They had to realize in a practical way that God is at the head of all things. Later, Joshua learned this same truth. The Bible says, "And it came to pass, when Joshua was by Jericho, that he lifted up his eyes and looked, and, behold, there stood a man over against him with his sword drawn in his hand: and Joshua went unto him, and said unto him, Art thou for us, or for our adversaries? And he said, Nay; but as captain of the host of the Lord am I now come. And Joshua fell on his face to the earth, and did worship, and said unto him, What saith my lord unto his servant? And the captain of the Lord's host said unto Joshua, Loose thy shoe from off thy foot; for the place whereon thou standest is holy. And Joshua did so" (Josh. 5:13-15).

This account shows how Joshua was taught that God is the head of everything. In effect, God said to Joshua, "Joshua, you need to know that this battle is not going to be your battle; I'm taking over, and I'm going to lead the forces." God uses men, but the men He uses must rely totally on Him.

This is what Moses had to learn also. He had to realize that nothing substitutes for surrendering to God personally. Moses had surrendered to a task and to a people, but he had not really surrendered to God Himself. Without question, Moses was sincere, but he still lacked knowledge of God's ways of working.

So often I've heard young missionaries say, "I surrendered to the Lord to go to Africa" or "I surrendered to the Lord to go to South America." No doubt they are sincere in what they say, and I do not wish to belittle their surrender to the Lord to go to a mission field. But I am concerned that we realize our surrender is to be to the Lord totally with no strings attached. If we surrender to the Lord with a specific place in mind, we're likely to question the leading of the Lord if we're unable to serve in that place. But if we surrender totally to God Himself, He may lead us anywhere according to His divine plan. The important thing is to be totally dependent on God and not challenge or question Him concerning where He leads us.

The Bible stresses the need of a believer to surrender himself to the Person of God. The following are some of the statements that emphasize this: "Submit yourselves therefore to God" (James 4:7); "Present your bodies a living sacrifice, holy, acceptable unto God" (Rom. 12:1); "Commit thy way unto the Lord; trust also in him" (Ps. 37:5); "Ye are complete in him" (Col. 2:10).

Job expressed what it is to surrender to the Person of God when he said, "I have heard of thee by the hearing of the ear: but now mine eye seeth thee. Wherefore I abhor myself, and repent in dust and ashes" (Job 42:5,6).

Responses to Surrender

It is interesting to study the responses of those who have seen the need to be totally surrendered to God alone. This caused Isaiah to say, "I am undone; because I am a man of unclean lips, and I dwell in the midst of a people of unclean lips: for mine eyes have seen the King, the Lord of hosts"

(Isa. 6:5). Before Jeremiah saw the Lord in this way, he said, "I cannot speak: for I am a child" (Jer. 1:6). But after Jeremiah realized the enabling power of God and the need to surrender to Him alone, he became one of the great prophets of the Old Testament.

Paul saw the Lord on the road to Damascus, and he "trembling and astonished said, Lord, what wilt thou have me to do?" (Acts 9:6). This should be the response of every person who sees the Lord in His holiness and surrenders to Him.

We, too, must realize that God is everything; He alone originates and forms the work, although He uses surrendered people. This is illustrated many times in the Scriptures. Later, at the crossing of the Red Sea, God used Moses, but it was God who performed the miracle and delivered Israel (Ex. 14). In Israel's battle with Amalek, God used Joshua on the battlefield and Moses up in the mountain praying, but it was God who won the battle (ch. 17). In the wilderness journeying of the Israelites, water came from a rock to quench their thirst. Although He used Moses, God gave the water (ch. 17). In the conquering of the first city after the Israelites entered Canaan, He used Joshua, but God was totally responsible for the destruction of the city (Josh. 6).

Earlier, we considered Gideon, who began with an army of 32,000 but had it trimmed down to 300. There was no doubt in this case that although Gideon was the instrument, the victory was totally of God (Judg. 7). As the Apostle Paul was on a ship during a storm at sea, he was able to tell the passengers and crew, "For there shall be no loss of any man's life among you, but of the ship. For there stood by me this night the angel of God, whose I am, and whom I serve, saying, Fear not, Paul, thou must be brought before Caesar: and, lo, God hath given thee all them that sail with thee" (Acts 27:22-24). God used Paul, but it was evident that God alone saved the lives of those involved.

Since God uses surrendered people, it is important that we be surrendered to Him for whatever He wants us to do, but we need to realize that the ultimate victory is due to Him alone.

So Moses fled into the desert where, instead of bemoaning his sad plight, he learned to know God. He had to become nothing so God could be all in all. May this be our desire also—to know God thoroughly so we will realize that He is all we need.

Chapter 7

Moses in God's Private School

Because Moses feared for his life, he fled to the desert, which really became his entrance into God's private school. Hebrews 11:27 says, "By faith he forsook Egypt, not fearing the wrath of the king." But this verse does not refer to Moses' leaving Egypt at this time. He was greatly afraid of the king, because the king was seeking to kill him. Hebrews 11:27 refers to a time 40 years later after God had accomplished His work with him. In his own strength, Moses had killed an Egyptian, but this accomplished nothing as far as Israel's deliverance was concerned. Forty years later, under the power of God, Moses was used to destroy all of Egypt. What a difference 40 years can make when they are spent under the private tutorship of God.

What caused this difference? First, there was the time element of 40 years. This, of course, is not the entire answer, because some people experience little spiritual progress in 40 years. If they found themselves in Moses' situation, many would give up in despair and say, "What's the use? I tried to serve the Lord, but it didn't work." I've seen this type of thing happen. Young people ready to go to the mission field have become completely overwhelmed by some obstacle that delayed their departure. Some immediately drew the conclusion that God didn't want them on the mission field after all.

This kind of thinking was not characteristic of Moses. During the 40 years he spent in God's private school, Moses received an even greater burden to deliver his people. At the end of the 40 years, he was God's choice instrument ready to be used in giving leadership to Israel.

The Big Difference

The key difference that 40 years made is seen in the first two words of Hebrews 11:27, "By faith." Because Moses learned to know God so well during the 40 years in the wilderness, he had sufficient faith to endure all that he had to face in later years.

Think of the faith that Moses had to have. He was willing to take the Israelites—numbering about 3 million—into the desert where there would be no provisions other than what God would miraculously give. Moses looked beyond this present world, "seeing him who is invisible" (Heb. 11:27). Moses had his eyes fixed on eternal values, not temporal values. In particular, he had his eyes fixed on God Himself.

If Moses had such faith after his return from the desert at age 80, why did he not have such faith when he first surrendered at age 40? Faith is impossible when we are not in God's direct plan and, therefore, cannot stand on God's promises. To have faith, we must fulfill the conditions of faith; we must meet the requirements that God says are necessary. This involves not only hearing God's Word but reckoning it to be true and then obeying what it says. This is faith in action.

This is true not only for salvation but also for the Christian life. Concerning salvation, John 5:24 says, "He that heareth my word, and believeth on him that sent me, hath everlasting life, and shall not come into condemnation; but is passed from death unto life." Notice the phrase, "He that heareth my word." It is necessary to know what God's Word is in order to know how to respond.

Believers often wonder how they can have a greater faith in God. Romans 10:17 answers this: "Faith cometh by hearing, and hearing by the word of God." If we want to increase our faith, we must increase our knowledge of the Word of God and thereby our knowledge of God Himself. Then we must act on what we know. We are to count God's Word as true—reckon on it, ponder it, and then act.

When Moses failed God by running ahead of Him, it would have been useless for him to have wept about his problem. Nothing is gained by shedding tears over failure that is due to unbelief or sin. The Bible records an example which proves this very fact. After the Israelites had been defeated at Ai, "Joshua rent his clothes, and fell to the earth upon his face before the ark of the Lord until the eventide, he and the elders of Israel, and put dust upon their heads" (Josh. 7:6). As Joshua cried out to the Lord, notice how the Lord responded: "The Lord said unto Joshua, Get thee up; wherefore liest thou thus upon thy face? Israel hath sinned, and they have also transgressed my covenant which I commanded them: for they have even taken of the accursed thing, and have also stolen, and dissembled also, and they have put it even among their own stuff" (vv. 10,11).

There are times to weep, but when sin is involved, confession and obedience are needed.

Faith becomes a natural matter when we have determined the will of God and firmly stand on His promises. Only as he took such a position could the Apostle Paul say, "I can do all things through Christ which strengtheneth me" (Phil. 4:13).

When the disciples came to Jesus and asked why they were not able to cast out a demon, He answered: "Because of your unbelief: for verily I say unto you, If ye have faith as a grain of mustard seed, ye shall say unto this mountain, Remove hence to yonder place; and it shall remove; and nothing shall be impossible unto you" (Matt. 17:20).

Alone With God

At the time Moses first tried to become Israel's deliverer, he was trained intellectually, militarily and socially in Pharaoh's court. But it took the desert experience to mold him into the man God needed. This was a time of solitude for Moses—alone with God. This is an extremely important kind of training. Too few people are willing to wait on God. As a result, many have zeal without knowledge. After Christ's resurrection, the disciples needed to wait on God rather than to immediately go out to preach the gospel. Christ "commanded them that they should not depart from Jerusalem, but wait for the promise of the Father, which, saith he, ye have heard of me" (Acts 1:4). The promise of the Father to which Christ referred was the coming of the Holy Spirit, which took place on the Day of Pentecost. Christ assured the disciples that when the Holy Spirit came upon them they would receive power and be witnesses for Him (v. 8). In these days, we do not need to wait for the Spirit of God to come since He is now here and indwells every person who receives Christ as Saviour (Rom. 8:9).

The "university" of Egypt had equipped Moses for his work with people in the upper class, but the private "university" of the desert was needed to qualify him for work with the lowly slaves whom he was destined to deliver. The former years of training in Egypt were valuable, and God used this training that Moses received. However, the training in the desert alone with God was not only valuable, it was also indispensable if he was to perform the work God had in mind for him. Those 40 years in the desert were Moses' best years. Because he was in the prime of his life at that time, some might ask, Why waste those years in such a place? According to the world's standards, they definitely seemed to be wasted years. But nothing compares with time spent alone with God. There is an extreme contrast between human and divine education. It is only as we spend time with God that we will really be what He wants us to be.

During the 40 years that He worked with Moses, such a close relationship developed between the two that God spoke with Moses face to face. God told the Israelites: "Hear now my words: If there be a prophet among you, I the Lord will make myself known unto him in a vision, and will speak unto him in a dream. My servant Moses is not so, who is faithful in all mine house. With him will I speak mouth to mouth, even apparently, and not in dark speeches" (Num. 12:6-8). The Bible records concerning Moses: "There arose not a prophet since in Israel like unto Moses, whom the Lord knew face to face" (Deut. 34:10).

In the years that followed the desert experience, there is much evidence that Moses had spent a great deal of time alone with God. Exodus 3:1 says, "Now Moses kept the flock of Jethro his father in law, the priest of Midian: and he led the flock to the backside of the desert, and came to the mountain of God, even to Horeb." This mountain was also known as Mount Sinai. But notice that in this verse it is referred to as the "mountain of God." It was precisely that to Moses, for there was probably a well-worn pathway to the mountaintop where Moses frequently went to meet God.

Have you spent time in the "backside of the desert" with the Lord? I'm not referring to a literal desert but to a place where you can be alone with God—where you can commune with Him and get to know Him better. I have found this to be extremely profitable on a daily basis, and I also occasionally spend two or three days alone with God, my Bible, and perhaps a devotional book. On such occasions I spend a great deal of time in prayer, and I can tell you from experience that nothing compares to being alone with God.

Knowing God Better

Moses knew God so intimately that he communed with Him face to face. Later, when Moses met God at the burning bush, it was evident that Moses had been alone with Him. No novice meets God as Moses met Him there. At the altar one may have a crisis experience, but the kind of knowledge Moses had about God comes only from spending much time together.

The Apostle Paul also had an intense desire to know God better. As Paul reflected on his life, he considered everything in the past as loss and then stated the purpose of his life: "That I may know him, and the power of his resurrection, and the fellowship of his sufferings, being made conformable unto his death" (Phil. 3:10). If we are not just as serious about wanting to know God, there is no way that we will become what He wants us to be.

Some think that Moses wrote the Book of Genesis during these years in the desert. There is no way of knowing for sure, but we do know as we study Moses' life that an important, gradual change took place in his life during those 10 years. He came to rely on the power of God rather than on himself or on armies or on any human resources. He learned to see the wisdom of God as superior to anything he had witnessed in all of Egypt. By the time God gave Moses his personal call at the burning bush, Moses was so deeply convinced of his nothingness that he gave excuse after excuse concerning why he wasn't qualified. But by then he was exactly as God wanted him. This really marked the third crisis of his life as he finally came to the place of settling the issue once and for all—it had to be none of self and all of

God. Realizing this important truth, the songwriter put it this way:

> O the bitter pain and sorrow,
> That a time could ever be,
> When I proudly said to Jesus,
> All of self and none of Thee.
>
> Yet He found me I beheld Him
> Bleeding on th' accursed tree,
> And my wistful heart said faintly,
> Some of self and some of Thee.
>
> Day by day His tender mercies,
> Helping healing full and free
> Brought me lower while I whispered,
> Less of self and more of Thee.
>
> Higher than the highest heaven,
> Deeper than the deepest sea,
> Lord Thy love at last has conquered,
> None of self and all of Thee.
> —Theodore Monroe

The Bible quickly passes over the 40 years that Moses spent alone in the wilderness. God chose to keep secret the intimate times He and Moses had, as well as the trials that Moses experienced in His private school.

Chapter 8

Moses' Call and Commission

When Moses saw the burning bush and decided to investigate why it was not consumed, the Bible says, "And when the Lord saw that he turned aside to see, God called unto him out of the midst of the bush, and said, Moses, Moses. And he said, Here am I" (Ex. 3:4).

Moses' Graduation Day

This dramatic means of catching Moses' attention was God's way of showing Moses that he was about to "graduate" from his 40 years of private schooling in the desert. He had spent those 40 years primarily alone with God, and now he had concluded this stage of his training. God knew that His man was now ready. The time had come, according to God's promise, to deliver Abraham's descendants from Egypt after 400 years of affliction (Gen. 15:13,14). The burning bush incident, therefore, became the setting of God's commissioning service for Moses. It was a "commencement exercise" for Moses, since he had completed his intensive training program in the desert. But even on this significant day, Moses was to learn several important lessons. This event became the great turning point in his life; he was never the same again after his commencement exercise.

There is no indication that the burning bush which caught Moses' attention was anything but an ordinary bush. Surely Moses had seen other bush fires before, but in this instance, the bush continued to burn and yet was not consumed by the fire. The bush shone with the emblem of deity, and from the heart of it came the voice of God addressed directly to Moses.

God called Moses' name twice, which arrested Moses' attention and underscored the need to listen. From that moment on, Moses' entire life would be different. That day brought the call of God on his life that would completely change the course of any plans he had.

In the backside of the desert, Moses had learned his lessons well. Until he had been banished to the desert, emphasis had been on his deeds—his was a life of doing. But his training in the desert had caused him to see the need of having his heart in right relationship with God—he saw the need of being what God wanted him to be. So a great change had taken place in Moses' life—he realized that being was more important than doing, and later he learned that the doing came from the being.

This sight of a bush aglow with inextinguishable fire was to become the occasion of a life-changing encounter with God. The knowledge of God by hearsay was to become knowledge by experience. When Job came to this crucial time in his life, he said, "I have heard of thee by the hearing of the ear: but now mine eye seeth thee" (Job 42:5). Such an experience brought a tremendous change in Job's life, and it was also to bring a tremendous change in Moses' life.

At the burning bush God transformed Moses from an unknown desert shepherd into the greatest and best known leader until Jesus Christ appeared. Moses probably did the greatest work that any person has ever done, including that of the Apostle Paul. Although Paul was a tremendous missionary, he was not called of God to lead about three million people into a desert where they would have to be taken care of by God Himself, or perish.

The years of seclusion and quiet meditation with God in the backside of the desert as a shepherd had really prepared Moses for this moment. God knew this, but Moses did not.

There is a beautiful symbolism in the burning bush. Throughout the Old Testament, fire is frequently a symbol of divine revelation. Later, when the Israelites were gathered around Mount Sinai, the sight of the glory of the Lord was like devouring fire on the top of the mountain in the eyes of the children of Israel (Ex. 24:17).

A lesson is also learned in that the bush which Moses saw burning without being consumed was just an ordinary bush.

However, this ordinary bush became extraordinary because of the glow of the divine presence which revealed itself through the bush. The important thing was not the bush itself, but the fire and the revealed presence of the Lord. Moses had learned that in spite of his colorful past in Egypt, he was really just a common bush in God's eyes. He came to realize that the important thing about his own life was not himself, but the glory of God that was revealed through him. If there was to be true greatness, it had to be God's greatness. If Moses was to stand out among others—even as the bush stood out among others—he had to be in right relationship with the Lord and let that relationship be reflected through his life.

The disciples, before they received the indwelling of the Spirit on the Day of Pentecost, denied the Lord and fled when the enemy surrounded Him. They were cowards. But later their lives were distinctively different. Jesus had foretold that day when He said, "Ye shall receive power, after that the Holy Ghost is come upon you: and ye shall be witnesses unto me" (Acts 1:8). And that is exactly what happened. When the Holy Spirit came upon those men on the Day of Pentecost, they became dynamic witnesses for Jesus Christ.

After God had twice called Moses' name and Moses had answered, God instructed: "Draw not nigh hither: put off thy shoes from off thy feet, for the place whereon thou standest is holy ground. Moreover he said, I am the God of thy father, the God of Abraham, the God of Isaac and the God of Jacob" (Ex. 3:5,6). When he heard this pronouncement, "Moses hid his face; for he was afraid to look upon God" (v. 6).

Qualifications for Service

Moses was soon to discover that the essential qualifications for serving God are unshod feet and a hidden face. Shoes, because they are related to the feet, remind us of self-activity. This characterized Moses in his early years in Egypt, for he had led an active life. During the 40 years in the desert, however, he had learned to wait on God and to be what he ought to be, rather than to be concerned about doing. This truth is also illustrated by Mary and Martha in the New Testament (Luke 10:38-42). Martha was concerned about doing, but Mary was concerned about being. Martha was busy doing something for the Lord, but Mary was concerned about spending time with Him. Jesus told Martha: "Martha, Martha, thou art careful and troubled about many things: but one thing is needful: and Mary hath chosen that good part, which shall not be taken away from her" (vv. 41,42).

So often in our churches today we are over-programmed because we think success lies in programs. But it is more important to spend time with God and to worship Him properly. Service is important, but we must realize that once we allow the Lord to make us what He wants us to be, service will be the natural result. Remember—doing comes from being.

When God spoke to Moses at the burning bush, Moses hid his face. By nature, man wants to turn his face to the limelight. Too often, we are guilty of working for the applause of men; we are too concerned about the reaction of others to what we are doing.

It is difficult for us to learn that we should serve only for the praise of God rather than for the praise of men. Although we at Back to the Bible have been sensitive to this issue over the years, we have had to learn some hard lessons also. And God usually lets us learn these lessons the hard way, because that's the way we remember them best. Like Moses, we, too, need to hide ourselves in the consciousness of our unworthiness. Moses was commanded to take off his shoes—indicating that God was not interested in his activity; and Moses hid his face—indicating that he was intensely aware of his unworthiness before God. These were extremely important lessons that Moses learned while in the desert alone with God.

Just as Moses' attention had to be arrested before God spoke to him, so it is with us—God speaks only to those whose hearts are quiet enough to hear His voice. A recurring phrase throughout the Scriptures is: "He that hath an ear, let him hear" (see Rev. 2:7). It takes quietness of soul and heart to allow the Lord to speak to one through His Word.

Upon hearing the voice of God, Moses trembled and hid his face. Do we react that way before the authoritative voice of God's Word? Moses soon learned that what he had failed to do by revolution, he would be able to do by revelation. That is, he would be able to deliver his fellow Israelites from the oppression of the Egyptians. What he could not accomplish by force, he was able to accomplish by faith.

The heart of the revelation at the burning bush was the ever-present nature of God. We will consider this in more detail later as we examine how God revealed Himself to Moses at this time.

When God spoke, Moses' immediate response was "Here am I" (Ex. 3:4). Are we as ready to hear the voice of God as Moses was? Such readiness results only from spending time alone with God. Only as we are ready to hear the voice of God will we be ready to give His Word to others. This is brought out in Paul's charge to Timothy: "Preach the word; be instant in season, out of season; reprove, rebuke, exhort with all longsuffering and doctrine. For the time will come when they will not endure sound doctrine; but after their own lusts shall they heap to themselves teachers, having itching ears; and they shall turn away their ears from the truth, and shall be turned unto fables" (II Tim. 4:2-4).

God's Plan for Moses and Israel

Having obtained Moses' undivided attention at the burning bush, God then outlined His plan for Moses and Israel. I always thrill when I read this portion of the Scriptures, because I imagine what God's words must have meant to Moses. When Moses was being trained in the Egyptian courts, he saw the terrible plight of his people and wondered how God might use him to deliver them. He had just spent 40 years on the backside of the desert, and undoubtedly, this was a growing burden to him. He must have talked to the Lord many times about the Israelites' need to be delivered from the Egyptians. So when God spoke to Moses at the burning bush and outlined His program for the deliverance of Israel, Moses was probably thrilled beyond words.

God told Moses: "I have surely seen the affliction of my people which are in Egypt, and have heard their cry by reason of their taskmasters; for I know their sorrows; and I am come down to deliver them out of the hand of the Egyptians, and to bring them up out of that land unto a good land and a large, unto a land flowing with milk and honey" (Ex. 3:7,8). Perhaps Moses broke down with emotion as he heard these words from God; he must have wept tears of joy as he heard God's pronouncement that Israel would finally be delivered from Egypt.

As God outlined His program, Moses was made to realize, as we need to realize, that God's work must always begin with God. We cannot plan something and then invite God to give us the power to do it; we are to seek God's will first. Unless a plan originates with God, it is not God's work. We are simply workers whom God has chosen so that He might do His work through us—it is not our duty to decide what work is to be done.

Although Moses must have been overjoyed about God's announcement to deliver Israel, the following statement probably was a shock to him: "Come now therefore, and I will send thee unto Pharaoh, that thou mayest bring forth my people the children of Israel out of Egypt" (v. 10).

From this we see that God always does His work through an individual. In effect, God was telling Moses, "I am going to do something, Moses, but I need a man, and you're the one I have chosen." What a difference there is between God sending a man and a man running ahead of God unsent.

The greatest test of Moses' life came at this point. This was the third crisis in his life. The first had been at his birth, when his parents met the situation by their faith in God. The second crisis was when Moses decided he could no longer be called the son of Pharaoh's daughter. In this third crisis, he was called on to make an extremely important personal decision which called for total commitment to God. To meet this crisis successfully, Moses had to put himself entirely at the disposal of God.

One of the hardest things anyone can do is to go back to the place and the people he once failed. God asked this of Moses. Once Moses thought he could deliver his people by his own power; now he is sent back to them by the hand of God.

When Moses attempted to deliver his people earlier, he was, in effect, asking God to be on his side. Now, however, God was asking Moses to be on His side. What a difference! All too often we are more concerned about God being on our side than we are about being on His side.

Trembling Before God

In the New Testament, when Stephen addressed the Israelites and rehearsed God's dealings with the nation, he told of the incident of the burning bush and specifically mentioned that "Moses trembled" (Acts 7:32). His fear no doubt stemmed from his awe for a holy God whom he had intimately come to know during his 40 years in the desert. Moses' meeting place with God became a special place; it was even known as the "mountain of God" (Ex. 3:1).

In this incident, God was speaking to Moses. The New Testament reveals how God has spoken to us: "God, after He spoke long ago to the fathers in the prophets in many portions and in many ways, in these last days has spoken to us in His Son, whom He appointed heir of all things, through whom also He made the world" (Heb. 1:1,2, NASB). Elsewhere the Book of Hebrews warns: "See that ye refuse not him that speaketh: for if they escaped not who refused him that spake on earth, much more shall not we escape, if we turn away from him that speaketh from heaven: whose voice then shook the earth: but now he hath promised, saying, Yet once more I shake not the earth only, but also heaven" (12:25,26).

On the Isle of Patmos, the Apostle John heard the voice of the Lord and said, "I was in the Spirit on the Lord's day, and heard behind me a great voice, as of a trumpet" (Rev. 1:10). John continued, "I turned to see the voice that spake with me" (v. 12). John then saw that it was the Lord speaking to him. Notice how he reacted: "I fell at his feet as dead" (v. 17). God's Word causes us to tremble when we realize His awesomeness and authority.

God speaks to us today through the Bible, His Word. That is why Romans 10:17 says, "Faith cometh by hearing, and hearing by the word of God." As we read the Word of God we should sense God's awesomeness, for it is as if He were speaking to us audibly. Therefore, we should be quick to hear and quick to obey.

We should also fear to miss the will of God. The Bible says, "Work out your own salvation with fear and trembling" (Phil. 2:12). The psalmist said, "Serve the Lord with fear, and rejoice with trembling" (Ps. 2:11). Isaiah referred to trembling at God's Word: "For all those things hath mine hand made, and all those things have been, saith the Lord: but to this man will I look, even to him that is poor and of a contrite spirit, and trembleth at my word. Hear the word of the Lord, ye that tremble at his word" (Isa. 66:2,5). The psalmist said, "My flesh trembleth for fear of thee; and I am afraid of thy judgments" (119:120).

God speaks to us as firmly today as He spoke to Moses. God says to us through His Word: "Ye have not chosen me, but I have chosen you, and ordained you, that ye should go and bring forth fruit, and that your fruit should remain; that whatsoever ye shall ask of the Father in my name, he may give it you" (John 15:16). Notice that we did not do the choosing; God did the choosing and has committed His ministry to us. Paul reminded all believers that they belong totally to God when he said, "For ye are bought with a price: therefore glorify God in your body, and in your spirit, which are God's" (I Cor. 6:20).

Commissioned by God

Moses was commissioned by God at the burning bush. Let us not forget that believers today are also commissioned by God. We have referred before to Acts 1:8, which records the clear declaration of Christ: "Ye shall receive power, after that the Holy Ghost is come upon you: and ye shall be witnesses unto me." Notice that the Lord did not say "You may be" or "I'm asking you to be"; He said "You will be." Each person who knows Jesus Christ as Saviour is a witness. Some are better witnesses than others, but all are witnesses.

The Apostle Paul also wrote concerning our commission by God to witness for Him. First, however, Paul reminded believers that they were a new creation in Jesus Christ: "Therefore if any man be in Christ, he is a new creature: old things are passed away; behold, all things are become new"

(II Cor. 5:17). Having become a new creature, the believer has been reconciled to God. Paul said that God has "reconciled us to himself by Jesus Christ" (v. 18).

But notice that Paul did not stop at that point. Having declared that we are reconciled to God, he went on to say what God has commissioned us to do: "And hath given to us the ministry of reconciliation; to wit, that God was in Christ, reconciling the world unto himself, not imputing their trespasses unto them; and hath committed unto us the word of reconciliation" (vv. 18,19). So we see that God has committed a definite ministry to us. It is undoubtedly more common for us to consider what we have committed to God, even as Paul said, "I know whom I have believed, and am persuaded that he is able to keep that which I have committed unto him against that day" (II Tim. 1:12). This is an important aspect of our relationship to God, but let us not forget that He has committed something to us—the ministry of reconciliation. He has given us the message of the gospel of Christ, which we are responsible to share with others. Isn't it strange that we are able to talk easily about so many other things, but often find it extremely difficult to talk about the one thing that God has committed to our responsibility? To exercise the ministry of reconciliation, you need not be a preacher, as we often think of preachers. It simply means that you know what God's Word says about the need of others to trust Jesus Christ as personal Saviour and that in your daily contacts you do all you can to communicate this message to them.

Because we have this awesome responsibility, Paul said, "Now then we are ambassadors for Christ" (II Cor. 5:20). When we realize this as we should, we will be desperately concerned—as was the Apostle Paul—that others be reconciled to God. As already indicated, we did not choose this ministry on our own—God chose us and chose this ministry for us, according to John 15:16. But let's also remember the promise that fruit will result as we carry out our responsibility—"that ye should go and bring forth fruit, and that your fruit should remain." How wonderful to realize that God has not only chosen us to carry out a responsibility for Him, but He has promised that fruit will result from what we do and that the fruit will remain.

In II Corinthians 5, where he stated that God has committed to us the ministry of reconciliation, Paul also mentioned the fact that believers would someday give account to God for what they do in this life. Paul said, "For we must all appear before the judgment seat of Christ; that every one may receive the things done in his body, according to that he hath done, whether it be good or bad" (v. 10). This is not a judgment of condemnation, but a judgment where believers' works are evaluated, and they are either rewarded or not rewarded according to what they have done for Christ. Although it is not a judgment of condemnation, Paul saw it as a time of giving serious accounting to God, for he said, "Knowing therefore the terror of the Lord, we persuade men" (v. 11). The word translated "terror" is the Greek word for "fear." So this phrase is really referring to "the fear of the Lord." We should have a reverential fear of the Lord and should fear to miss His will for our lives.

At the burning bush, Moses was intensely aware of his previous failures. "Moses said unto God, Who am I, that I should go unto Pharaoh, and that I should bring forth the children of Israel out of Egypt?" (Ex. 3:11). Moses was aware that he had tried this once and it hadn't worked. He had so thoroughly mastered the lesson of human inadequacy that he was too timid, too reserved and too nonaggressive to respond to the call of God. Before, he had been confident of his own ability, but now he had absolutely no confidence. This is what God had taught him during his 40 years in the desert, but God wanted Moses to respond to Him and to His ability.

The verses following Exodus 3:11 record a deeply revealing dialogue between God and Moses. The once self-sufficient Egyptian prince pleaded total lack of qualification for the task God was calling him to do. Moses was negative, but God was now dealing with him to be positive.

Moses had yet to understand what God meant when He said, "Certainly I will be with thee" (v. 12), and "Thus shalt thou say unto the children of Israel, I Am hath sent me unto you" (v. 14). Before, Moses had been too quick and impetuous; now he was too slow and reluctant. But what a lesson God had for Moses and for us; His purpose will not be thwarted by the whims and moods of His servants.

Chapter 9

The Burning Bush:
The Conquest of Inferiority

Having been given God's call and commission at the burning bush, Moses entered into a deeply revealing dialogue with God. In this dialogue, the once self-sufficient, Egyptian-trained prince pleaded before God that he lacked every qualification to accomplish the task to which God was calling him.

Moses' Excuses

Moses gave seven reasons why he wasn't the man for God's task: lack of capability, lack of message, lack of authority, lack of eloquence, lack of fitness or adaptation, lack of previous success, and lack of previous acceptance. Each of these will be considered in detail as we carefully examine this crucial time in Moses' life.

Without question, all of the excuses Moses gave originated from a genuine sense of insufficiency. Because of this, his reluctance seemed extremely humble and pious—but God was not impressed.

Instead of receiving God's approval, the excuses Moses gave only kindled God's anger. The Bible says, "The anger of the Lord was kindled against Moses" (Ex. 4:14). This does not mean that God had a fit of temper; rather, it means that God was not pleased with the excuses Moses offered. In effect, God was saying, "Moses, you have no right to make these excuses, and if your faith were in the right place and Person, you would not be making them."

Just as God became angry with Moses because of his excuses, so He becomes angry with any believer who limits Him by a lack of faith. Actually, the excuses Moses gave were the exact reasons why God had selected him for the task. Through God's private training of Moses in the desert, Moses was now emptied of self-confidence and self-dependence. This was the kind of person God needed to fulfill His promises. But along with this, Moses had to exercise the genuine faith that would cause him to lean totally on God. Moses had learned well the negative aspect of denying self-dependence; he needed to learn the positive aspect of relying only on God.

For each lack that Moses expressed, God had a satisfying and abundant provision. What Moses failed to understand at this time was that when God calls, He always guarantees and furnishes all that is needed to accomplish His will. This is also true of believers today. When God calls you to do something, He always guarantees and furnishes all you need to do what He asks.

Moses' weaknesses would have been his strengths if he had only learned to rely completely on God. God wanted Moses to rely on Him so He could supply all he needed. To Moses' excuse of lack of capability, God said, in effect, "I'm your capability." To the lack of a message, God said, "I'll give you the message." To the lack of authority, God said, "I'll be your authority." To the lack of eloquence, He said, "I'll be with your mouth, for I made it in the first place." To the lack of fitness or adaptation, God said, "I'll take care of that; I'm all the fitness you need." To the lack of previous success, God said, "I'll be your success." And to the lack of previous acceptance, He said, "That's My responsibility; I'll take care of all these things for you if you will only rely totally on Me. Learn to trust Me completely for every need."

Every believer needs to realize that he is not sufficient in himself to do what God calls him to do. Paul realized this. He said, "Not that we are sufficient of ourselves to think any thing as of ourselves; but our sufficiency is of God" (II Cor. 3:5). But recognizing what we are in Christ caused Paul to write: "I can do all things through Christ which strengtheneth me" (Phil. 4:13). In their time of need, Paul told the Corinthians: "God is able to make all grace abound toward you; that ye, always having all sufficiency in all things, may abound to every good work" (II Cor. 9:8). God is able to do whatever He desires, so we can count on the fact that when He calls He will also supply what is needed to accomplish His will.

God's reassuring promise to Moses was: "Certainly I will be with thee; and this shall be a token unto thee, that I have sent thee: When thou hast brought forth the people out of Egypt, ye shall serve God upon this mountain" (Ex. 3:12). This reassuring promise of God and His later, more complete revelation of Himself were eventually sufficient to convince Moses that all the resources of God were backing him up. He had to learn, and we must learn also, that all of God's work must really begin with Him and must be accomplished by Him, using believers as instruments.

It is God's business to choose the human instrument and then to furnish him with all that is necessary to perform the task He calls him to do. This is the lesson Moses had to learn, and it is the lesson we have to learn. We never have a right to challenge God's choice of His instrument. God tells us: "Ye have not chosen me, but I have chosen you" (John 15:16).

When Moses began his excuses with the statement, "Who am I" (Ex. 3:11), he revealed something other than humility on his part. These words indicated that Moses still lacked the unconditional faith that he needed. He had not yet really seen the Person of God in His program.

Exodus 3:6-10 reveals God's program, but Moses did not fully see the Person of God revealed in the outworking of this program. It is evident throughout this passage that God, by His own power, was going to accomplish the entire work, yet Moses had failed to catch this point.

We are the weakest instrument, but we need to remember that God can take what is weak and accomplish the greatest task if we will only listen to Him and allow Him to do what He wants. The excellency of the instrument does not matter, but it is vitally important that the instrument be invested with the presence and power of God. If it is, it can be used to accomplish tremendous tasks.

Elements in God's Program

Four elements stand out in the program God outlined to Moses. First, God said, "I am the God of thy father, the God of Abraham, the God of Isaac, and the God of Jacob" (Ex. 3:6). This identified God as the same One served by Moses' ancestors. Second, concerning the Israelites, God said, "I have surely seen the affliction of my people which are in Egypt" (v. 7). Third, God revealed His purpose to Moses when He said, "I am come down to deliver them out of the hand of the Egyptians" (v. 8). Fourth, God revealed the specific job He had for Moses when He said, "Come now therefore, and I will send thee unto Pharaoh" (v. 10).

When Moses saw that God's attention focused on him as the individual to be used to deliver Israel, he began to make excuses. Moses had learned that he could not accomplish God's purpose by relying on himself. Even a consecrated self is still only self. But a greater lesson than self-emptying had to be learned by Moses, although the step of self-emptying is basic before one can be filled with God's power. God does not share His glory with another, so He does not fill with power the one who is full of self.

The burning bush serves as a picture of Moses' life. Although the bush continued to burn, it was not consumed. It was an earthly bush aglow with a heavenly fire. In reality, the bush was only fuel for the fire, yet the supply was constantly being renewed.

So, too, Moses was only a common bush to be used by God's power. When Moses was in Egypt, he thought of himself as being a special, uncommon bush. He had special training, ability and authority which he thought would cause his own people to understand how God would use him to deliver them. But they did not understand. Moses had to learn that he was really only a common bush. He had to learn that the significance was not in the bush but in whether it was invested with the presence and power of God. Any bush would have served God's purpose when God chose to set one afire. And any person would have served God's purpose if He had chosen to use him to deliver Israel.

God had promised Moses that He would be with him. God was actually saying, "You are going to be my bush, but

I'm the One who will cause you to burn with the glow of My presence." The evident presence of God is an indication of the authority of God.

God's authority is promised to every believer in the present age. The Lord Jesus Christ said, "All power [authority] is given unto me in heaven and in earth. Go ye therefore, and teach all nations, baptizing them in the name of the Father, and of the Son, and of the Holy Ghost: teaching them to observe all things whatsoever I have commanded you: and, lo, I am with you alway, even unto the end of the world" (Matt. 28:18-20). All authority belongs to Christ, and He has promised to be with us and to give us that authority as we take the gospel to everyone. As He spoke these words to the disciples, they possibly thought, How can we go—we won't be accepted by the people. But the promise of the presence of Christ made all the difference, because it meant that they had His authority.

The writer of Hebrews reminds us of Christ's words: "I will never leave thee, nor forsake thee" (13:5). Because of this promise, the writer said, "So that we may boldly say, The Lord is my helper, and I will not fear what man shall do unto me" (v. 6). No wonder he could conclude his letter with the wonderful benediction: "Now the God of peace, that brought again from the dead our Lord Jesus, that great shepherd of the sheep, through the blood of the everlasting covenant, make you perfect in every good work to do his will, working in you that which is wellpleasing in his sight, through Jesus Christ; to whom be glory for ever and ever" (vv. 20,21). The word translated "perfect" in this passage can have the meaning of "make correct adjustment." This meaning is in keeping with what the Bible says about God working in the believer. This was what Moses had to learn—not only that God would be with him but also that God would be working in him and through him. What a marvelous God we have! Not even a sparrow falls to the ground without Him knowing it, and even the hairs on our heads are numbered. This same God told Moses and tells us: "I will be with you, I will work in you, and I will work through you."

Moses' inferiority was the result of fear—he was afraid he would fail. Moses looked back at his past and was intensely aware that he had failed previously. As God made it clear that he was His man to deliver the Israelites, Moses was afraid he would fail again. He made a wrong estimate of God's promises and provisions. Such a lack of faith is sin. Fear is turned into confidence when a believer realizes that, through the enablement of God, he can do anything God wants him to do. Paul realized this (Phil. 4:13), and we need to realize it also. Not only does such a realization turn fear into confidence, but it also turns weakness into power. Moses also had the fear of man—he was afraid of what others would say or think.

Lessons Moses Had to Learn

Moses had to learn several major lessons before he could be used of God. These are significant lessons for us to consider, because we need to learn them too.

First, Moses had to learn that God's work is to be done by God, not man. God had clearly instructed Moses that He had come to deliver Israel and that He would lead them out. But as Moses realized that God had him in mind as the instrument to lead the people out, he gave excuses as if it all depended on him rather than on God. God did not say, "This is what I want you to do—now do it." Rather, He said, "I'm going to do this, but I want to use you to do it." Moses did not fully understand this at the time, for his attention was still focused on himself rather than on God's mighty power.

We who have trusted Jesus Christ as Saviour also need to remember that we are not working for God; Christ is working in us to accomplish what He desires. This truth is evident from the benediction of Hebrews 13: "Now the God of peace . . . make you perfect in every good work to do his will, working in you that which is wellpleasing in his sight, through Jesus Christ; to whom be glory for ever and ever" (vv. 20,21).

Second, Moses had to learn that the task at hand depended on God's power, not on man's eloquence. Moses had to resolve the problem of whether God uses man's ability or whether God exercises His own ability through man's personality. Was God going to use Moses with all of his ability and training, or was God going to accomplish the task

Himself through Moses' personality, using Moses' talents and training by His own ability? This is a tremendous distinction, and we will consider it further as we look at other details in Moses' life.

Third, Moses had to learn that God accomplishes His will by His own authority, not by man's authority. In other words, who is really in charge? Pharaoh had to be persuaded to let the people go, and as Moses thought about his past, he was intensely aware of his inability to persuade Pharaoh of anything. Moses had to learn who was in charge and who persuades whom. Moses was brought face to face with the issue of God's sovereignty as he was confronted with the question of who sees that a purpose is accomplished. As we observe in these studies God's further revelation of Himself and His power, we will learn what Moses learned.

If we are only looking at ourselves, then we will say what Moses said, "Who am I" (Ex. 3:11). If we are looking to ourselves, we will accomplish nothing. But God's answer to such a question is always: "I will be with thee" (v. 12). It makes little difference who we are when God says, "I will be with you" or "I will send you."

As Moses reflected on his own ability and training, he said to God, in effect, "Why do you want to send me? Don't you know I'm just a shepherd? Don't you know that I'm a nobody?" But that's exactly the kind of person God looks for—one who considers himself a nobody so that what is accomplished through his life will bring glory to God, not to the individual. As long as we think we are somebody, God may let us attempt to do things in our own strength. But not until we see ourselves as nobody and God as all in all will He take over and accomplish His will by His strength.

The Message in the Name

Moses had some deep misgivings about what would happen if he went to his own people and tried to deliver them from the Egyptians. He had tried it once in his own way and had failed. Now he was extremely reluctant to try it again. In his reluctance, Moses made an inquiry of God. He asked: "Behold, when I come unto the children of Israel, and shall say unto them, The God of your fathers hath sent me unto you; and they shall say to me, What is his name? what shall I say unto them?" (v. 13).

Previously, Moses knew God by the name Elohim, but now God revealed Himself to Moses by a new name. God answered his question by saying, "I Am That I Am: and he said, Thus shalt thou say unto the children of Israel, I Am hath sent me unto you" (v. 14).

The name God used in referring to Himself contained a message in itself. In Old Testament times names were especially significant. God would often reveal to parents what they should call their children and thus prophetically reveal the character of the person in his name. For example, Jacob's name meant "a supplanter," which involves scheming. Jacob's entire life was one of scheming until God finally captured him for Himself. God then told Jacob, "Thy name shall be called no more Jacob, but Israel: for as a prince hast thou power with God and with men" (Gen. 32:28).

It was also prophetically significant that Mary and Joseph named the virgin-born child "Jesus," for the name means "Saviour." God instructed Joseph about Mary and the Child in these words: "She shall bring forth a son, and thou shalt call his name Jesus: for he shall save his people from their sins" (Matt. 1:21).

So, as God revealed Himself to Moses as "I Am That I Am" (Ex. 3:14), He was really giving a new revelation of Himself. The voice simply declared His essential being but gave no explanation. The words "I Am" are related to God's name, "Jehovah." This name, as do the words "I Am," reveal that God is the self-existent One. He always exists—past, present and future.

God's revelation of Himself as "I Am That I Am" affirmed His power to lead His people out of Egypt and to bring them into the Promised Land. The revelation of Himself by this name revealed that He had the ability to become to His people whatever their needs required. It was an all-inclusive name. God was declaring, "I will be to you whatever you need." By referring to Himself as "I Am That I Am," God was saying, "I am everywhere all the time—within, without, before, behind, past, present and future."

Moses had to learn that the I Am was in charge of all and that He was the power for all. Moses was to do nothing of his own volition in delivering the Israelites—it was all done by God through Moses.

Moses learned his lesson well, as was evident later when the Israelites were in the wilderness after being delivered from Egypt. When the authority of Moses was challenged by Korah, Moses said to him: "Hereby ye shall know that the Lord hath sent me to do all these works; for I have not done them of mine own mind" (Num. 16:28). In other words, Moses was saying, "You're not quarreling with me; you're quarreling with God." By this time, Moses realized that the deliverance of Israel from Egypt and their entrance into Canaan was God's work, not his.

So sure was Moses of God's authority that he told Korah and his followers: "If these men die the common death of all men, or if they be visited after the visitation of all men; then the Lord hath not sent me. But if the Lord make a new thing, and the earth open her mouth, and swallow them up, with all that appertain unto them, and they go down quick into the pit; then ye shall understand that these men have provoked the Lord" (vv. 29,30). Moses had no sooner finished speaking, and the Bible says, "The ground clave asunder that was under them: and the earth opened her mouth, and swallowed them up, and their houses, and all the men that appertained unto Korah, and all their goods. They, and all that appertained to them, went down alive into the pit, and the earth closed upon them: and they perished from among the congregation" (vv. 31-33).

But at the time of the burning bush incident, Moses had not yet thoroughly learned that all authority was from God. He had not yet learned that God is the unchangeable God who lives in the eternal present. As F. B. Myers said of God: "He is the self-sufficient God who alone is His own equal." But at this time, Moses looked at himself and could only say, "Who am I?"

The Application of Knowledge

For 40 years in the desert, Moses had lived and communed with God, so he had come to know Him in an intimate way. Now Moses faced putting into practical experience what he had learned God to be. He had learned that God was the almighty God, and now he was to put this knowledge into practice as he faced a specific situation—leading the Israelites out of Egypt. Knowledge of God is not enough; one must put into practice what he knows to be true concerning God.

This was pointed out to me several years ago when I came to a new understanding of what it meant to be indwelt by the living Christ. I had been preaching for years that Christ indwells every believer, but somehow this truth took on a new meaning for me. I had knowledge of it, but I had not really integrated this knowledge into my practical experience. Do you have knowledge of the teaching of the Scriptures concerning the indwelling Christ? If so, are you living in daily consciousness of this truth? I encourage you to meditate prayerfully on Ephesians 1:17,18.

Moses asked God, "Who am I?" (Ex. 3:11). He did not realize that the most crucial question was not who he was but who God was. Moses was just a shepherd, despised by the Egyptians. He realized he was nothing, and that is what God wanted him to realize so He could use him. As mentioned previously, I Corinthians 1:27 says, "God hath chosen the foolish things of the world to confound the wise; and God hath chosen the weak things of the world to confound the things which are mighty."

So the question Moses should have been concerned about answering was, "Who are You?" God was revealing this to Moses by revealing Himself as "I Am That I Am."

Moses realized that he needed authority—God's authority—if he was to go to his fellow Israelites and claim to be their deliverer. That is why Moses needed an answer to give the people when they asked, "What is his name?" (Ex. 3:13). In other words, Moses was asking, "By what authority am I going? Who really is sending me? Who will provide the needs?"

This matter is mentioned in John 10:4: "And when he putteth forth his own sheep, he goeth before them." This verse states the timeless principle that God goes before His own when He sends them out. God accepts the responsibility. This fact is also seen in Matthew 4:19, which records the words of Christ: "Follow me, and I will make you fishers of men."

The Scope of the Name

In revealing Himself to Moses as I Am, God was telling
him: "I will be to you whatever you need." Notice, God was
not saying that He would give Moses whatever he needed but
that He would be to Moses whatever he needed.

Many names and combinations of names are used of God
in the Bible, but in referring to Himself as the I Am, God
was including all that is involved in the other names. It was as
if He were furnishing His people with a blank check to fill out
in any amount they needed to fulfill His commission to
them. Then they were to cash it in the bank of heaven.

God does the same for us. The check can only be filled in
by faith, however, for "without faith it is impossible to
please him" (Heb. 11:6). Notice what is promised to the one
who comes to God by faith. The Lord Jesus said, "If any
man thirst, let him come unto me, and drink" (John 7:37).
The Apostle Paul revealed God's promises in these words:
"What shall we then say to these things? If God be for us,
who can be against us? He that spared not his own Son, but
delivered him up for us all, how shall he not with him also
freely give us all things?" (Rom. 8:31,32). This is why Paul
was able to say: "I can do all things through Christ which
strengtheneth me" (Phil. 4:13).

Our knowledge of God is much too limited. In effect,
Christ has said to us: "If you are in darkness, I am the Light;
if you need righteousness, I am the Lord of Righteousness; if
you are hungry, I am the Bread of Life; if you are
defenseless, I am the Good Shepherd; if you need peace, I am
the Peace; if you need wisdom, sanctification and
redemption, I am all of that to you." It is evident from the
Scriptures that Jesus Christ is all we need. No wonder the
Bible says, "In him dwelleth all the fulness of the Godhead
bodily" (Col. 2:9).

In considering God's revelation of Himself to Moses as "I
Am That I Am" (Ex. 3:14), it is also interesting to notice
that the same name is used of Christ in the New Testament.
"Before Abraham was, I am" (John 8:58); "I am the
resurrection, and the life" (11:25); "I am the way, the truth,
and the life" (14:6); "I am the true vine" (15:1); "I am
Alpha and Omega" (Rev. 1:8); "I am . . . the bright and

morning star" (22:16). The Lord Jesus Christ is the believer's great I Am.

The name "I Am" was used only in connection with God's people, Israel. When addressing Pharaoh, Moses did not emphasize this name because it would have meant nothing to him. When talking to Pharaoh, he used the commanding name, "The Lord God of Israel" (Ex. 5:1); that is, the God of the same people Pharaoh was attempting to crush. It is important to realize that the name "I Am" means nothing to the unbeliever.

Moses' Credentials

Moses was still not convinced that the people would believe he was sent from God, even if he told them that God's name was "I Am That I Am." Moses told God: "But, behold, they will not believe me, nor hearken unto my voice: for they will say, The Lord hath not appeared unto thee" (Ex. 4:1). Moses obviously feared because of his lack of authority. He felt the need of having some kind of special credentials as he went to the people. He thought he needed something that would set him off in such a way that the people would say, "Ah, here comes the man who can do the job."

Earlier, when Moses endeavored to deliver the Israelites by his own efforts, he came to them with plenty of credentials from the courts of Egypt, but his own people rejected him. In the New Testament, the credentials of Moses are referred to in Stephen's message: "Moses was learned in all the wisdom of the Egyptians, and was mighty in words and in deeds" (Acts 7:22) He had his titles, degrees and honors. But Stephen went on to say that though Moses thought his people would understand his desire to deliver them, "they understood not" (v. 25). Yes, Moses had considerable prestige, as far as the world was concerned, the first time he tried to deliver them, but now he had been in the desert for 40 years and had no credentials of any kind—he was only a shepherd. Authority was important for Moses' task, but he needed to determine whose authority was important—his or God's.

Moses' concern about authority did not go unanswered. The Lord asked Moses: "What is that in thine hand?" (Ex. 4:2). Moses answered: "A rod" (v. 2).

Moses' rod was a shepherd's rod, and since shepherds were despised by the Egyptians, the presence of the rod would be a constant reminder of his despicableness to others. Although it was a symbol of foolishness to the world, God used it as a symbol of His authority. Moses' rod was to have a great future in the events of Moses' life. How significant that when God chose an instrument for His service, He did not choose a golden scepter but a shepherd's rod.

We have seen previously that this is the principle by which God operates—He uses the weakest instruments to accomplish the mightiest of deeds. And when He does this, it is obvious that the work was accomplished by His power, not by the instrument itself. God used rams' horns in the hands of Joshua and the priests (Josh. 6:1-21), the jawbone of an ass in Samson's hand (Judg. 15:14-20), earthen pitchers in the hands of Gideon and his 300 men (7:16-25), and a shepherd's sling in David's hand (I Sam. 17:31-58). These incidents prove that when anything—no matter how insignificant—is used by God, it can perform His appointed task. This is also true of people—God can use any of us to accomplish His will if we are wholly committed to Him.

So a rod with God behind it is mightier than the greatest army without God. In Moses' case, the rod reminded him that he was really nobody. However, because it was the rod of God, it served as a scepter of God's authority. In Moses' hand, the plain staff was only a shepherd's rod; but when used as God's rod in a man's surrendered hand, it was a symbol of omnipotence.

All of us need to be reminded of our nothingness without God. There is always the tendency for us to think that we are more than we really are. This can be a special danger to the person who God seems to use significantly. The person may begin to think that part, or much, of what is being accomplished is because of his own ability or training. The Devil has a way of appearing as an angel of light, patting us on the back and saying, "My, you're doing a wonderful work." Soon, pride enters in, and God is unable to use us as He wants to.

Moses could never become proud as long as he had the shepherd's staff and was reminded of how he was despised by the Egyptians. So with that rod, God was able to use Moses in a significant way, because it reminded Moses that he had to rely on God if anything was to be accomplished.

As a rod of God, the shepherd's staff served as a scepter of God's authority. In Moses' hand it was only a shepherd's rod, but in God's hand it was a symbol of omnipotence. What a difference! The rod became to Moses what the name of Jesus Christ is to us today. It is the symbol of authority, although despised by the world. Christ has all authority, and He promises to be with us in all of that authority as we tell the world about Him (Matt. 28:18-20).

The name Jesus Christ represents all that He is. The Book of Ephesians not only reveals who He is but also what we are in Him. Ephesians 1:19-23 says, "And what is the exceeding greatness of his power to us-ward who believe, according to the working of his mighty power, which he wrought in Christ, when he raised him from the dead, and set him at his own right hand in the heavenly places, far above all principality, and power, and might, and dominion, and every name that is named, not only in this world, but also in that which is to come: and hath put all things under his feet, and gave him to be the head over all things to the church, which is his body, the fulness of him that filleth all in all."

Notice also the great truths of Ephesians 2:4-6: "But God, who is rich in mercy, for his great love wherewith he loved us, even when we were dead in sins, hath quickened us together with Christ, (by grace ye are saved;) and hath raised us up together, and made us sit together in heavenly places in Christ Jesus." How I love that sixth verse! "And hath raised us up together, and made us sit together in heavenly places in Christ Jesus." This means that even though we are nothing, after we were raised from spiritual death, we were placed with Christ in all of His authority. We do not actually wield His authority, but He uses us in exercising His authority.

The Rod and The Serpent

Concerning the rod, God told Moses: "Cast it on the ground" (Ex. 4:3). Moses obeyed and "it became a serpent;

and Moses fled from before it. And the Lord said unto Moses, Put forth thine hand, and take it by the tail" (vv. 3,4). Think how dangerous it would be to pick up a serpent by its tail! Those who know anything about snakes, as Moses would have after his years in the desert, realize that you pick up a snake near the head, not by the tail. But Moses had learned his lessons of faith so well during his 40 years in the desert that he explicitly followed God's command to pick up the serpent by the tail. Moses had confidence that if God said to pick up the snake by the tail, then it was all right to do so. Moses' confidence was rewarded, for when he picked up the snake, it turned into the rod.

As we consider God's way of dealing with Moses in commanding him to pick up the serpent by the tail, we should be impressed also with the fact that God's methods do not always seem logical to us. Once we are sure of the Lord's will, our responsibility is not to question the logic of it but to obey it, regardless of the obstacles. God instructed Joshua and the Israelite army, as they entered the land of Canaan and tried to take the fortified city of Jericho, to do something that was contrary to logic. He told them to march around the city once each day for six days and seven times on the seventh day. At the completion of the seventh trip on the seventh day, the priests were to sound a loud blast with their horns, and the wall was to fall. The Israelites did precisely what God instructed, and the walls fell just as He had promised. The account of this incident is found in Joshua 6.

Inasmuch as the Egyptians worshiped serpents, the act of Moses fleeing from the serpent symbolized the might of Egypt, from which he had fled and was a fugitive. Nevertheless, at God's command, Moses picked up the serpent by the tail, and it became a harmless staff.

In this way, God instructed Moses that he, by faith, should return to Egypt. God also made it known to Moses that He would take care of him if he were obedient through faith. God was also showing Moses that He would eventually render Egypt harmless, even as He had the serpent, and that He would destroy its power to hurt Israel anymore.

When God displayed His authority to Moses, it is of interest that the rod turned into a serpent. Not only were serpents worshiped by the Egyptians, but a serpent also reminds us that the one seeking to discourage Moses was Satan, since he is frequently pictured throughout the Bible as a serpent. He approached Eve in the form of a serpent (Gen. 3:1). The last book of the Bible also refers to Satan as a serpent: "And the great dragon was cast out, that old serpent, called the Devil, and Satan, which deceiveth the whole world" (Rev. 12:9). Although Satan desires to exercise control over people, his power to do this was broken when Christ died on the cross. Hebrews 2:14 says, "Forasmuch then as the children are partakers of flesh and blood, he [Christ] also himself likewise took part of the same; that through death he might destroy him that had the power of death, that is, the devil."

As God demonstrated to Moses His authority over the serpent, He was showing Moses that He would eventually crush the power of Egypt, as well as completely destroy the power of Satan.

Remember that the miracle-working power was not in Moses' rod itself. There was no magic in the wood fiber; its value lay only in its complete surrender to God's will. By the act of surrendering the rod to God, the rod of Moses became the rod of God. Someone has well said: "There was no power in the wood to provide dry land in the midst of water at the Red Sea or water in the midst of dry land in the desert, but there was power in the God who commanded it to do so. When the man of the rod yielded to God, and the rod was yielded to the man, it accomplished what otherwise could not have been done." So we, too, are taught in Ephesians 6:10: "Be strong in the Lord, and in the power of his might."

Later, when Moses was completely surrendered to God, his personality, training and gifts were all used by God, but they were used in God's strength. All Moses really needed was status with God—not prestige with men. Status with God gives any man more power and more prestige than he can acquire from any other source, and it makes him worthy to stand anywhere before anyone at any time in the power of God.

Another Sign

But the rod turning into a snake and then back into a rod was not the only sign God gave Moses. God told Moses: "Put

now thine hand into thy bosom" (Ex. 4:6). Moses obeyed
God, and when he took his hand out of his bosom, it was
"leprous as snow" (v. 6).

God then instructed Moses: "Put thine hand into thine
bosom again" (v. 7). Moses did so, and when he took it out,
"it was turned again as his other flesh" (v. 7).

Leprosy is used in the Bible as a symbol of sin. Just as
God took away the leprosy from Moses' hand, so the Second
Man took away the sin which was brought by the First Man.
The Bible says, "For since by man came death, by man came
also the resurrection of the dead. For as in Adam all die, even
so in Christ shall all be made alive" (I Cor. 15:21,22). On this
same subject, Romans 5:17-19 says, "For if by one man's
offence death reigned by one; much more they which receive
abundance of grace and of the gift of righteousness shall reign
in life by one, Jesus Christ. Therefore as by the offence of
one judgment came upon all men to condemnation; even so
by the righteousness of one the free gift came upon all men
unto justification of life. For as by one man's disobedience
many were made sinners, so by the obedience of one shall
many be made righteous."

So, not only will the Serpent (Satan) be eternally
defeated, but every trace of his abominable work will be
eradicated by the atoning sacrifice of Christ, who "was
manifested, that he might destroy the works of the devil"
(I John 3:8). As we have mentioned previously, Christ broke
Satan's power at the cross (Heb. 2:14), and Christ will
eventually confine Satan to the lake of fire forever. The Bible
says that at the end of the millennial rule of Christ, "the devil
that deceived them was cast into the lake of fire and
brimstone, where the beast and the false prophet are, and
shall be tormented day and night for ever and ever" (Rev.
20:10). Satan is the prince of this world now, but he will not
rule in hell—he will be tormented forever.

Consider the personal applications from this
incident—Moses placing his hand in his bosom. The bosom
reminds us of a person's heart; thus, it represents what he is.
The hand is associated with a person's activity; thus, it
represents what he does. As we consider this comparison,
Luke 6:45 makes an important point: "A good man out of
the good treasure of his heart bringeth forth that which is

good; and an evil man out of the evil treasure of his heart bringeth forth that which is evil: for of the abundance of the heart his mouth speaketh." Thus, the hand that holds the rod of God's power must be a cleansed hand, which evidences a cleansed heart.

Jesus used another analogy when He said: "I am the vine, ye are the branches" (John 15:5). In other words, Christ was saying, "The fruit that you're going to bear comes from within Me." And just as Christ was clean, so the believer has to be clean in order to bear fruit as God desires.

Thus, the rod of God in the cleansed hand of a cleansed man becomes the scepter of God's authority. Although at the time that God performed the miracle with Moses' rod there was nothing unique about the rod, it was later referred to as "the rod of God" (Ex. 4:20).

Another lesson can be learned from the fact that Moses' hand became leprous. This occurred when he put his hand into his bosom, representing his heart. God was showing Moses something very important. Because man's heart is evil, the activities he performs with his hands are also evil. When God later cleansed Moses' hand it was indicative of a cleansed heart. In effect, God was telling Moses: "Now with a pure heart and a pure hand, I want you to take this rod and do My work."

Lack of Eloquence

After God gave Moses signs of authority in response to his excuse of lack of authority, Moses offered another excuse—the lack of eloquence. Again, we should remind ourselves that Moses was not being belligerent or rebellious toward God in offering these excuses; rather, he was so convinced of his nothingness that he did not think he was of any use to God. He was in need of fully realizing that God had said He would accomplish the deliverance of Israel but that He would use Moses to accomplish this because he had recognized his nothingness.

Moses told the Lord: "I am not eloquent, neither heretofore, nor since thou hast spoken unto thy servant: but I am slow of speech, and of a slow tongue" (Ex. 4:10). Probably like the great Cromwell of old, Moses had no ready supply of words. Or, like other men, such as D. L. Moody, he lacked oratorical ability. But notice God's answer to Moses' excuse: "Who hath made man's mouth? or who maketh the dumb, or deaf, or the seeing, or the blind? have not I the Lord? Now therefore go, and I will be with thy mouth, and teach thee what thou shalt say" (vv. 11,12). With these words, God let Moses know that He was not looking for eloquence; He was looking for a man. This was a key truth that God had to teach Moses, and it is a key truth He wants to teach us today.

This truth is seen in Ezekiel 22:30, which records the words of the Lord: "I sought for a man among them, that should make up the hedge, and stand in the gap before me for the land, that I should not destroy it: but I found none." Because God could not find such a person He said, "Therefore have I poured out my indignation upon them; I have consumed them with the fire of my wrath: their own way have I recompensed upon their heads" (v. 31).

Later, Moses proved to be such a person, for he stood in the gap for his people as God threatened to pour out His wrath against them. The psalmist wrote concerning this incident: "Therefore he said that he would destroy them, had not Moses his chosen stood before him in the breech, to turn away his wrath, lest he should destroy them" (Ps. 106:23).

While men seek better methods, God seeks better men. Men are so prone to trust methods or organizations to accomplish certain goals, but God wants better men, who are surrendered completely to Him, through whom He can accomplish His goals. *Men are God's methods.* God wants men who are mighty in the Word, mighty in faith, and mighty in prayer. He delegates responsibility to such men and performs great works through their lives. It is only to such men that God is able to entrust His authority to accomplish His work. Concerning this matter, II Chronicles 16:9 says: "For the eyes of the Lord run to and fro throughout the whole earth, to show himself strong in the behalf of them whose heart is perfect toward him." The word "perfect" in this verse refers to those who are wholeheartedly devoted to God. It involves a singlemindedness in serving God.

God is not seeking for a man with great ability but for a man He can use in His ability. This is why Ephesians 6:10

says, "Be strong in the Lord, and in the power of his might."
Zechariah 4:6 emphasizes the same thought: "Not by might,
nor by power, but by my spirit, saith the Lord of hosts."

Because God does His work through man, He told Moses:
"I am come down to deliver them [the Israelites] out of the
hand of the Egyptians" (Ex. 3:8). And then God added:
"Come now therefore, and I will send thee unto Pharaoh"
(v. 10). God was going to deliver the Israelites from the
Egyptians, but He was going to use a man—Moses—to do it.

God had revealed Himself to Moses as "I Am That I Am"
(v. 14); so, if eloquence was necessary, all Moses had to do
was trust the great I Am to supply the eloquence. If Moses
had only been willing to trust Him, God would have had no
difficulty in adding the gift of persuasive oratory to Moses'
other talents.

The Sufficiency of God

Remember that when we recognize the indwelling Lord,
our deficiencies and infirmities become the occasion for the
display of His all-sufficient grace to perfect. We need to
realize, as the apostle did, that "[God's] strength is made
perfect in weakness" (II Cor. 12:9). But Paul did not come to
this realization until he was assured by God, "My grace is
sufficient for thee" (v. 9). Like Paul and Moses, we need to
recognize that God's grace is sufficient for whatever we need.

Moses' doubting heart still placed far more confidence in
an eloquent tongue than in the One who created it; namely,
the great I Am. As we reflect on the verses we have already
seen regarding the sufficiency of God in our need, let us re-
view by quoting some of them from the New American
Standard Bible: "Not that we are adequate in ourselves to
consider anything as coming from ourselves, but our
adequacy is from God" (II Cor. 3:5). "I am the vine, you are
the branches; he who abides in Me, and I in him, he bears
much fruit; for apart from Me you can do nothing" (John
15:5). "For it is God who is at work in you, both to will and
to work for His good pleasure" (Phil. 2:13). "I can do all
things through Him who strengthens me" (Phil. 4:13). "For
in Him all the fulness of Deity dwells in bodily form, and in

Him you have been made complete, and He is the head over all rule and authority" (Col. 2:9,10).

How wonderful it is to realize that Christ is made to us all that we need. This is particularly emphasized in I Corinthians 1:30,31: "But of him are ye in Christ Jesus, who of God is made unto us wisdom, and righteousness, and sanctification, and redemption: that, according as it is written, He that glorieth, let him glory in the Lord." If you need wisdom, He is that wisdom; if you need righteousness, He is that righteousness; if you need sanctification, He is that sanctification; if you need redemption, He is that redemption.

Because Christ is all we need, nothing is more important than knowing Him and making Him known to others. We see Paul's priority in making Christ known to others, for he said to the Corinthians: "And I, brethren, when I came to you, came not with excellency of speech or of wisdom, declaring unto you the testimony of God. For I determined not to know any thing among you, save Jesus Christ, and him crucified. And I was with you in weakness, and in fear, and in much trembling. And my speech and my preaching was not with enticing words of man's wisdom, but in demonstration of the Spirit and of power: that your faith should not stand in the wisdom of men, but in the power of God" (I Cor. 2:1-5).

With Christ being all we need, we see the *hope* of our calling: "The eyes of your understanding being enlightened; that ye may know what is the hope of his calling, and what the riches of the glory of his inheritance in the saints" (Eph. 1:18). And then we also see the *potential* of our calling: "And what is the exceeding greatness of his power to us-ward who believe, according to the working of his mighty power, which he wrought in Christ, when he raised him from the dead, and set him at his own right hand in the heavenly places, far above all principality, and power, and might, and dominion, and every name that is named, not only in this world, but also in that which is to come: and hath put all things under his feet, and gave him to be the head over all things to the church, which is his body, the fulness of him that filleth all in all" (Eph. 1:19-23).

Christ is elevated above every name, and we are also seated together with Him: "And hath raised us up together, and made us sit together in heavenly places in Christ Jesus" (2:6).

Moses Reluctantly Consents

After God explained to Moses that He had made man's mouth, Moses said, "O my Lord, send, I pray thee, by the hand of him whom thou wilt send" (Ex. 4:13). This verse has frequently been misunderstood. Many have interpreted it to mean that Moses was saying, "It's no use, Lord, I'm not going, so You may as well send somebody else." Such an interpretation considers Moses' response to be one of rebellion. This is not necessarily true, however, for the meaning is obscured somewhat in the King James Version. The New American Standard Bible translates this verse: "Please, Lord, send now the message by whomever Thou wilt." Rather than expressing rebellion, Moses was saying, "Since You are determined to send me, and since I must undertake this mission, then let it be so; but I would rather You had chosen someone else. But I will go because I am compelled to go."

Another translator expresses it this way: "Send me, if there is no alternative." So we see that Moses' attitude was one of reluctant consent—finally giving in to what the Lord wanted him to do. This type of attitude is often heard in testimonies today. It seems especially prevalent among young people, who tell of knowing God's will, but of being unwilling to do it at first and then finally giving in.

God is not pleased with consent that is given reluctantly, or grudgingly. Concerning Moses, the Bible says, "And the anger of the Lord was kindled against Moses, and he said, Is not Aaron the Levite thy brother? I know that he can speak well. And also, behold, he cometh forth to meet thee; and when he seeth thee, he will be glad in his heart" (v. 14).

God was not pleased at all with Moses' reluctant consent to go only if He insisted. Because of his excuse of lack of eloquence, the Lord let Moses know that someone else would be provided, and that person would be his brother Aaron. Although Aaron would go along with Moses to supply the skill that Moses thought he lacked, Aaron would still be in a secondary position. But even the need for Aaron to go was brought about because Moses failed to appropriate all that was involved when God said, "I Am That I Am" (3:14). Moses still failed to realize that God would be to him whatever he needed.

Although Aaron would do the public speaking, Moses was the one who would receive the message from God and pass it on to Aaron. God had a special relationship with Moses, and He would continue to communicate directly to him. In turn, Moses was to share this communication with Aaron, who would then be his spokesman.

Moses' concern about lack of eloquence is a lesson that I have had to personally apply. In the early years of the Back to the Bible ministry, I was particularly sensitive about my inability to speak as I should to effectively reach the listeners of the broadcast. I was bothered by my inability to the extent that I told God, "Lord, You picked the wrong man. You know I don't have command of the English language as I should; nor do I have the kind of vocabulary I need to reach all of these people. I'm not an orator; You know I cannot really persuade men."

As I continued to think and talk that way to the Lord, He finally made very clear to me—and I think it was through the study of Moses—that Back to the Bible was not my undertaking, it was His. Thus, the messages were not really mine, they were His. He caused me to realize that I was only the mouthpiece that He wanted to use to deliver His message, and as I remained sensitive to Him, He would tell me what to say. I was to say it in the best way possible—no matter how stammering that might be. Needless to say, I realized more than ever that it was to be His power in the message, not my oratory.

I often think of D. L. Moody in this regard. It is said that when he was preaching in England on one occasion, a university student came to him after the service and said, "Mr. Moody, do you realize that you made 18 grammatical mistakes in your sermon today?" D. L. Moody—who always had a quick reply—said to the young man, "Yes, I may have made that many mistakes. But listen, young man, I use all the grammar I have for the Lord—what are you doing with yours?"

God made clear to Moses what his relationship would be to Aaron: "Thou shalt speak unto him, and put words in his mouth: and I will be with thy mouth, and with his mouth, and will teach you what ye shall do. And he shall be thy spokesman unto the people: and he shall be, even he shall be to thee instead of a mouth, and thou shalt be to him instead of God" (Ex. 4:15,16).

So a whole new program was initiated because of Moses' reluctance to appropriate all that God wanted to be to him. Such reluctance seemed very humble on the surface, but it only served to kindle God's anger. And it always does when God's servant limits His ability to supply. Such reluctance is simply a lack of faith. Romans 14:23 says, "Whatsoever is not of faith is sin." It is interesting to contrast Romans 14:23 with Exodus 3:14, where God revealed Himself to Moses as "I Am That I Am." With such a revelation of God as this, it is easy to see why a lack of faith is sin. No wonder God was angered when Moses kept insisting that he was unable to do the task God wanted to enable him to do. Moses evaded his God-entrusted responsibilities merely because he felt inadequate. So at Moses' request, God displaced him as His spokesman and appointed a weak Aaron, who later became oppressive and caused many problems for Moses.

Aaron's Weakness

Aaron's weakness was especially revealed in the incident of the golden calf. This incident took place after Moses had led the children of Israel out of Egypt, and they were gathered at Mount Sinai. While Moses was on the mountaintop talking with God, the people became restless because Moses had been gone for some time. The people went to Aaron and said, "Up, make us gods, which shall go before us; for as for this Moses, the man that brought us up out of the land of Egypt, we wot [know] not what is become of him" (Ex. 32:1).

With Moses gone, Aaron was next in charge, but he seriously failed in his responsibility of leadership. Notice what he told the people: "Break off the golden earrings, which are in the ears of your wives, of your sons, and of your daughters, and bring them unto me" (v. 2). The people did as instructed, and Aaron "fashioned it with a graving tool, after he had made it a molten calf" (v. 4). Aaron was so weak spiritually that he even built an altar before the golden calf (v. 5). Because of this idolatry, God became angry with Aaron and the Israelites and immediately ordered Moses to descend the mountain and get things straightened out. This illustrates what a thorn Aaron was to Moses during these years. But Moses had to remember that it was only because of his excuse to the Lord that Aaron was assigned to him in the first place.

Moses' Imitation Humility

Moses' excuse of lack of eloquence (4:10) was not genuine humility. It is wonderful when a person has a divinely given humility, but it is obnoxious when a person has a self-produced humility. Divine humility comes only by the grace of God; it cannot be achieved by saying, "I will be humble" or "I'm going to humble myself." Moses' attitude obviously was not genuine humility because the Lord became angry with his excuse. Such would not have been the case if Moses' attitude had been genuine humility.

As we have indicated, Moses' attitude should not be classified as rebellion; rather, it was excessive timidity and lack of the necessary faith to trust God for the task at hand. Moses had not yet seen God as the true "captain of the host of the Lord" (Josh. 5:14). Moses had not yet seen that the deliverance of Israel had to be God's undertaking alone, although God wanted to use Moses to accomplish the task.

Nothing is more dishonoring to God, and more dangerous for us, than to possess an imitation humility. If we refuse to occupy a position because we do not think we have the qualifications, yet God, in His grace, has assigned it to us, it is not genuine humility. Such an attitude puts too much value on personal ability and qualifications and, in effect, actually rejects God. But we, like Moses, must remember that God is the great I Am. God will be to us precisely what we need in a given situation.

Suppose that Moses did possess the eloquence he thought he needed to persuade the Israelites that he was the one to deliver them. Do you think he would have readily accepted

God's call? On the basis of what he did 40 years earlier in his own strength, it seems that he would have quickly responded to God's call. Forty years earlier he set out to deliver Israel in his own strength, so it would be assumed that if he thought he was equal to the task when God later called him, he would have tried it. But he had no feeling of superiority—no overestimate of his authority, training and ability.

Consider this question: How much eloquence did Moses think he needed before he would be qualified to accept God's call? Without God, no amount of eloquence could have accomplished the purpose. With God in control, however, the most stammering tongue could prove to be sufficient. So it is apparent that Moses was relying too much on his own ability and too little on God. Such an attitude does not believe God; it does not find in self a reason for believing God. This is really the height of presumption.

Refusing to believe God is really calling God a liar. This is what the Bible says: "He that believeth on the Son of God hath the witness in himself: he that believeth not God hath made him a liar" (I John 5:10). In contrast to being a liar, the Bible says that "God is not a man that he should lie; neither the son of man, that he should repent: hath he said, and shall he not do it? or hath he spoken, and shall he not make it good?" (Num. 23:19).

When God assigns a task to us, He will always furnish the grace and power to perform it. This fact is evident from II Corinthians 9:8: "God is able to make all grace abound toward you; that ye, always having all sufficiency in all things, may abound to every good work." What more do we want?

God has committed certain things to us. Second Corinthians 5:19 reveals that one of these things is the "word of reconciliation." But whenever God commits something to us, He also provides what we need to perform His will. The Lord Jesus Christ told His disciples: "Follow me, and I will make you fishers of men" (Matt. 4:19). The responsibility of these men was to follow Jesus; His responsibility was to make them fishers of men. Having provided salvation for us, God graciously gives us whatever we need to perform His will. This is evident in Romans 8:32: "He that spared not his own

Son, but delivered him up for us all, how shall he not with him also freely give us all things?"

God's enabling grace is also revealed in John 15:16: "Ye have not chosen me, but I have chosen you, and ordained you, that ye should go and bring forth fruit, and that your fruit should remain; that whatsoever ye shall ask of the Father in my name, he may give it you." By these statements, the Lord Jesus Christ was simply saying, "I'm sending you, but if anyone has any lack or any need, just ask the Father in My name and it will be supplied to you."

To leave our study of Moses at this point, after emphasizing his weaknesses, would be doing him a great injustice and dishonor. We must remember that after God's thorough training of His instrument during those 40 years, God knew Moses well and was using the incident at the burning bush to put Moses through his final examinations. God had to bring Moses to the point of realizing that he was nothing in himself. When Moses realized that, God gave him the great revelation of Himself. God opened Moses' inner eyes to see who He truly was, and is. This is the kind of enlightening that we need, and this is why Paul prayed as he did for believers: "The eyes of your understanding being enlightened; that ye may know what is the hope of his calling, and what the riches of the glory of his inheritance in the saints" (Eph. 1:18).

At this point, I want to underscore something that is tremendously important: Spiritual truths can be perceived only by the Spirit of God working in us; He has to open our spiritual eyes to them. It is possible to accumulate many facts about what the Bible teaches, but that is all they are unless one has his spiritual eyes opened to understand the true significance of those facts.

Identification With God

It was one thing for Moses to recognize the negative aspect of denying himself; but it was quite another thing for him to recognize the positive aspect of being identified with God. It is also crucial that we recognize what it means to be identified with God. For this to become a realization in our own lives, we must know three truths.

First, we must know God and our position in Him. Philippians 3:10 reveals the Apostle Paul's concern to know his identifying relationship with God: "That I may know him, and the power of his resurrection, and the fellowship of his sufferings, being made conformable unto his death."

Identification by means of God's name is seen in Exodus 3:13,14: "And Moses said unto God, Behold, when I come unto the children of Israel, and shall say unto them, The God of your fathers hath sent me unto you; and they shall say to me, What is his name? what shall I say unto them? And God said unto Moses, I Am That I Am: and he said, Thus shalt thou say unto the children of Israel, I Am hath sent me unto you."

Our position in Christ is especially revealed in the Book of Ephesians: "Blessed be the God and Father of our Lord Jesus Christ, who hath blessed us with all spiritual blessings in heavenly places in Christ" (1:3). Also notice this tremendous statement: "And hath raised us up together, and made us sit together in heavenly places in Christ Jesus" (2:6).

Second, we must know that God seeks for a man, but that whatever work is done is God's undertaking. This is identification with His power. We have seen this in Moses' case in such verses as Exodus 3:12: "He [God] said, Certainly I will be with thee; and this shall be a token unto thee, that I have sent thee: When thou hast brought forth the people out of Egypt, ye shall serve God upon this mountain." The need for identification with God's power is also seen in verses 19 and 20 of the same chapter: "I am sure that the king of Egypt will not let you go, no, not by a mighty hand. And I will stretch out my hand, and smite Egypt with all my wonders which I will do in the midst thereof: and after that he will let you go." Identification with God's power is referred to in Exodus 6:1, where God told Moses, "Now shalt thou see what I will do to Pharaoh." God also told Moses, "The Egyptians shall know that I am the Lord, when I stretch forth mine hand upon Egypt, and bring out the children of Israel from among them" (7:5). What a display of God's power, and what a need there is for us to be identified with it.

The New Testament emphasizes God's power in such verses as Ephesians 6:10: "Be strong in the Lord, and in the

power of his might." God's power is also referred to in the
Great Commission: "All power [authority] is given unto me
[Christ] in heaven and in earth. Go ye therefore, and teach
all nations, baptizing them in the name of the Father, and of
the Son, and of the Holy Ghost" (Matt. 28:18,19).

Third, we must know God's ample provision. This is
identification with God's methods. In Moses' case, this was
seen particularly concerning the rod that God used to
perform miracles and thus convince Moses that His methods
were best (Ex. 4:1-7). It did not seem logical to Moses that
God would attach any significance to a rod, since it was a
symbol of a despised shepherd, but God does not always
work in ways that seem logical to men.

Although the methods of God seem foolish to an
unbeliever, they do not seem foolish to a believer. The New
Testament says, "For the preaching of the cross is to them
that perish foolishness; but unto us which are saved it is the
power of God" (I Cor. 1:18). The Apostle Paul was
concerned that others not put their confidence in his wisdom
and ability but in God's wisdom and power. Paul said, "My
speech and my preaching was not with enticing words of
man's wisdom, but in demonstration of the Spirit and of
power: that your faith should not stand in the wisdom of
men, but in the power of God" (2:4,5).

When we know these three things concerning God, we
will be more effective in our Christian lives because we will
be depending on our identification with God rather than on
our own ability and training.

Chapter 10

Moses Returns to Egypt

After Moses reluctantly accepted God's call, and God allowed Aaron to be his spokesman, God said, "Thou shalt take this rod in thine hand, wherewith thou shalt do signs" (Ex. 4:17). Verse 20 says, "And Moses took the rod of God in his hand." This reveals that his shepherd's staff was later referred to as "the rod of God." Because a shepherd was despised by the Egyptians, Moses may have wanted to leave his staff behind, but this was an explicit and binding order concerning the rod—he was to take it with him wherever he went.

As Moses turned to leave the place where God called him, we can imagine what it must have been like for him. As the fire faded from the bush and the voice was hushed, he must have gazed about him at the countryside and looked at the sheep and mountains. Perhaps he came to himself like the Prodigal Son the Bible tells about in Luke 15. This was a crucial hour in Moses' life. Eighty years had preceded this moment, and his graduation was practically over except for a couple more tests to firmly establish in his mind what God wanted to do through him. A great future lay before him because he had seen God in a new way.

This reminds us of what Jesus said concerning our future when we are in right relationship to Him. He said, "Follow me, and I will make you fishers of men" (Matt. 4:19). He has also told us: "If any man thirst, let him come unto me, and drink. He that believeth on me, as the scripture hath said, out of his belly shall flow rivers of living water" (John 7:37,38).

124

Moses Announces His Plans

As Moses left the place of the burning bush, he returned to his home in the desert to announce his plans. "Moses went and returned to Jethro his father in law, and said unto him, Let me go, I pray thee, and return unto my brethren which are in Egypt, and see whether they be yet alive. And Jethro said to Moses, Go in peace" (Ex. 4:18). In discussing his desire to return to Egypt, there is no indication that Moses shared with the others the intimate dealings he had experienced with God. This is usually a good policy to follow, so the freshness and delicacy of one's personal fellowship with God will not be lost. Often when we talk to others about what we have experienced with the Lord, their ideas and thoughts tend to dissipate some of the precious things we have seen as we have spent time with God. So as a rule, when God deals with us as He dealt with Moses, it is best not to be quick about sharing it with others. There will probably come a time when we will be able to share it with others, but often others are not able to understand the deep things we have personally experienced with God.

Have you ever noticed how little the Lord reveals to others about His private dealings with His servants? Hardly anything is said in the Bible concerning the 40 years of His personal dealing with Moses. Even this reveals the grace of God. I feel this has been true of my own relationship with the Lord. I have experienced His dealing with me in an intimate way, and there are some secrets that only God and I will ever know.

Even though almost nothing is revealed of the 40 years of Moses' private schooling, there is evidence that he spent much time with God. And we must remember that such a relationship with God does not occur in one major experience or crisis. Too many people talk about a great experience they have had in life as though that is everything. But we are not to live the present on the basis of the past. The key issue is whether we are walking close to God at the present.

Although God's anger was revealed against Moses for making excuses, it was tempered by His mercy, for God knows the problems of His servants.

In this regard, I love Psalm 103 and never tire of reading it and meditating on it. Verses 8-14 are especially precious: "The Lord is merciful and gracious, slow to anger, and plenteous in mercy. He will not always chide: neither will he keep his anger for ever. He hath not dealt with us after our sins; nor rewarded us according to our iniquities. For as the heaven is high above the earth, so great is his mercy toward them that fear him. As far as the east is from the west, so far hath he removed our transgressions from us. Like as a father pitieth his children, so the Lord pitieth them that fear him. For he knoweth our frame; he remembereth that we are dust."

God manifested this kind of graciousness toward Moses. Though God was angered by Moses' excuses which revealed his doubts, He was full of mercy in bringing Moses to see his need of relying on Him alone.

To strengthen and encourage Moses' faith, God revealed two matters to Moses—first, his brother Aaron was already on his way to meet him (v. 14), and the men who sought his life in Egypt were dead (v. 19).

God Works on Both Ends

It is important to realize that God always works on both ends. Not only did He need to prepare Moses, but also He needed to cause Aaron to go into the desert to meet Moses. The ability of God to work at both ends to accomplish His will is seen in the case of Philip and the Ethiopian eunuch (Acts 8). God prepared Philip to go to the eunuch, and He made the eunuch ready for Philip's coming. The same principle is also seen in the case of Saul (Paul) and Ananias (Acts 9). God had to prepare Ananias and give him the courage to be willing to go to Saul, and God needed to prepare Saul to receive Ananias. God's working on both sides is also evident when a person responds to the gospel. God motivates His servants to give the gospel message, and he motivates others to respond to the message (John 16:8-11). Cornelius and Peter (Acts 10) also serve as a beautiful illustration of God's ability to work at both ends to accomplish His will.

The fact that Moses said nothing of his private dealings with the Lord in the desert as he announced to his father-in-law his plans to return to Egypt may have more than one explanation. As already indicated, God's dealings with him might have been too intimate to share with others. But it is also possible that Moses still lacked full assurance that God would really be able to use him in delivering Israel. Moses was intensely aware of the inconsistencies in his life, and he was only then becoming fully aware of God's ability to make up for his lack. The tests that God gave Moses after this incident reveal that Moses still needed to learn about God. Moses was still looking too much at himself and not enough at the sufficiency of God. The final death blow to self had not yet fallen.

At this point Moses was, in the New Testament sense, the type of Christian described in Romans 7. In other words, he knew what he should do, but he did not have the ability to carry it out in his own strength. Moses needed to be the type of person described in Romans 8—and so do we. This chapter reveals that victory is possible as one relies entirely on God.

Moses' Titles

However, one significant change took place during the experience that Moses had at the burning bush. After this time, he was described by such phrases as "the man of God" (Deut. 33:1) or "the servant of God" (Deut. 34:5).

A special title given to Moses that is so significant is "friend" of God (Ex. 33:11). Exodus 33 reveals the face-to-face communion that God had with Moses. Verse 9 says, "It came to pass, as Moses entered into the tabernacle, the cloudy pillar descended, and stood at the door of the tabernacle, and the Lord talked with Moses." Verse 11 says, "The Lord spake unto Moses face to face, as a man speaketh unto his friend." The close relationship we have with Jesus Christ is explained in His words of John 15:15: "Henceforth I call you not servants; for the servant knoweth not what his lord doeth: but I have called you friends; for all things that I have heard of my Father I have made known unto you." The title "friend" implies trust in every respect.

It is evident from the Scriptures that Abraham was also a friend of God. When God was considering the destruction of Sodom because of its wickedness, He said, "Shall I hide from Abraham that thing which I do?" (Gen. 18:17). What a privilege to be the friend of God! Nothing compares to true friendship and the understanding that results from it. Someone has described it in these words:

> O the comfort,
> the inexpressible comfort
> of feeling safe with a person.
> Having neither to weigh thoughts
> nor measure words;
> but pouring them all right out
> just as they are—
> chaff and grain together—
> certain that a faithful hand
> will take and sift them;
> keep what is worth keeping,
> and with a breath of kindness
> blow the rest away.
> —Author Unknown

After Moses' announcement to his father-in-law, "the Lord said unto Moses in Midian, Go, return into Egypt: for all the men are dead which sought thy life" (Ex. 4:19). Moses' response to God's command is seen in the following verse: "So Moses took his wife and his sons and mounted them on a donkey, and he returned to the land of Egypt. Moses also took the staff of God in his hand" (NASB).

The Lord gave further instructions to Moses: "When thou goest to return into Egypt, see that thou do all those wonders before Pharaoh, which I have put in thine hand: but I will harden his heart, that he shall not let the people go" (v. 21) Many have stumbled over the statement, "I will harden his heart," and this will be discussed in detail at a later time. God continued His instructions: "Thou shalt say unto Pharaoh, Thus saith the Lord, Israel is my son, even my firstborn: and I say unto thee, Let my son go, that he may serve me: and if thou refuse to let him go, behold, I will slay thy son, even thy firstborn" (vv. 22,23). Although Pharaoh was to experience ten plagues, God here alluded only to the tenth plague—the killing of the firstborn. At this point, God did not tell Moses that there would be ten plagues, but He did allude to the climaxing plague that would be brought on Pharaoh and the Egyptians. This brings us to the final tests that Moses experienced.

Chapter 11

Moses' Final Test: Complete Separation

The first of Moses' final tests was for the purpose of complete separation—we might call it sanctification or a setting apart from the world. God had given Israel the sign of separation, which was circumcision. It was first given to Abraham, as recorded in Genesis 17:9-14. Through Abraham, this sign was communicated to his descendants, Israel. Although Moses was preparing to bring the Israelites into the land God promised them, he had not been obedient to the sign of the covenant, circumcision.

The Bible says, "It came to pass by the way in the inn, that the Lord met him, and sought to kill him. Then Zipporah took a sharp stone, and cut off the foreskin of her son, and cast it at his feet, and said, Surely a bloody husband art thou to me. So he let him go: then she said, A bloody husband thou art, because of the circumcision" (Ex. 4:24-26). How strange that Moses had neglected circumcision for his son. But now that God was about to deliver Israel, He reminded Moses that without circumcision an Israelite was cut off from the covenant.

Although the rite of circumcision is not part of the Church Age, there is a circumcision of the heart. Colossians 2:10-12 says, "And ye are complete in him, which is the head of all principality and power: in whom also ye are circumcised with the circumcision made without hands, in putting off the body of sins of the flesh by the circumcision of Christ: buried with him in baptism, wherein also ye are risen with him through the faith of the operation of God, who hath raised him from the dead." So as we appropriate the death of the Lord Jesus Christ and die to sin, we

130

appropriate that which counts for our separation. This fact is also mentioned in Romans 6:4: "Therefore we are buried with him by baptism into death: that like as Christ was raised up from the dead by the glory of the Father, even so we also should walk in newness of life."

Moses was attacked suddenly with a serious illness because he had neglected circumcising his son. In his illness, his conscience caused him to see that he had not taken care of this important sign of the covenant.

Apparently his foreign wife objected to such an ordeal, and perhaps he had previously conceded to her objections and so had not circumcised his son. As long as Moses was not among his people, this was not a particular problem to him, but now that he was returning as a citizen and leader of Israel, he dared not go back with an uncircumcised son. How could he be involved in seeking to fulfill the covenant promises of God if he had not even kept the sign of the covenant? Because Moses was to be so intimately used among his people, he came under God's thorough disciplining.

Here we see another principle. The more responsibility an individual has, the more God expects of him and chastens him so he will be the kind of person God wants him to be. But this chastening is because of God's love and because He wants to be able to do even more through us. Hebrews 12:6 says, "For whom the Lord loveth he chasteneth, and scourgeth every son whom he receiveth." Verse 11 says, "Now no chastening for the present seemeth to be joyous, but grievous: nevertheless afterward it yieldeth the peaceable fruit of righteousness unto them which are exercised thereby."

Because Moses was severely ill, it was necessary for his wife to circumcise their son. Although she seemed to have despised the rite and the act itself, she did it, apparently because she realized that Moses' serious illness was because of his disobedience. It was not the mother's normal duty to perform the circumcision. This was the responsibility of the father, for God had appointed him head of the home.

The New Testament emphasizes the responsibility of the man as the head of the household. In fact, if he does not serve well in this capacity, he is disqualified from certain church offices. Paul instructed Timothy that one of the qualifications for an elder, or overseer, is that he "ruleth well his own house, having his children in subjection with all gravity [dignity]" (I Tim. 3:4).

God has never changed his order. He placed the man—the father—at the head of the family to govern the family. This seems to have been another reason for God's judgment of Moses—he had not taken his proper place in the home. His wife had to perform the circumcision because Moses was too ill, and yet if it was not performed, there was the possibility that Moses would die. With no alternative, Moses' wife performed the circumcision.

Before God could use Moses to carry out His commission, Moses had to set his house in order. Obedience at home must precede the display of power to the world. This is always true. Moses' experience with his wife revealed to him that she would not be in complete sympathy as he went before Pharaoh for the release of the Israelites. The indication is that he sent her back home because when the Israelites were later delivered from Egypt, Jethro brought her and her sons to meet Moses in the wilderness (Ex. 18:1-5).

Let us consider the lessons God has for us from the incident of Moses' test of separation from the world. First, we must consider the things of the world as refuse in comparison to what we have in Jesus Christ. Paul said, "Whatever things were gain to me, those things I have counted as loss for the sake of Christ. More than that, I count all things to be loss in view of the surpassing value of knowing Christ Jesus my Lord, for whom I have suffered the loss of all things, and count them but rubbish in order that I may gain Christ" (Phil. 3:7,8, NASB). Paul desired to know Jesus Christ not only as Saviour but also as Lord. He wanted Christ to be in first place in every area of his life. Only when we have this same desire can we say, as did Paul, "I can do all things through Him who strengthens me" (4:13, NASB).

Romans 12:1 reveals what every believer needs to do: "Present your bodies a living sacrifice." A "sacrifice" means death—in the believer's case, death to self. But the believer is to be a "living" sacrifice. Although we are to be dead to self, we are to be alive to God.

Our attitude toward Jesus Christ determines what the Holy Spirit's attitude is toward us. This fact is revealed in

John 7:37,38: "If any man is thirsty, let him come to Me and drink. He who believes in Me, as the Scripture said, 'From his innermost being shall flow rivers of living water' " (NASB). The following verse reveals that Christ was speaking of the Holy Spirit: "But this He spoke of the Spirit" (NASB).

After dealing with Moses, God was ready to send him on to Egypt. After Moses' son was circumcised, the Bible says that God let Moses go (Ex. 4:26). The Lord then spoke to Aaron and said, "Go into the wilderness to meet Moses. And he went, and met him in the mount of God, and kissed him. And Moses told Aaron all the words of the Lord who had sent him, and all the signs which he had commanded him" (vv. 27,28). These two verses tell of the meeting of two brothers who had not seen each other for at least 40 years. How different things were now because Moses was so different after being in the private school of God. He was no longer the disappointed man, smarting with a sense of failure and gloomily looking into the future as he had when he first fled from Pharaoh. Now he was strong in the Lord, even as Ephesians 6:10 tells us: "Be strong in the Lord, and in the power of his might."

Moses was conscious that he had a great mission before him, and he sensed God's presence with him, which would enable him to be equal to every emergency. Moses told Aaron all the instructions of the Lord, and one can imagine these brothers rejoicing together as they realized that God at last was going to deliver the Israelites from Egypt. Moses and Aaron had plenty of time to discuss what God was going to do through them, since it was a 40-day journey from the mountain of God (Horeb) to Egypt. Imagine what Moses must have shared with Aaron concerning his 40 years in the wilderness in God's private school, which was climaxed with his experience at the burning bush. No doubt they rehearsed joyfully the fact that they could finally understand how God had worked with Moses in his early training in Pharaoh's court and how this would now be useful background for the task God had for him to do. Aaron was probably very impressed with how much God had come to mean to Moses because of his years alone in the desert with God.

With joyful hearts Moses and Aaron returned to Egypt and "gathered together all the elders of the children of

Israel" (v. 29). Immediately Aaron worked in his capacity as Moses' spokesman, for verse 30 says, "Aaron spake all the words which the Lord had spoken unto Moses." Notice that Aaron did not communicate what God had spoken to him but what God had spoken to Moses. Not only did Aaron communicate God's message to the people, but he also "did the signs in the sight of the people" (v. 30). Aaron performed miracles to confirm that the message communicated through Moses was really of God.

Note the response of the people: "The people believed: and when they heard that the Lord had visited the children of Israel, and that he had looked upon their affliction, then they bowed their heads and worshipped" (v. 31). A revival broke out among the people, and they worshiped God because of the good news of deliverance.

As is so often asked concerning a specific revival, one would ask in this case, How long did it last? They bowed their heads and worshiped God, but they were a people who had often compromised and backslidden—some were even worshiping the idols of the Egyptians. It was only to be expected that when they heard of the possibility of being delivered from Egyptian bondage, they would immediately respond to Aaron and Moses. It is almost impossible to determine the genuineness of revival when it is occurring. As a college administrator said when asked to appraise the genuineness of the revival that had broken out among the student body, "Ask me that question six months from now, and I will be better able to answer it."

It is quite possible that even Moses wondered how long the revival of the Israelites would last, since he could vividly remember how they had rejected him previously when he had been so intent on delivering them from Egypt. He had thought then that they would understand, "but they understood not" (Acts 7:25). Would the revival last? What did the future hold?

Chapter 12

Moses' Final Test: Total Rejection

The second part of Moses' final test was the rejection by Pharaoh and his own people, which forced him to rely on God alone.

Moses and Aaron Before Pharaoh

According to the fifth chapter of Exodus, Moses and Aaron went before Pharaoh. The Bible does not mention how these two men were able to enter the presence of Pharaoh. All we can conclude is that Moses and Aaron could not possibly have gotten a hearing with Pharaoh except by the enablement of God. When things look impossible, we need to remember the words that occur often in the Scriptures: "but God."

Remember that Moses was to carry his shepherd's rod with him wherever he went and that the Egyptians considered shepherds to be an abomination. Only God could work it out in such a way that Pharaoh would permit an abominable shepherd to enter his presence.

The Bible says, "Moses and Aaron went in, and told Pharaoh, Thus saith the Lord God of Israel, Let my people go, that they may hold a feast unto me in the wilderness" (Ex. 5:1). These words must have seemed like a thunderclap to Pharaoh. Moses and Aaron came with more than their own authority—they came with the authority of God. Later, God told Moses, "See, I have made thee a god to Pharaoh" (7:1). So as Moses and Aaron first appeared before him, Pharaoh was listening as if God were speaking to him. Pharaoh should have recognized his responsibility. And note how God gave

Pharaoh the opportunity for obedience. Even this was the evident grace of God being manifested to Pharaoh.

God did not immediately launch his judgments on the haughty king and his subjects. Before God deals in judgment and wrath, He acts in mercy. This principle is in accordance with the character of God. For examples of God's extending mercy before His judgment, consider Noah, who preached righteousness for 120 years before the flood came (Gen. 6). Consider also the prophets of Israel who warned again and again of coming judgment before Israel's captivity. Consider, too, that the Lord Jesus Christ Himself foretold the destruction of Jerusalem and warned people to turn to God. The destruction came in A.D. 70, but the Lord had foretold the judgment about 40 years earlier. So we see the principle that God extends His mercy before He sends judgment.

Even in our day we see the mercy of God being extended. Because of radio programs such as Back to the Bible, there is no place in the world where the Word cannot be heard. People are being warned of coming judgment, and the warning itself is an indication of the longsuffering of God. In referring to coming judgment, Peter told believers, "Since all these things are to be destroyed in this way, what sort of people ought you to be in holy conduct and godliness" (II Pet. 3:11, NASB). Peter also said, "Beloved, since you look for these things, be diligent to be found by Him in peace, spotless and blameless, and regard the patience of our Lord to be salvation" (vv. 14,15, NASB).

No one will ever be able to say that God did not extend mercy before judgment. Unbelievers have been warned over and over again. Backslidden Christians, who must give account to the Lord, have also been warned through the teaching and preaching of God's Word. Surely the mercies of the Lord are abundantly extended to us. Lamentations 3:22,23 says, "It is of the Lord's mercies that we are not consumed, because his compassions fail not. They are new every morning: great is thy faithfulness."

Pharaoh's Response

When Moses and Aaron appeared before Pharaoh and said, "Thus saith the Lord God of Israel, Let my people go"

(Ex. 5:1), Pharaoh responded with statements that revealed his true character. He said, "Who is the Lord, that I should obey his voice to let Israel go? I know not the Lord, neither will I let Israel go" (v. 2). Obviously, Pharaoh had heard about Jehovah, but he did not know Him in a personal way, so he refused to obey His commands. How firmly Pharaoh's heart was set against God and the Israelites was revealed in his last statement: "Neither will I let Israel go."

Pharaoh was quick to assert himself against God. We must remember that Egyptian monarchs possessed unbridled power and authority. Each pharaoh was considered a child of the sun and to be worthy of the worship given the greatest Egyptian gods. The highest oath of any Egyptian was, "By the life of Pharaoh." Without the permission of the pharaoh no one had a right to do anything. All Egypt existed just for him. People lived, suffered and died for him. The armies, priests and magicians served and ministered to only him. From his exalted throne he looked down on his wretched subjects and on Israel as a slave nation under the dominion of those subjects. He considered the tears, groans and wails of bondage of the Israelites to be only a fitting sacrifice to one in his exalted position.

When Pharaoh refused to grant his request, Moses replied that even the king of Egypt could not defy the God of Israel. Later, the Lord assured Moses, "Now shalt thou see what I will do to Pharaoh" (6:1). But the Lord also told Moses: "But Pharaoh shall not hearken unto you, that I may lay my hand upon Egypt, and bring forth mine armies, and my people the children of Israel, out of the land of Egypt by great judgments. And the Egyptians shall know that I am the Lord, when I stretch forth mine hand upon Egypt, and bring out the children of Israel from among them" (7:4,5). This was the kind of man that God and Moses had to deal with.

Moses and Aaron told Pharaoh, "The God of the Hebrews hath met with us" (5:3). Note the way they referred to God—"the God of the Hebrews." The Almighty One of Israel was not requesting a favor of Pharaoh; He was commanding obedience. But Pharaoh's reply revealed that he did not know the God of the Hebrews.

Since Pharaoh did not know God, he might have asked, "Who dares to command me; am I not a god with authority

over everyone?" The key element in Pharaoh's response is
seen in the word "obey" (5:2). It must have stung Pharaoh to
the quick to think that he would be expected to obey
anyone. He considered himself to be a god; therefore, he
needed to obey no one. Was this other god stronger than he?
Who dared to issue such a summons? Was not the God of
Moses and Aaron only a God of mere slaves? How dared they
speak of their paltry God in the presence of almighty
Pharaoh?

Although Pharaoh said he did not know God, it was
apparent that he was going to learn of God in one way or
another. The plagues that came on him and the Egyptians
revealed the power of the true God. And this true God was
represented by Moses. This is why God told Moses, "I have
made thee a god to Pharaoh: and Aaron thy brother shall be
thy prophet" (7:1). When Moses and Aaron first stood before
him, Pharaoh said that he did not know God. But eventually
he would not only recognize God, he would also consider
Moses to be a god.

Pharaoh had to learn all of this the hard way. Not only
did he refuse to let the people go when Moses and Aaron first
requested it, but he also considered the request itself to be
merely an excuse for idleness. This shows the extent to which
Pharaoh disbelieved Moses and Aaron, who said, "The God of
the Hebrews hath met with us: let us go, we pray thee, three
days' journey into the desert, and sacrifice unto the Lord our
God; lest he fall upon us with pestilence, or with the sword"
(5:3).

Although the request was to allow the Israelites to
worship, Pharaoh was sure its purpose was only to get out of
work. He said, "Moses and Aaron, why do you draw the
people away from their work? Get back to your labors!"
(v. 4, NASB). Pharaoh refused to let the people go and
essentially accused Moses and Aaron of lying concerning why
they wanted to go.

Pharaoh was obviously threatened by the growing
number of Israelites, for he said, "Behold, the people of the
land now are many, and ye make them rest from their
burdens" (v. 5). Pharaoh thought he knew what would teach
the people a lesson, so he issued a new decree to those
responsible over the Israelites: "You are no longer to give the

people straw to make brick as previously; let them go and gather straw for themselves. But the quota of bricks which they were making previously, you shall impose on them; you are not to reduce any of it. Because they are lazy, therefore they cry out, 'Let us go and sacrifice to our God' " (vv. 7,8, NASB).

Pharaoh was evidently afraid of losing his clutch on the Israelites, so he made their burdens heavier instead of lighter. Satan also does everything he can to keep from losing his grasp on those who serve him. However, those who know Jesus Christ as Saviour possess the indwelling Holy Spirit, who can give victory over the Devil. This is why I John 4:4 says, "Greater is he that is in you, than he that is in the world." Hebrews 2:14 tells of the victory of Christ over Satan: "Since then the children share in flesh and blood, He Himself likewise also partook of the same, that through death He might render powerless him who has the power of death, that is, the devil" (NASB).

Jesus drew an analogy between Satan and Himself and said, "When a strong man armed keepeth his palace, his goods are in peace: but when a stronger than he shall come upon him, and overcome him, he taketh from him all his armour wherein he trusted, and divideth his spoils" (Luke 11:21,22). This was the Lord's explanation of how He was able to conquer Satan and his emissaries.

The Israelites' Appeal to Pharaoh

The news that Pharaoh refused to let them go and that he had also increased their burdens came as an almost unbearable shock to the Israelites. When the Israelites were not able to maintain their quota of bricks while gathering their own straw, the Israelite foremen were beaten (v. 14). Since Moses and Aaron had not helped matters any, these Israelite foremen decided to present their own case before Pharaoh. They came before Pharaoh and said, " 'Why do you deal this way with your servants? There is no straw given to your servants, yet they keep saying to us, "Make bricks!" And behold, your servants are being beaten; but it is the fault of your own people' " (Ex. 5:15,16, NASB). Pharaoh was not impressed by what the Israelites had to say. He responded,

" 'You are lazy, very lazy; therefore you say "Let us go and sacrifice to the Lord." So go now and work; for you shall be given no straw, yet must deliver the quota of bricks' " (vv. 17,18, NASB).

After this visit with Pharaoh, the Israelite foremen realized that their case was hopeless. "The officers of the children of Israel did see that they were in evil case" (v. 19). These officers, or foremen, gained nothing by going to Pharaoh themselves. Yet, they insisted on representing themselves before Pharaoh rather than letting Moses do so. God often lets people try their own way first to show them that they cannot solve their own problems. It is often the case, too, that God lets people try their own way so they will learn that it is not really best in the long run.

After their visit with Pharaoh, the foremen of Israel and the Israelites realized they were locked into their misery with no relief in sight.

This account reveals two things that the Israelites did not yet realize. First, they were not really ready to leave Egypt, as Moses and Aaron were seeking permission for them to do. Later, after they were out of Egypt, they grumbled often against Moses and wished they were back in Egypt (Ex. 14:11,12; Num. 11:5). Especially revealing is Exodus 14:12, which records the grumbling of the people after they had left Egypt. They said, "Is not this the word that we did tell thee in Egypt, saying, Let us alone, that we may serve the Egyptians? For it had been better for us to serve the Egyptians, than that we should die in the wilderness." Even though the Israelites wanted to be delivered from their Egyptian bondage, they feared what was outside the land worse than they feared what was inside.

Second, the Israelites had to learn that it was absolutely necessary for deliverance to come from without, not from within. They had neither the resources to pay their own ransom nor the power to break their own chains of bondage. In addition, the will to go was lacking.

So it is evident that the Lord still had to work in the lives of the Israelites to show them the need to completely depend on Him. They needed both the will and the enablement that only He could provide. That God had the ability to accomplish both is evident from Philippians 2:13: "For it is

God which worketh in you both to will and to do of his good pleasure." God not only puts the desire in a person to do something, but He also gives the enablement to accomplish those things that are His will.

As we later study the plagues on Pharaoh and the Egyptians, we will see how God made His people willing to forsake all in Egypt and to follow Moses into the wilderness.

Have you wondered why you may be having certain testings in your life? It could be for the same reason God brought testings on the Israelites—to make them willing to do His will. Although this is not always the purpose of testing, it can be. Once you become willing to do God's will by depending on Him completely, you never regret the testing because of the lesson it has taught you.

Moses Learns to Stand Alone

As Moses was rejected by Pharaoh and then by his own people, he was learning what it meant to stand alone with God. Not only did Pharaoh refuse his request, but he essentially called Moses a liar. And the Israelites went around Moses by taking their case directly to Pharaoh. It was one thing to be rejected by Pharaoh, an unbeliever, but it was quite another thing to be rejected by his own people. Moses experienced a bitter and painful lesson in learning to trust God alone. Every vestige of hope in others was ripped away, and he had no other choice than to stand alone with God.

Moses was deeply sensitive to the failure he had experienced 40 years earlier when he tried to deliver the Israelites and was rejected by them. His one ray of hope now was that they had seemingly recognized him as the instrument of God's deliverance. The revival that had taken place when he came back from the desert must have greatly encouraged him. But as he and Aaron waited outside the court of Pharaoh while the foremen of Israel presented their case, Moses was about to receive his greatest blow. As these foremen came out from the presence of Pharaoh, they met Moses and Aaron and said to them, "The Lord look upon you, and judge; because ye have made our savour to be abhorred in the eyes of Pharaoh, and in the eyes of his servants, to put a sword in their hand to slay us" (Ex. 5:21). What an accusation!

The entire plan of delivering Israel seemed to have backfired. Once again his own people were bitter toward him and accused him of being directly responsible for their troubles, even though Moses had been willing to give his life for them. How those words must have cut deeply into his heart.

Notice again what the Israelites told Moses and Aaron: "The Lord look upon you, and judge" (v. 21). They were calling down the judgment of God on Moses and Aaron! What a heartbreaking accusation after his years of agonizing over the need of delivering his people. The Israelites also said, "Ye have made our savour to be abhorred in the eyes of Pharaoh." This phrase could literally be translated: "Ye have made our savour to stink in Pharaoh's sight."

As we look back at this scene from today's vantage point, we can understand why these things happened, but at the time, neither the Israelites nor Moses knew how God was working behind the scenes. This should be a lesson to us. In our own difficult circumstances, we cannot see through the whys except by faith. But God always knows what is in the future, so He, being sovereign, is never caught off guard. But it was necessary for both the Hebrews and Moses to see that their case was humanly hopeless—that no logic of theirs nor appeals to Pharaoh could alter their circumstances.

One's heart goes out to Moses because his troubles were only beginning. He had been prepared for the rebuff which he received from Pharaoh because he had been warned of this by God. But no warning had been given him concerning the rebuff by his own people, which was much harder to take. How discouraging it is when one is criticized by those he is trying to help. This teaches us, too, that it is easier to take criticism from unbelievers than it is to take it from believers.

Facing Opposition

The Lord Jesus Christ warned us about rebuff. He said, "If ye were of the world, the world would love his own: but because ye are not of the world, but I have chosen you out of the world, therefore the world hateth you" (John 15:19).

The Lord went on to remind us, "Remember the words that I said unto you, The servant is not greater than his lord. If they have persecuted me, they will also persecute you; if they have kept my saying, they will keep your's also" (v. 20). The Lord revealed the purpose of such opposition directed toward Him and His followers: "But this cometh to pass, that the word might be fulfilled that is written in their law, They hated me without a cause" (v. 25).

Opposition to Jesus came frequently from those who claimed to be in right relationship with God, such as the scribes and Pharisees. But those who opposed Him revealed that they actually were not in right relationship with God, and Christ referred to them as "the world" (v. 19). As the Lord Jesus sought to comfort His disciples concerning the trouble they would have to endure, He said, "These things I have spoken unto you, that in me ye might have peace. In the world ye shall have tribulation: but be of good cheer; I have overcome the world" (16:33).

The opposition that Moses received from his own people taught him not to expect their enthusiastic loyalty. This was what he needed, because they frequently murmured against him as he led them through the wilderness. Thus, we see that God was training Moses to be the kind of person he needed to be later. Even though, on the surface, the opposition of Moses' own people seemed to go against him, it was actually accomplishing what God wanted. This was the outworking of the principle that is specifically stated in Romans 8:28: "We know that all things work together for good to them that love God, to them who are the called according to his purpose." But have you ever wondered why God works all of these things together for our good? The answer is found in the next verse—that we might "be conformed to the image of his Son" (v. 29).

Not only was God teaching Moses something, but He was also teaching the Israelites something. They needed to look beyond Moses—they needed to trust in God alone for deliverance. They were not to trust in a human instrument but in the God who was using that instrument.

Undoubtedly, Moses gained the most from the lesson as he stood alone with God, unable to depend any longer on the support of his people for his own encouragement. Moses

stood at the point where God wanted him. In my Bible, I have
written the word "arrived" at Exodus 5:21, because it was
the opposition of the Israelites that caused Moses to stand
alone with God. In the desert, Moses had learned not to rely
on himself; now he learned not to rely on others.
Recognizing both of these truths is the basis for progress. He
was now prepared for what was to come in the future. Moses
had learned that there was no good thing in his flesh, and
now he learned that this applied to others also; therefore, he
should not put his trust in others. That there is nothing good
in the flesh was stated specifically by the Apostle Paul: "For
I know that in me (that is, in my flesh,) dwelleth no good
thing" (Rom. 7:18).

We must remember as we study the Old Testament, and
in particular the nation of Israel, that God intends for us to
learn important lessons from what we study. The experiences
of the Israelites serve as examples to individual believers and
reveal pitfalls that should be avoided. Referring to the
incidents that happened to the Israelites, the New Testament
says, "Now these things happened to them as an example,
and they were written for our instruction" (I Cor. 10:11,
NASB). This is why we are carefully examining the Old
Testament account of Moses and Israel; what we learn from
these events serves as an example to the individual believer
today.

Although Moses realized that he could not depend on
others, he was baffled about what God was trying to
accomplish. Having been opposed by his fellow Israelites,
Moses said to the Lord, "Wherefore hast thou so evil
entreated this people? why is it that thou hast sent me? For
since I came to Pharaoh to speak in thy name, he hath done
evil to this people; neither hast thou delivered thy people at
all" (Ex. 5:22,23).

As a leader, Moses was frustrated because he realized his
responsibility. Others found it easy to criticize and oppose,
but Moses knew he had no one to criticize or oppose, so he
had to rely totally on God. This is why he poured out his
heart to God, asking what he should do. Anyone who holds
the highest position in a group or organization knows a little
about what Moses went through. Many times a leader can
turn to no one else but God. When Moses was faced with

opposition 40 years earlier, he fled. Now, instead of fleeing, he went to the Lord. Moses was convinced that he was doing God's will as revealed to him in the desert, but things did not go as he expected.

And isn't this often the way it is with us? God lays a burden on our hearts to do a particular thing for Him, but when the response is not what we expected, we become discouraged. At such times, we need to go to God's Word, which tells us: "Cast not away therefore your confidence, which hath great recompence of reward. For ye have need of patience, that, after ye have done the will of God, ye might receive the promise" (Heb. 10:35,36). Also, Galatians 6:9 tells us: "Let us not be weary in well doing: for in due season we shall reap, if we faint not."

Although Moses was baffled by what was happening, his confidence in God remained firm. Commenting on this incident, Hebrews 11:27 says, "By faith he forsook Egypt, not fearing the wrath of the king: for he endured, as seeing him who is invisible." Although Moses was tremendously perplexed by the rejection of his brethren, he had his eyes fixed on God alone.

Moses Experiences Death to Self

The agony of soul through which Moses passed must have been as death to him. Earlier, he had tried to persuade the Lord that he was nothing, but he agreed to go to Pharaoh with Aaron as his spokesman. Then Pharaoh rejected him—which God had forewarned that he would—and then his own people rejected him. What an agonizing death to self it was! Everything that a leader might naturally long for, Moses had to die to. As he lay there on the ground alone before God, perhaps Moses even wished himself back in the desert, for he asked God, "Why is it that thou hast sent me?" (Ex. 5:22). Earlier it had been difficult for him to imagine that God could really use him, and the question came to his mind again. But in the process, he was seeing that he must rely totally on God. He was like a corn of wheat falling into the ground and dying. And that is exactly what God wanted, as John 12:24 says, "Except a corn of wheat fall into the ground and die, it abideth alone: but if it die, it bringeth forth much fruit."

Moses was no longer to abide alone; he was to bear much fruit for God. Moses clearly saw the hopelessness of relying on himself and on others and was casting himself entirely on God. It is not easy to die to one's own plans and work. It is extremely difficult to be renounced by one's own people—even despised by them. This was more than Moses could personally take, and that's why he cried out to God.

Moses had learned deep lessons on the backside of the desert, but he learned something now that climaxed these lessons—he learned to put away self completely and to rely totally on God. This was a sentence of death to him.

In the New Testament, Paul said concerning the sentence of death, "Yes, I felt within my very self the sentence of death, to keep me from depending on myself instead of God who raises the dead" (II Cor. 1:9, Williams). Every successful servant of God must learn the significance of the death sentence on self. Only then can he be dead to self and alive to God.

Jeremiah recorded the words of the Lord on this subject: "Cursed be the man that trusteth in man, and maketh flesh his arm, and whose heart departeth from the Lord.... Blessed is the man that trusteth in the Lord, and whose hope the Lord is" (17:5,7).

How interesting it is that Moses had a sentence of death for Pharaoh, yet he himself had to experience the sentence of death on self. Before Moses could communicate a message of life, or deliverance, to Israel, he had to experience a message of death on self. And before we can effectively communicate the message of salvation and the essentials of Christian growth to others, we must experience death to self. This is not physical death but death to one's selfish desires. We must be weaned from relying on our own strength.

The Old Testament had much to say about Israel relying on the strength of others rather than on the strength of God. Isaiah said it this way: "Woe to them that go down to Egypt for help; and stay on horses, and trust in chariots, because they are many; and in horsemen, because they are very strong; but they look not unto the Holy One of Israel, neither seek the Lord!" (31:1). The same kind of warning and encouragement is revealed in II Chronicles 32:7,8: "Be strong and courageous, be not afraid nor dismayed for the king of Assyria, nor for all the multitude that is with him: for there be more with us than with him: with him is an arm of flesh; but with us is the Lord our God to help us, and to fight our battles."

The Lord Himself gave us an example to follow in self-denial. Philippians 2:5 says, "Let this mind be in you, which was also in Christ Jesus." The following verses describe the mind, or attitude, that the Lord Jesus Christ had: "Who, although He existed in the form of God, did not regard equality with God a thing to be grasped, but emptied Himself, taking the form of a bond-servant, and being made in the likeness of men. And being found in appearance as a man, He humbled Himself by becoming obedient to the point of death, even death on a cross" (vv. 6-8, NASB).

Of course, the Lord's death was a physical one, whereas we are to die to self that we might be fruitful. Using the analogy of death, the Apostle Paul said, "That which you sow does not come to life unless it dies" (I Cor. 15:36, NASB). This is a tremendous lesson we need to learn if we are to be fruitful—we must appropriate our death to self. Moses had to learn this, and we have to learn this. In the case of the Lord Jesus Christ there was death before resurrection, and in our case there must be death to self before we can live for God as He desires.

Because Paul had died to self and was living to God, he was able to write: "That I may know him, and the power of his resurrection, and the fellowship of his sufferings, being made conformable unto his death" (Phil. 3:10). We must recognize that we have died with Christ as Romans 6 tells us, and we need to learn to appropriate the benefits that result.

God Encourages Moses

In Moses' deep discouragement, he even blamed God for not fulfilling His promise. Moses said, "Neither hast thou delivered thy people at all" (Ex. 5:23). But in spite of this accusation, there is no indication that God reprimanded Moses in any way. God knew what Moses was going through at this time; He saw the heart of His servant.

How wonderful to know that God understands. He never overlooks sin, but when a believer is going through difficulty, God looks on him with sympathy. The psalmist realized this and wrote: "He has not dealt with us according to our sins, nor rewarded us according to our iniquities. . . . Just as a father has compassion on his children, so the Lord has compassion on those who fear Him. For He Himself knows our frame; He is mindful that we are but dust" (Ps. 103:10,13,14, NASB). Man sees only the outward appearance, but God sees the heart and is understanding when His children become frustrated.

God knew Moses' heart. He knew that His man was totally committed to Him. God also knows every detail about us. If we are not totally committed to Him, He knows it. But if we are, He knows that too.

Moses had been slapped down from every side and was now flat on his face before God. He was not running from God but to God. He was completely broken; that is, he was dead to self. He did not need another slapping down but something that would jolt him to the reality of God and life.

This is often what we need too. Frequently, so much emphasis is placed on dying to the old man that we forget that we are really alive in Christ and are to be vibrantly living for Him. Our death with Christ is a past act appropriated by faith; we participated in His death when we trusted Him as personal Saviour. Then, as Romans 6 tells us, we were raised together with Christ, so we are to be living to Him.

As Moses prayed to God, he was not in need of another rebuke but of encouragement. This encouragement was given to Moses, and the verse that records it is one of the key verses concerning Moses' life.

In our studies we have carefully considered how God was preparing His man from birth to age 80 to be the instrument He could use to deliver Israel. We have seen Moses in the courts of Pharaoh, in the desert alone with God, and rejected by Pharaoh and his brethren as he returned to Egypt. He stands alone now before God, discouraged and defeated. But notice God's encouraging words! Exodus 6:1 says, "Then the Lord said unto Moses, Now shalt thou see what I will do to Pharaoh." Notice the key words: "then," "now" and "I." "Then" reveals that it was not until Moses realized he must never trust in himself or in others that God gave him the encouragement he needed. "Now" reveals that having come to this point, a different course of action would be taken. "I" reveals who would take that action—God Himself. God refused to use Moses as an instrument until Moses realized that only God could perform the task.

Moses was finally dead to self and alive to God; the true combination was complete. It was no longer Moses *and* God but God *through* Moses.

God then told Moses what would happen concerning Pharaoh: "For with a strong hand shall he let them go, and with a strong hand shall he drive them out of his land" (6:1).

Moses could forget all the bitter words of his brethren and his own personal defeat before Pharaoh. Deliverance was sure because God not only had promised it, but Moses, for the first time, seemed to realize that God also was undertaking the task. As Moses considered the faithfulness of God, he realized that the I Am was sufficient for everything. Moses realized this only as he came to know God intimately as the great I Am.

It is more important to know God than to merely rely on His promises. No man has ever been greatly used of God until he has known God personally. For responses of those who have come to this point, be sure to read again Philippians 3:10, Job 42:5,6 and Joshua 5:14,15.

When Moses passed the test and relied on the Lord alone, the Lord then restated His purpose, which Moses was to share with Israel. He rescheduled Moses' meeting with Pharaoh and renewed Moses' commission.

From the life of Moses we can see that the man God uses is the one who dies to himself, as a kernel of grain must die before it can reproduce (John 12:24,25). We have seen that one cannot really live for God and be used as God desires until he denies self (Luke 9:23,24). But even the very desire to quit relying on self and to begin relying totally on God comes from God Himself (Phil. 2:13).

Conclusion

We have followed Moses from the time of his birth when his parents exercised their faith and hid him in the reeds by the bank of the Nile. We saw how he had the best training Egypt could offer under the tutelage of Pharaoh's daughter. We have seen the defeat he suffered because he relied on himself rather than on God. But God allowed Moses to experience defeat so that he would come to the end of himself and rely totally on God.

We have seen Moses in the loneliness of the desert, where he spent 40 years in God's private school. There, as he saw the holiness of God, he came to abhor himself, even as Job did (Job 42:5,6). At the burning bush, God gave Moses His call and commission, and Moses had to adjust his understanding of God to his ideas of the man God uses. Because Moses had come to the end of himself and had no confidence in himself, he thought it impossible for God to use him. But this is precisely the kind of person God uses, and that is why He called and commissioned Moses to the gigantic task of delivering 3 million Israelites from Egypt.

Although Moses met defeat and discouragement before Pharaoh and before his own people when he returned to Egypt, God encouraged him by giving him a revelation of Himself, restating His purpose for Moses, rescheduling Moses' meetings with Pharaoh, and renewing His commission to Moses. How patient God was with Moses all those years. Now that Moses was to the point that God wanted him, He was about to use him in a phenomenal way.

God prepared His man by allowing circumstances in his life to bring him to the end of himself and to total commitment to God, just as we must recognize that it is "not I, but Christ" (Gal. 2:20).

From this time forward, obedience characterized Moses' life. In such obedience of faith, he accomplished what no other person has before or since as he led 3 million people through the wilderness for 40 years. There is such a difference between the Moses of the account we have considered and the Moses of the account that follows that one wonders if it is the same person. But he was used so mightily because God had thoroughly prepared him for what was ahead. And we, too, will be greatly used of God as we allow Him to mold us into what He wants us to be.

Chapter 13

God Strengthens His Man

The emancipation of Israel from Egypt was in reality an intense conflict between two great personalities—God and Satan. Each person had prepared his man for this conflict.

Key Men—Moses and Pharaoh

For 80 years God had been preparing Moses to be His key person in this conflict. The time of preparation was so long because this was a gigantic task such as no other person had been called upon to do. Moses probably had a high IQ and many natural talents, as well as training in the courts of Egypt, but he had to have 40 years of special training alone with God in the desert. Those 40 years gave Moses his final preparation as God's man for emancipating Israel from Egypt.

But Satan also had his man—the God-defying Pharaoh. When Moses first appeared before him, Pharaoh said, "Who is the Lord, that I should obey his voice to let Israel go? I know not the Lord, neither will I let Israel go" (Ex. 5:2). Pharaoh's heart was hardened against God. God had forewarned Moses of this when He told him, "When thou goest to return into Egypt, see that thou do all those wonders before Pharaoh, which I have put in thine hand: but I will harden his heart, that he shall not let the people go" (4:21). However, God had also promised Moses, "I will stretch out my hand, and smite Egypt with all my wonders which I will do in the midst thereof: and after that he will let you go" (3:20). The subject of the hardening of Pharaoh's heart will be discussed in detail later as we examine the plagues that God brought on Pharaoh and Egypt.

The conflict between God and Satan was really a one-sided conflict, for God had already told Moses, "Thou shalt say unto Pharaoh, Thus saith the Lord, Israel is my son, even my firstborn: and I say unto thee, Let my son go, that he may serve me: and if thou refuse to let him go, behold, I will slay thy son, even thy firstborn" (4:22,23). So these verses clearly indicate that the outcome of the conflict was already determined in the mind of God.

The Lord had told Moses, "Now shalt thou see what I will do to Pharaoh: for with a strong hand shall he let them go, and with a strong hand shall he drive them out of his land" (6:1). Even the Egyptians would know that Jehovah was God: "The Egyptians shall know that I am the Lord, when I stretch forth mine hand upon Egypt, and bring out the children of Israel from among them" (7:5).

Just as God and Satan conflicted concerning the emancipation of Israel from Egypt, so there will be conflict between them during a future time known as the Tribulation. This conflict is recorded in Revelation 4—20. Satan's man at that time will be the Antichrist, who will exalt himself as God.

Moses' Need for Strengthening

In considering the emancipation of Israel from Egypt, the early chapters of Exodus tell how God prepared His man for this task. Chapters 5—15 reveal how God strengthened His man. Moses needed to be strengthened so Pharaoh would realize that he was being confronted by God's man. Pharaoh needed to realize that he could not just ignore Moses because God was speaking through him.

Moses also needed to be strengthened because of his new position. He had been elevated from a shepherd, who was considered an abomination by the Egyptians, to God's personal spokesman against Pharaoh. Moses had to be strong as he was used by God in completely breaking the stubbornness of Pharaoh.

Pharaoh claimed to be a powerful god, but he soon discovered that he was no match for Moses and his God.

Later, God told Moses, "See, I have made thee a god to Pharaoh" (7:1). Although Pharaoh claimed to be a powerful god, he needed to realize that he was only a tool of God's enemy, Satan. When he refused the request to let Israel go, Moses replied that even the emperor of Egypt could not defy the God of Israel. It took a long time—possibly a year—before Pharaoh came to the same conclusion. God needed a strong man to make Pharaoh realize this, so it was necessary for Him to strengthen Moses for this great task.

As Moses came before Pharaoh to seek the emancipation of Israel, he conveyed more than a request of God that Pharaoh let the people go—it was a command. Since Pharaoh did not know God, he refused to recognize any power higher than himself. Moses assured him, however, that he would learn to know God in one way or another. Pharaoh chose the hard way. It took ten severe judgments, or plagues, to cause Pharaoh and his people to recognize the power of God and to understand that God meant what He said. The plagues continued until Pharaoh and his people were broken and destroyed, for they had set their wills against God. Pharaoh needed to know that God Almighty was undertaking the emancipation of Israel and that Moses was God's man of the hour. In studying the plagues that were brought on Pharaoh and the Egyptians, we will see that Pharaoh became progressively hardened against God while Moses became progressively stronger for God.

Israel's Preparation

On the other hand Israel, too, had to be prepared for the journey from Egypt to Canaan. In Genesis 15 the Israelites had been promised that after 400 years the nation would be brought out of captivity with a strong hand. This time element was completely fulfilled, so they needed to be prepared for the journey. At first they were unwilling because their faith in God was very weak. Although they had many problems in Egypt, they preferred to stay there rather than risk having nothing once they left.

There were two aspects to God's work in preparing the Israelites for what was ahead. First, three of the judgments, or plagues, were experienced by the Israelites as well as by the Egyptians. The Israelites experienced God's mercy and were spared from the last seven plagues. They saw the goodness of God in this, which led them to repent of their evil ways. Romans 2:4 states the scriptural principle: "The goodness of God leadeth thee to repentance."

Second, God also prepared Israel by revealing that Moses was His chosen leader. The Israelites had to be convinced that their deliverance was all God's undertaking, not their's. Little by little, God was able to teach them to rely on Moses as His representative. Moses himself became progressively bolder in his faith and more powerful in his leadership. One experience of faith led to another, just as one step leads to another. As Romans 1:17 says, "Therein is the righteousness of God revealed from faith to faith." The study of Moses' life and how he was strengthened by God is a study of how a believer progresses from faith to faith.

Chapter 14

Preparation for Israel's Exodus

As we study concerning the Israelites and what happened to them, let us remember the sobering words of I Corinthians 10:11: "Now these things happened to them as an example, and they were written for our instruction, upon whom the ends of the ages have come" (NASB). Thus, we need to carefully study what occurred during Old Testament times so that we can learn lessons for today.

Just as Moses needed to be prepared and strengthened by God for the task he was to accomplish we, too, need to be ready for what God wants us to do.

The Announcement to the Elders

When God first made it clear to Moses that he was the man He wanted to use to deliver Israel, Moses was reluctant because he was so sensitive about his deficiencies. Finally, however, Moses agreed to be God's representative, after he was convinced that the deliverance of Israel was to be God's work, not his. But because of Moses' insistence on his lack of eloquence, God permitted his brother Aaron to be his spokesman.

It was a memorable time when Moses and Aaron first announced to the Israelites that God was going to deliver them from Egypt. Exodus 4:29-31 records this significant time: "And Moses and Aaron went and gathered together all the elders of the children of Israel: and Aaron spake all the words which the Lord had spoken unto Moses, and did the signs in the sight of the people. And the people believed: and when they heard that the Lord had visited the children of

Israel, and that he had looked upon their affliction, then they bowed their heads and worshipped." Notice that Moses and Aaron presented their credentials. As the spokesman, Aaron "did the signs in the sight of the people." These signs were miracles that confirmed the fact that the message which Moses and Aaron delivered originated with God.

Moses must have been greatly encouraged by the response of the people, for they "bowed their heads and worshipped" (v. 31). Although this was a good response from the people, there were to be rough days ahead as the Israelites spoke out against Moses and his leadership.

But even though there were discouraging times later, the goodness of God allowed Moses and Aaron to see the favorable response of the people at this time. Although Moses and Aaron had confidence in God, their faith was rather weak, so this initial response of the people was highly significant. They saw God's ability to work in the lives of the Israelites and were tremendously encouraged. A rebuff at this point might have been a tragedy in Moses' life.

God did not test Moses beyond what he was able to endure. The New Testament tells of God's goodness in regard to this matter: "No temptation has overtaken you but such as is common to man; and God is faithful, who will not allow you to be tempted beyond what you are able; but with the temptation will provide the way of escape also, that you may be able to endure it" (I Cor. 10:13, NASB). When God allows a temptation, or testing, He also makes available sufficient grace for the Christian to be able to stand in spite of it. He does not allow the believer to be tested beyond what he is able to bear. The trial of our faith is very important, but only God knows how much trial we can take at any one time. And because of His faithfulness and goodness, He does not push the believer beyond his limit.

First Meeting With Pharaoh

Having had their first meeting with the elders of Israel, Moses and Aaron then had their first meeting with Pharaoh. God had already told Moses that Pharaoh would not listen to him, but He made it clear to Moses that by the time God was through with Pharaoh, he would listen. Although God had told Moses about the eventual slaying of the firstborn if Pharaoh did not let the Israelites go, Moses and Aaron did not mention this to Pharaoh when they first appeared before him. They simply announced to Pharaoh, "Thus saith the Lord God of Israel, Let my people go, that they may hold a feast unto me in the wilderness" (Ex. 5:1).

Pharaoh was far from being impressed by Moses and Aaron or by the God of Israel. Pharaoh said, "Who is the Lord, that I should obey his voice to let Israel go? I know not the Lord, neither will I let Israel go" (v. 2).

Had Moses and Aaron immediately told Pharaoh that the firstborn of Egypt would be killed if he did not let Israel go, the hardness of Pharaoh's heart might not have been demonstrated. But even this simple request which they made of him caused the hardness of Pharaoh's heart to become immediately apparent. Pharaoh was considered a god, and, as such, worship was directed to him. God would eventually break him of his haughtiness, but first He was going to reveal to Israel, to Moses and Aaron and to us today that Pharaoh was a hardened individual to begin with. Pharaoh failed to recognize that God puts on the throne whomever He wills, and He removes from the throne whomever He wills. God could have immediately taken care of Pharaoh, but He did not do so, for there were many lessons to be taught through the hardness of this individual.

The key to understanding all that was involved is Exodus 5:2, which records Pharaoh's refusal to recognize anyone higher than himself. He was considered a god, and he was not about to let any other being receive greater recognition than himself. In essence, he told Moses and Aaron, "I do not recognize your God. I will not obey Him. No one is going to tell me what I can or cannot do!"

Pharaoh thus hardened his own heart against God Almighty. Concerning Pharaoh the New Testament says, "For the scripture saith unto Pharaoh, Even for this same purpose have I raised thee up, that I might shew my power in thee, and that my name might be declared throughout all the earth" (Rom. 9:17). Verse 22 adds, "What if God, willing to shew his wrath, and to make his power known, endured with much longsuffering the vessels of wrath fitted to destruction." Inasmuch as Pharaoh hardened his own heart against God, he became one of the "vessels of wrath fitted to destruction."

God did not make Pharaoh a vessel fit for destruction; Pharaoh did that himself. God had much longsuffering, or patience, with him. God only added to the hardening process already evident in Pharaoh's life.

We sometimes say that, because of His foreknowledge, God knew that all of this was going to take place. However, it is not as if God sees things as future. Since God knows everything, it is as if everything were in the present tense to Him. We think of events as being past, present or future, but the whole future is before God just as though it were present. In other words, everything to God is in what I like to call the "ever-present tense." We are creatures of time, but He works with everything in constant view before Him. That is why Romans 8:28 is such a precious verse: "All things work together for good to them that love God, to them who are the called according to his purpose." God knows what is ahead, so He can cause all things to work together for our good.

Pharaoh's rejection of God's command to let Israel go was allowed by God for several other reasons. First, Pharaoh's behavior was tolerated so the world would know that the God of heaven has thoroughly subdued everything that is called god. Second, it was allowed so that Israel might be brought to a singular knowledge of God. The nation was in a backslidden condition and needed a greater respect of God's hatred of sin. Third, Pharaoh's rejection of God's authority made Israel willing to leave Egypt. Even though they were oppressed by the Egyptians, they were not ready and willing to leave. Thus, God had to make them willing (see Phil. 2:13). Fourth, Moses and Aaron needed to realize that the task of delivering Israel was hopeless if they relied on their own strength. Only the God of heaven could cause Pharaoh to change his mind. Fifth, the Israelites needed a greater concept of who God is and what He wanted to do for them. Their estimate of God was far too low. They needed to learn the truth that "God is our refuge and strength, a very present help in trouble" (Ps. 46:1).

God's Mercy and God's Judgment

The nation of Israel realized that it did not have answers to the problems it faced. Most nations today also recognize the same thing. They have many overwhelming problems which they do not know how to cope with—population explosions, inflation, famine. The tendency is for one nation to rise up against another nation in an attempt to satisfy its needs and solve its problems. The Scriptures indicate that world conditions are going to get much worse before they get better. In fact, we will not really have world peace until the Prince of Peace comes to establish His kingdom on earth. When Christ comes to set up His earthly kingdom, He will first bring judgment on the nations. But as is customary in God's manner of working, grace is always abundantly manifested before judgment.

Although a day of judgment is coming, as described in the Book of the Revelation, God is abundantly extending His mercy at the present time. Just as God gave 120 years of mercy before the judgment of the flood in Noah's time, so now the nations are being given a chance to repent and return to God as the preaching of the gospel is heard in all parts of the world. Never in the history of the world has there been a time when the gospel has been preached as much and as clearly as it is today—from one end of the world to the other. This is being accomplished through a variety of means such as missionaries, radio, literature and Bible translators.

But we must remember that God's salvation is more than just an invitation to get right with God. God's plan of salvation involves a declaration of what God demands of the sinner. Of course, He demands it in love, but it is still a demand. Just as God was demanding Pharaoh to let His people go, so God demands certain things of us. Acts 17:30 says that God "commandeth all men every where to repent." This is not an option; if we are to be right with God, we must repent. The word "repent" includes more than sorrow; it is actually a change of mind. No one can come into right relationship with God until he changes his mind about who God is, about his sin and about the need to have that sin taken care of. Those who never change their minds about these things never come to God trusting in Jesus Christ alone for salvation.

Having trusted Jesus Christ as Saviour, the believer's life will be drastically different. This is especially true as he looks forward to the coming of Christ. Concerning the return of Christ, I John 3:3 says, "And every man that hath this hope in him purifieth himself, even as he is pure." What a wonderful hope the believer has once he has placed his trust in Jesus Christ!

But how sad it will be for those who continue to reject Christ as Saviour. Second Thessalonians 1:8 refers to those unsaved who will be living at the time of Christ's return to earth: "In flaming fire taking vengeance on them that know not God, and that obey not the gospel of our Lord Jesus Christ." The following verse reveals the awful judgment that these people will experience: "Who shall be punished with everlasting destruction from the presence of the Lord, and from the glory of his power" (v. 9). If the gospel is not obeyed, judgment is sure. The more light that is given and rejected, the more terrible will be the judgment on the unbeliever.

To turn away from the light and the truth of God causes one to become more and more hardened in sin. Whereas the manifestation of the grace and mercy of God causes some to respond to Him, it seems to cause others to rebel all the more. The same sun that melts the ice hardens the clay. And often, the sun of God's mercy and grace melts some hearts but hardens others.

Pharaoh was one who turned his face against Almighty God and continued to reject Him. Any manifestation of the grace of God only served to harden Pharaoh's heart all the more until he was one of "the vessels of wrath fitted to destruction" (Rom. 9:22).

Background for God's Action

The fifth and sixth chapters of Exodus provide the background for all that followed. Exodus 5:9 reveals how lightly Pharaoh thought of the words of God. As Pharaoh instructed his men to make the Israelites' work load heavier, he said of the Israelites, "Let them not regard vain words." Pharaoh was referring to the words spoken to him by Moses and Aaron, which were the words of God. Pharaoh considered the mandate given to him by God through Moses as "vain words." No one can think this lightly of the words of God and escape judgment.

So God worked with Pharaoh not only to reveal that he was a vessel "fitted to destruction" but also to make Israel willing to leave the land of Egypt. When Moses and Aaron first met with the elders of Israel, they gladly accepted God's promise of deliverance, and "they bowed their heads and worshipped" (4:31). But later it was evident that the Israelites were not really willing to leave Egypt. Thus, even Pharaoh's response and his act of increasing the work load of the Israelites were used by God to make the Israelites willing to leave Egypt.

The foremen of the Israelites were so upset with the increased work load that they bypassed Moses and went directly to Pharaoh. When Pharaoh refused to lighten their work load, the foremen lashed out at Moses and said, "The Lord look upon you, and judge; because ye have made our savour to be abhorred in the eyes of Pharaoh, and in the eyes of his servants, to put a sword in their hand to slay us" (5:21). The people were far from ready at that time to forsake Egypt for the uncertainty of the desert trip ahead of them. So God was preparing them in a special way, even though they could not understand it at the time. God was allowing them to experience grief so He could bring about His will in their lives. This reminds us of Lamentations 3:32: "But though he cause grief, yet will he have compassion according to the multitude of his mercies." Although God may allow believers to experience grief for a time, it is for the purpose of later showing His mercy.

After Moses had been rejected by Pharaoh and by his own people, he was left alone with God. "Moses returned unto the Lord, and said, Lord, wherefore hast thou so evil entreated this people? Why is it that thou hast sent me? For since I came to Pharaoh to speak in thy name, he hath done evil to this people; neither hast thou delivered thy people at all" (Ex. 5:22,23). Moses was completely at the end of himself; he had nowhere to turn but to God. This set the stage for all that followed. Pharaoh defied God; Israel rejected God's plan and saw no hope; Moses saw himself as helpless and cast himself on God alone. Then God was ready to act.

God's Promise

This significant statement follows: "Then the Lord said unto Moses, Now shalt thou see what I will do to Pharaoh: for with a strong hand shall he let them go, and with a strong hand shall he drive them out of his land" (Ex. 6:1).

Although these words of God to Moses sounded as if they might be fulfilled the next day, it was actually several months, maybe even a year, before they were fulfilled. Several steps were involved in the process, and Moses had to learn to wait on God.

One of the key words in this verse is "now." God was, in effect, telling Moses, "Now that you are where you ought to be, Moses, I will begin to act." Israel had been crushed under Pharaoh's inhuman work assignments, and Pharaoh had essentially challenged God to a duel.

Another key word is "I"—"what I [God] will do." Since Moses had learned that he was not to rely on anyone except God Himself, God promised that Moses would see what He would do to Pharaoh. And when God was finished with Pharaoh, He would show Moses what He was going to do with Israel. Moses' responsibility was to simply rest on the promises of God. During his 80 years of preparation, Moses had learned to know God.

The words of Exodus 6:1 amounted to God giving His final word to Moses. The word of God is just as reliable as God is. Because God has complete integrity, He always honors His word. Isaiah 55:11 records this promise of God: "So shall my word be that goeth forth out of my mouth: it shall not return unto me void, but it shall accomplish that which I please, and it shall prosper in the thing whereto I sent it."

Exodus 6 emphasizes the importance of the name of God. God told Moses, "I am the Lord: and I appeared unto Abraham, unto Isaac, and unto Jacob, by the name of God Almighty, but by my name Jehovah was I not known to them" (vv. 2,3); "Wherefore say unto the children of Israel, I am the Lord" (v. 6).

The words "I am the Lord," appearing in verses 2 and 6, serve as brackets for all that is in between. What is said between these statements pledges the very nature of God Himself to accomplish what is promised. What God promised is indicated by seven "I wills" in verses 6-8. "I will bring you out from under the burdens of the Egyptians" (v. 6); "I will rid you out of their bondage" (v. 6); "I will redeem you with a stretched out arm" (v. 6); "I will take you to me for a people" (v. 7); "I will be to you a God" (v. 7); "I will bring you in unto the land" (v. 8); "I will give it you for an heritage" (v. 8).

The words that serve as brackets, "I am the Lord," clinch the promises of God. He had revealed Himself to Moses as "I Am That I Am" (3:14). All that Moses needed, God would be to him, and this was what God emphasized in His promises recorded in Exodus 6. Whatever was needed to fulfill the promises, God was more than able to supply. This was true concerning Israel, and it is also true concerning us. Whatever our need is, He is able to meet it.

In analyzing the "I wills" in Exodus 6:6-8, it is possible to group them into three categories. The first three, which appear in verse 6, have to do with emancipation. The Lord said, "I will bring you out from under the burdens of the Egyptians, and I will rid you out of their bondage, and I will redeem you with a stretched out arm, and with great judgments."

The next two "I wills," which appear in verse 7, have to do with God's taking the nation of Israel to Himself. He said, "I will take you to me for a people, and I will be to you a God: and ye shall know that I am the Lord your God, which bringeth you out from under the burdens of the Egyptians."

The last two statements, which appear in verse 8, have to do with assurance of victory in the spiritual warfare that Israel faced. God said, "I will bring you in unto the land, concerning the which I did swear to give it to Abraham, to Isaac, and to Jacob; and I will give it you for an heritage: I am the Lord."

Reactions of Israel and Pharaoh

These promises of God were delivered by Moses to the Israelites, but they rejected his message. The Bible says,

"Moses spake so unto the children of Israel: but they hearkened not unto Moses for anguish of spirit, and for cruel bondage" (v. 9). It is important to remember, however, that Moses discharged his responsibility by passing on God's message to the people. What they did with the message was their responsibility. So, too, in witnessing our responsibility is to give others the message of salvation; how they respond to it is their responsibility. So we need not answer the question, How many have responded to the message? The question we must answer is, Have I been faithful to my responsibility in giving out the message?

During his years of walking with the Lord, Moses had learned that he was not responsible for the reactions of others. He had learned that his responsibility was to discern God's message and to faithfully deliver it to others. The Lord had promised to bring the nation of Israel out of Egypt, but in order for an individual to participate in the fulfillment of that promise, he had to respond by faith. Studying how God took care of Israel in the wilderness proves that God was faithful to every promise He had made to them.

Although the Israelites rejected Moses' message, God instructed Moses to go before Pharaoh once again. God told Moses, "Go in, speak unto Pharaoh king of Egypt, that he let the children of Israel go out of his land" (v. 11). But Moses had problems with this commission of God. Since the Israelites had not accepted his message, what was the use of going before Pharaoh? Moses told God, "Behold, the children of Israel have not hearkened unto me; how then shall Pharaoh hear me, who am of uncircumcised lips?" (v. 12). But, in effect, God told Moses, "You leave Pharaoh to me. Remember, I told you that you would see what I was going to do with Pharaoh."

Then, the Bible records, "The Lord spake unto Moses and unto Aaron, and gave them a charge unto the children of Israel, and unto Pharaoh king of Egypt, to bring the children of Israel out of the land of Egypt" (v. 13).

Pharaoh disregarded any other god speaking to him; he made that very clear (see 5:2). Pharaoh was not going to have anyone telling him what to do—not even God!

But Pharaoh was in for a surprise! God told Moses, "See, I have made thee a god to Pharaoh: and Aaron thy brother shall be thy prophet" (7:1). Before God was through dealing with Pharaoh, Pharaoh would recognize Moses' power over him, because Moses was God's representative. Moses had authority because he spoke for God and with God's authority.

In the New Testament the authority of God is seen in the words of Christ: "All power [authority] is given unto me in heaven and in earth" (Matt. 28:18). In the same passage the Lord promised believers: "I am with you alway, even unto the end of the world [age]" (v. 20).

Exodus 7:1 indicates that Aaron was to be Moses' prophet; that is, he was to be Moses' mouthpiece. So as far as Pharaoh was concerned, Moses would be in the place of God over him, and Aaron would be Moses' prophet, or spokesman.

As a god over Pharaoh, Moses would rule Egypt in that he would have Egypt under his domination as he controlled Pharaoh. Moses was to tell Pharaoh what he must do, what he should expect to happen, and that he must appeal to Moses for relief from the plagues. As we study the plagues later, we will see how God made Moses a god to Pharaoh.

God told Moses, "Thou shalt speak all that I command thee: and Aaron thy brother shall speak unto Pharaoh, that he send the children of Israel out of his land" (v. 2). The words were not to be of Moses' choosing—he was to speak what God told him to speak.

We, too, are to be faithful in delivering God's message to an unbelieving world. Through the Apostle Paul God commands us, "Preach the word; be instant in season, out of season" (II Tim. 4:2). The reason for the urgency is stated in verse 3: "For the time will come when they will not endure sound doctrine." No wonder Paul told Timothy earlier in the same epistle to "hold fast the form of sound words, which thou hast heard of me" (1:13). It is a principle with God that when He gives a charge, He also gives the power to accomplish it. So we may be sure that when we act on His Word, the power to perform the task will be provided.

God told Moses, "I will harden Pharaoh's heart, and multiply my signs and my wonders in the land of Egypt" (Ex. 7:3). Although God announced that He would harden Pharaoh's heart, He did not say when He would do it. It seems, however, from the context that God did not harden Pharaoh's heart until the latter part of Moses' dealing with him. It is not until Exodus 9:12 that we read: "The Lord hardened the heart of Pharaoh," and this was after the sixth plague. Until that time God exercised His mercy and gave Pharaoh every opportunity to turn to Him.

The Contest

The total commitment of Moses and Aaron to God's will is seen in Exodus 7:6: "And Moses and Aaron did as the Lord commanded them, so did they." They did exactly as God said. So the contest began in earnest.

Although it appeared to be Moses and Aaron against Pharaoh, it was really God against Satan. Because of the omnipotence of God, the outcome of the contest was never in question. From the human viewpoint, however, it was a real contest, and people had to decide whether they would be on the side of God or Satan. All that God asked of His servants was absolute obedience so He could work through them to accomplish His will.

In total obedience to God's command, Moses and Aaron went before Pharaoh. The Bible says, "They did so as the Lord had commanded: and Aaron cast down his rod before Pharaoh, and before his servants, and it became a serpent" (v. 10). For Moses and Aaron this amounted to the presentation of their credentials. They represented a miracle-working God, and they had come to speak in His behalf.

But notice what Pharaoh did—he called the "wise men and the sorcerers: now the magicians of Egypt, they also did in like manner with their enchantments. For they cast down every man his rod, and they became serpents" (vv. 11,12).

The ability of the magicians of Egypt to imitate the miracles of Moses and Aaron should teach us many important lessons. One crucial lesson that we especially need to learn today is that everything supernatural is not necessarily of God. Today, experience and unusual happenings are emphasized, but it takes much wisdom to know whether or not the unusual is really of God.

In referring to the contest between Pharaoh's magicians and Moses and Aaron, the Apostle Paul said, "Now as Jannes and Jambres withstood Moses, so do these also resist the truth: men of corrupt minds, reprobate concerning the faith" (II Tim. 3:8). These two names, "Jannes" and "Jambres," were apparently part of Jewish tradition that had been handed down since the time of Pharaoh. As Paul wrote, the Holy Spirit superintended so he did not select erroneous details from Jewish tradition. In selecting these names, Paul identified the two men who exercised leadership among the magicians of Egypt in opposing Moses and Aaron. Notice what Jannes and Jambres had in common with the false teachers of Paul's day: "Men of corrupt minds, reprobate concerning the faith" (v. 8).

The Power of Satan

Even though the magicians of Egypt were able to perform some miracles, there were many miracles they could not perform. But let us not miss the point that there were *some* they were able to perform. No doubt they were able to do these by the power of Satan, who energized them.

During the coming Tribulation Satan's man will be the Antichrist. The Antichrist will be the prominent personality during the seven-year Tribulation, and he will exercise control over the entire world. A person known as the "false prophet" will direct worship to the Antichrist. In referring to the false prophet, Revelation 13:13-15 says, "He doeth great wonders, so that he maketh fire come down from heaven on the earth in the sight of men, and deceiveth them that dwell on the earth by the means of those miracles which he had power to do in the sight of the beast; saying to them that dwell on the earth, that they should make an image to the beast, which had the wound by a sword, and did live. And he had power to give life unto the image of the beast, that the image of the beast should both speak, and cause that as many as would not worship the image of the beast should be killed." Thus, we see how Satan will deceive the world through miracles.

Referring to the Antichrist, II Thessalonians 2:9,10 says, "Even him, whose coming is after the working of Satan with

all power and signs and lying wonders, and with all
deceivableness of unrighteousness in them that perish;
because they received not the love of the truth, that they
might be saved."

From the Book of Job we also see that Satan has definite
powers. Satan came before the presence of God and
challenged Him concerning Job. Satan told God that the only
reason Job was serving Him was that God had given him so
much. Satan asked, "Does Job fear God for nothing? Hast
Thou not made a hedge about him and his house and all that
he has, on every side? Thou hast blest the work of his hands,
and his possessions have increased in the land. But put forth
Thy hand now and touch all that he has; he will surely curse
Thee to Thy face" (Job 1:9-11, NASB).

At that point God allowed Satan to take away what Job
had, but God did not allow him to touch Job himself. God
said, "All that he hath is in thy power; only upon himself put
not forth thine hand" (v. 12). First, Job's oxen and donkeys
were stolen and his servants killed by the attacking Sabeans
(vv. 14,15). Then fire fell from heaven and burned up his
sheep and the servants that were with them (v. 16). Next, the
Chaldeans attacked and stole his camels and killed the
servants who were tending them (v. 17). But the worst of all
was the great wind which struck the house where his sons and
daughters were gathered, killing them all (vv. 18,19).

These incidents demonstrate the power that Satan was
able to exercise as God permitted him to do so. But Job still
did not curse God as Satan thought he would, so Satan
challenged God to let him touch Job's body. God also
permitted this, and the Book of Job is an account of how
God proved His ability to hold on to Job even in the midst of
Job's intense suffering.

The Power of God

Just as God allowed Satan to go only so far in attacking
Job, so He allowed the magicians of Egypt to go only so far
and no further. Notice what happened when their rods
became serpents: "Aaron's rod swallowed up their rods" (Ex.
7:12). That which makes this entire incident so significant is
the fact that the serpent was worshiped in Egypt. It was

considered a god, and the fact that Aaron's rod consumed the rods of the Egyptians revealed that God was pronouncing doom on the lying wonders and the serpent gods of Egypt. In addition to teaching the lesson God intended for the Egyptians, this act was no doubt of great encouragement to Moses and Aaron as they realized that God was working through them to perform miracles in order to accomplish His will. This was a fulfillment of God's promise that they would have power over the Egyptians and, in particular, that Moses would be made a "god to Pharaoh" (v. 1). In this first real encounter, it was evident that the gods of Egypt could not stand before the God of Moses and Aaron.

Chapter 15

The Progressive Strengthening

In considering how God strengthened Moses, we learn that Moses progressed in faith, boldness and power with both God and man.

It is important to reflect on how God had already worked with Moses before considering how God strengthened him further. After spending 40 years in God's special school in the wilderness, Moses was told, "Go, return into Egypt: for all the men are dead which sought thy life. And Moses took his wife and his sons, and set them upon an ass, and he returned to the land of Egypt: and Moses took the rod of God in his hand" (Ex. 4:19,20). Notice that he took with him the shepherd's rod, which would always remind him of his nothingness and of the need to depend entirely on God.

Going Backward With God

At that time God warned Moses that Pharaoh would refuse to let the Israelites go. The Lord told Moses, "When you return into Egypt, see that you do before Pharaoh all those miracles and wonders which I have put in your hand; but I will make him stubborn and harden his heart, so that he will not let the people go" (v. 21, Amplified) In a sense, this warning that Pharaoh would reject his plea let Moses know that he had to experience defeat before he could experience victory. Moses had to know what it was to go backward before he could go forward!

I will never forget an incident that taught me this lesson in relation to Back to the Bible in the early 1940s. I had invited a minister to preach a series of evangelistic messages

170

on the radio, and during that time we were having some extremely difficult financial struggles. Things certainly looked as if they were going backward. One day he and I met to pray especially about these matters. Before we prayed, he made this significant statement: "Brother Epp, it takes more faith to go backward with God than to go forward with God." I have never forgotten that statement!

It was necessary for Moses to be so committed to God that he could go backward with Him before going forward. Moses needed to have an unshakable faith in God, and this is what he acquired during the 40 years in the desert alone with God.

As Moses experienced the expected refusal of Pharaoh and the unexpected reaction of his own people, he saw that he was not to put trust in man but only in God. This was the key to Moses' future success. Had he not learned this lesson, God could not have used him as He later did.

As Moses experienced these setbacks, he actually went forward in his confidence in God. He had to learn the same lesson that the nation of Israel learned later when its armies were endangered. Hezekiah told the people, "Be strong and courageous, be not afraid nor dismayed for the king of Assyria, nor for all the multitude that is with him: for there be more with us than with him" (II Chron. 32:7). The Israelite army was smaller than the Assyrian army, but the significant difference was not in size but in the one in whom they were trusting. Referring to the king of Assyria, Hezekiah said, "With him is an arm of flesh; but with us is the Lord our God to help us, and to fight our battles" (v. 8).

Jeremiah warned against trusting in the arm of flesh when he said, "Thus saith the Lord; Cursed be the man that trusteth in man, and maketh flesh his arm, and whose heart departeth from the Lord. Blessed is the man that trusteth in the Lord, and whose hope the Lord is" (Jer. 17:5,7). We need to learn this lesson also. We must not put our confidence in people—good as they may be. This does not mean that we should not trust others, but it means that in the final analysis our confidence must be in God alone. We should never think when we encounter a problem that it can be automatically solved just by getting enough people to help with it. The Bible tells us: "Trust in the Lord with all thine heart; and lean not unto thine own understanding. In all thy ways acknowledge him, and he shall direct thy paths" (Prov. 3:5,6).

It was a horrible expression of ingratitude on the part of Israel for them to turn against Moses after Pharaoh had made their work load heavier. They told Moses, "The Lord look upon you, and judge; because ye have made our savour to be abhorred in the eyes of Pharaoh" (Ex. 5:21). But this, as well as Pharaoh's rejection, drove Moses to depend on the Lord alone. Verse 22 says, "Moses returned unto the Lord." I love that statement—Moses had nowhere else to turn, so he was forced to turn to the Lord.

The experiences Moses had at this time enabled him to take a firm stand for the Lord later when Israel was before the Red Sea with seemingly no way of crossing or escaping from the pursuing Egyptians. Moses courageously told the people, "Fear ye not, stand still, and see the salvation of the Lord, which he will shew to you to day: for the Egyptians whom ye have seen to day, ye shall see them again no more for ever. The Lord shall fight for you, and ye shall hold your peace" (14:13,14). Had it not been for Moses' previous training, he would not have been able to stand so confidently as God's representative at that time.

Examples of Progressive Strengthening

There are many scriptural examples of individuals who were progressively strengthened. For example, Jacob was overcome at Peniel that he might overcome! Joseph went down to prison before he rose to one of the highest positions in Egypt. Even Christ came down to the cross and then was exalted above every name.

In all of these examples we see the principle stated in John 12:24: "Except a corn of wheat fall into the ground and die, it abideth alone: but if it die, it bringeth forth much fruit." We are also reminded of Revelation 3:21: "To him that overcometh will I grant to sit with me in my throne, even as I also overcame, and am set down with my Father in his throne." It is no wonder that Colossians 3:1-3 tells us: "If [since] ye then be risen with Christ, seek those things which are above, where Christ sitteth on the right hand of God. Set your affection on things above, not on things on the earth. For ye are dead [have died], and your life is hid with Christ in God." The Apostle Paul experienced these truths also. Paul said, "For when I am weak, then am I strong" (II Cor. 12:10). He also stated, "I am crucified with Christ: nevertheless I live; yet not I, but Christ liveth in me: and the life which I now live in the flesh I live by the faith of the Son of God, who loved me, and gave himself for me" (Gal. 2:20).

Thus, it was necessary for Moses to have experienced the disciplining hand of God so that he would be ready for fruit bearing. He was progressively strengthened and was ready for God to begin His real work through him. This is why the Lord was able to tell him, "Now shalt thou see what I will do to Pharaoh" (Ex. 6:1). Moses had been very discouraged by the rejection of his own people, and having come to a complete end of himself, he turned to God. Because of this God was able to announce that His real work with Pharaoh could begin. This was actually the beginning of the end for Egypt, and in a sense it was the beginning of the nation of Israel. Also, it was the beginning of the greatest life ever lived by an individual except Christ Himself.

Some say that life begins at 40, but for Moses life began at 80. The 80 years were required for him to be precisely where God wanted him to be so he could be mightily used. Moses' desire was the same as that later expressed by the Apostle Paul: "That I may know him, and the power of his resurrection, and the fellowship of his sufferings, being made conformable unto his death" (Phil. 3:10).

"I Am the Lord"

For Moses death was the way to life. The pendulum in his life had swung past center. Too often, we want God to move according to our time schedule, but God has His own schedule. Moses was concerned earlier that God would deliver Israel immediately, but God did not choose to do so. What Moses did not realize was that Israel was far from ready to be delivered. Moses had to learn that God is always on time and that He has a purpose for His precise time schedule.

Another important aspect of Moses' progressive strengthening was that he realized that God—the great I

Am—was doing the work. Exodus 6:2-4 records God's words to Moses: "I am the Lord: and I appeared unto Abraham, unto Isaac, and unto Jacob, by the name of God Almighty, but by my name Jehovah was I not known to them. And I have also established my covenant with them, to give them the land of Canaan, the land of their pilgrimage, wherein they were strangers."

Moses saw God in a way that he had never seen Him before—his inner eyes were opened. In the New Testament Paul prayed that believers would have the eyes of their understanding enlightened (Eph. 1:18), for he also was concerned that we might see God in a new way. In another of Paul's prayers, he prayed, "That he would grant you, according to the riches of his glory, to be strengthened with might by his Spirit in the inner man; that Christ may dwell in your hearts by faith; that ye, being rooted and grounded in love, may be able to comprehend with all saints what is the breadth, and length, and depth, and height; and to know the love of Christ, which passeth knowledge, that ye might be filled with all the fulness of God" (3:16-19).

Moses was being prepared for spiritual warfare, and we, also, need to be prepared for it. This is why Paul told us, "Be strong in the Lord, and in the power of his might" (6:10). Note that the strength is "in the Lord," not in us, and that it is the power of "his" might, not ours.

Exodus 6:6-8 records God's renewed commission to Moses in which the original commission was enlarged and strengthened. As previously stated, it included seven "I wills" and was strengthened by the statement, "I am the Lord."

Notice these verses as translated in the Amplified Bible: "Accordingly, say to the Israelites, I am the Lord, and I will bring you out from under the burdens of the Egyptians, and I will free you from their bondage, and I will rescue you with an outstretched arm—with special and vigorous action—and by mighty acts of judgment. And I will take you to Me for a people, and I will be to you a God; and you shall know that it is I, the Lord your God, Who brings you out from under the burdens of the Egyptians. And I will bring you into the land concerning which I lifted up My hand and swore that I would give it to Abraham, Isaac, and Jacob; and I will give it to you for a heritage. I am the Lord [you have the pledge of My changeless omnipotence and faithfulness]."

The foundation was laid for Moses' real spiritual progress—everything had been set on solid bedrock, and Christ was that Rock. All of the experiences that Moses had after that time rested on this sure foundation.

Standing Alone With God

After Moses had cast himself completely on the Lord and the Lord had assured Moses of what He would do, "Moses spake so unto the children of Israel: but they hearkened not unto Moses for anguish of spirit, and for cruel bondage" (Ex. 6:9).

This reaction must have been very hard for a leader like Moses to accept, but it only verified that he had to learn to stand alone with God. Every true leader has to come to the realization that at times he will have to stand alone. The person unwilling to stand alone with God will never be the kind of leader that God wants him to be. God is looking for a person who will be obedient regardless of what others say. Because Moses was learning to stand alone with God, he was making progress in his relationship with God.

Throughout biblical history men have stood alone with God—men like Noah, Abraham, Joseph and Elijah. Although their friends turned against them and they had no one to lean on for support at times, they stood strong for God because they were willing to stand alone. And Moses' successor was no exception. After the death of Moses, Joshua faithfully led the people of Israel, but at the end of his life he presented the people with a decision they had to make. Joshua told the people, "Choose you this day whom ye will serve; . . . but as for me and my house, we will serve the Lord" (Josh. 24:15). Whether we are in a high position of leadership or not, it is important for us to realize that there will be times when we must stand alone with God for the convictions He has given us through His Word.

When Moses received no response from the Israelites, God told him, "Go in, speak unto Pharaoh king of Egypt, that he let the children of Israel go out of his land" (Ex. 6:11). Notice Moses' response to God's command. Although Moses' faith had been growing by leaps and bounds, there is evidence that his faith was still too small. Moses told God, "Behold, the children of Israel have not hearkened unto me; how then shall Pharaoh hear me, who am of uncircumcised lips?" (v. 12).

Moses had not yet gained complete victory over his introspective nature. He was quick to see his deficiencies and was sure that Pharaoh would not listen to him since his own people would not heed his words. But God did not lose patience with Moses; He continued to work with him until Moses gained the complete victory. God knew Moses' heart, and He did not give up on Moses, although others might have.

How well God knew Moses is indicated in Exodus 7:1 where God promised to make Moses "a god to Pharaoh." Imagine, God had more faith in Moses than Moses had in God! As Moses learned to stand alone with God, he was mightily used in His hands and had power over Pharaoh as if he were one of Pharaoh's gods.

As we consider how Moses acted on the authority of God, we are reminded of a privilege we have that even Moses did not have. Since the Day of Pentecost, as recorded in Acts 2, Christ lives within every believer. This is why Colossians 1:27 says, "Christ in you, the hope of glory." Verse 29 reveals that the power of Christ works mightily in each believer. So if we are in God's will when we speak or act, then we speak and act with His authority because He lives within us.

As God was preparing Moses to go before Pharaoh again, He left no room for Moses to falter. God told Moses what would happen when he went before Pharaoh. In His omniscience God saw the future and total victory, but time was an element Moses had to contend with, so he needed patience. Time is always a significant element for man, but it is not for God. God is not a creature of time; He is the Creator of time.

What God has promised concerning Israel will all be fulfilled even though thousands of years have now gone by without the final fulfillment. Although this may cause some to doubt the promises of God, the fulfillment of these promises is not less certain just because much time has elapsed. God is not affected by time.

God told Moses, "I will harden Pharaoh's heart, and multiply my signs and my wonders in the land of Egypt. But Pharaoh shall not harken unto you, that I may lay my hand upon Egypt, and bring forth mine armies, and my people the children of Israel, out of the land of Egypt by great judgments" (Ex. 7:3,4).

God then made this solemn promise to Moses: "And the Egyptians shall know that I am the Lord" (v. 5). All of Egypt would finally know God's sovereign power and would have to submit to Him, even though they would not place their faith in Him. God would eventually prove Himself to be far greater than any of the gods of Egypt.

Total Obedience

Then we read this beautiful statement: "Moses and Aaron did as the Lord commanded them, so did they" (v. 6). They demonstrated total obedience, and it is this kind of obedience that is the key to complete success. Although there were obstacles and Moses and Aaron would have reservations, yet they completely obeyed the Lord.

As we obey the Lord, we will experience success also. The Lord Jesus Christ has told us, "If ye abide in me, and my words abide in you, ye shall ask what ye will, and it shall be done unto you" (John 15:7). Note what this verse really says. The words "if ye abide in me" indicate complete trust and commitment to Him. We are to get our orders from Him—"and my words abide in you." Then, and only then, is it true that "ye shall ask what ye will, and it shall be done unto you." This is the key to spiritual success.

This reminds us of what God told Joshua: "Only be thou strong and very courageous, that thou mayest observe to do according to all the law, which Moses my servant commanded thee: turn not from it to the right hand or to the left, that thou mayest prosper whithersoever thou goest. This book of the law shall not depart out of thy mouth; but thou shalt meditate therein day and night, that thou mayest observe to do according to all that is written therein: for then thou shalt make thy way prosperous, and then thou shalt have good success" (Josh. 1:7,8).

But the Bible contains many examples of those who did not obey the Lord completely. Perhaps one of the best examples is Saul, the first king of Israel. Through Samuel the prophet God had instructed Saul to completely destroy the Amalekites and all of their possessions. Yet, Saul went against God's clear instructions and spared the best of the livestock, as well as the king of the Amalekites. When Samuel faced Saul with his disobedience to the Lord, Saul blamed his people for taking the best of the livestock, but he explained that it was so they could make sacrifices to the Lord (see I Sam. 15:21). Think of it. Saul had disobeyed the Lord and was going to use what he had gained in his disobedience to make a sacrifice to the Lord! Samuel told Saul, "Hath the Lord as great delight in burnt-offerings and sacrifices, as in obeying the voice of the Lord? Behold, to obey is better than sacrifice, and to hearken than the fat of rams" (v. 22).

Moses went before Pharaoh, and from this point forward we see unquestioned obedience on his part. Total obedience is really recognition of God's absolute sovereignty, and this is what Moses finally recognized.

The complete obedience of Moses is also seen in Exodus 7:10: "And Moses and Aaron went in unto Pharaoh, and they did so as the Lord had commanded." Verse 20 emphasizes the same theme: "And Moses and Aaron did so, as the Lord commanded." Twelve times God gave the orders, and twelve times Moses and Aaron did as God said. Miracles began to happen one after another as they gave unquestioned obedience to the Lord.

This teaches us that we must be where God wants us to be at the time He wants us to be there, and we must do what He says, if we expect to see things happen. As the believer desires to act and obey, he will see God work mightily in and through him.

Moses' Increased Boldness

It is interesting to see how Moses' faith continued to grow. This was especially apparent during the plague of the frogs that, through Moses and Aaron, had been brought on Egypt because of Pharaoh's refusal to let the people go. "Moses said to Pharaoh, 'The honor is yours to tell me: when shall I entreat for you and your servants and your people, that the frogs be destroyed from you and your houses, that they may be left only in the Nile?' Then he said, 'Tomorrow.' So he said, 'May it be according to your word, that you may know that there is no one like the Lord our God. And the frogs will depart from you and your houses and your servants and your people; they will be left only in the Nile' " (Ex. 8:9-11, NASB).

Moses was becoming bolder as he spoke to Pharaoh. Moses knew the Lord intimately, and he was walking with the Lord, so he was bold in speaking to Pharaoh about these matters. It is not enough just to have faith; one must act on his faith. True faith produces boldness.

Many times I'm reminded of this as I pray about a certain matter. I tell the Lord what I need or what I feel might be done, and then the Lord seems to say to me, "Will you tell Me to do it?" Telling the Lord, in faith, to do something is far different than asking for a particular matter. Mark 11:22,23 gives us the basis for telling the Lord to do something for us. These verses say, "Jesus answering saith unto them, Have faith in God. For verily I say unto you, That whosoever shall say unto this mountain, Be thou removed, and be thou cast into the sea; and shall not doubt in his heart, but shall believe that those things which he saith shall come to pass; he shall have whatsoever he saith." Notice that we are not to ask the mountain to move; we are to tell it to move. When our faith is based on a definite promise of God, He desires that we tell Him to do certain things for us.

As Moses spoke to Pharaoh about the frogs, he said, "Be it according to thy word: that thou mayest know that there is none like unto the Lord our God" (Ex. 8:10). Moses had only one purpose in mind, and that was to glorify God. Moses sought to honor God alone, and this is why God used him so mightily.

Because Moses and Aaron had been completely obedient to the Lord's command, the Lord responded to Moses' prayer. The Bible says, "And Moses and Aaron went out from Pharaoh: and Moses cried unto the Lord because of the frogs which he had brought against Pharaoh. And the Lord did according to the word of Moses; and the frogs died out of the houses, out of the villages, and out of the fields" (vv.

12,13). Because Moses had obeyed the word of the Lord, the Lord acted according to the word of Moses. The Lord loves to act in behalf of the person who dares to believe Him, who dares to venture out in faith, seeking only to glorify God.

Second Chronicles 20 records a striking example of how the Lord responds to those who glorify Him. Jehoshaphat was surrounded by enemies, and he prayed earnestly to the Lord. The Lord made it clear to him that he would not have to really fight the battle, for He told him, "The battle is not your's, but God's" (v. 15). Jehoshaphat took God at His word and put singers in front of his army as it went to meet the enemy. As the singers offered praise to Him, God miraculously worked in behalf of Israel.

It is important, however, that we guard against presumption—we must not expect Him to do something when He has not specifically indicated that it is His will to do so. But when we have done God's will and seek only to glorify Him, we can be bold in our prayer life. Jesus told the Father, "I have glorified thee on the earth; I have finished the work which thou gavest me to do" (John 17:4). Psalm 37:4 promises, "Delight thyself also in the Lord; and he shall give thee the desires of thine heart." If we have God in first place in our lives, we may be confident that He will act in our behalf.

The Weakening of Pharaoh

As the plagues came on Pharaoh and the Egyptians, he began to weaken a little bit. We will later study the plagues in detail, but at this point we want to especially notice how Moses was strengthened along the way. At one point during the plagues Pharaoh said to Moses, "Go, sacrifice to your God [here] in the land [of Egypt]. And Moses said, It is not suitable or right to do that; for the animals the Egyptians hold sacred and will not permit to be slain, are those which we are accustomed to sacrifice to the Lord our God; if we did this before the eyes of the Egyptians, would they not stone us? We will go three days' journey into the wilderness and sacrifice to the Lord our God, as He will command us" (Ex. 8:25-27, Amplified).

This was Pharaoh's first offer, but Moses was bold in faith and refused to compromise. Moses spoke for God and completely refused anything less than what God demanded. Moses even exposed Pharaoh's false religion as he mentioned that the Egyptians held certain animals to be sacred. Moses made it clear that his firm intention was to obey God completely.

That Moses' faith was becoming bolder and bolder is also seen in that he prayed for an end to the plague of flies: "Moses went out from Pharaoh, and intreated the Lord. And the Lord did according to the word of Moses; and he removed the swarms of flies from Pharaoh, from his servants, and from his people; there remained not one" (vv. 30,31). This was not presumption on Moses' part because he already had assurance from God that such a prayer was in accordance with His will.

Consider another incident from chapter 9. Moses had announced that a great hailstorm was coming and that everything not under a roof would be destroyed. Verses 20 and 21 say, "He that feared the word of the Lord among the servants of Pharaoh made his servants and his cattle flee into the houses: and he that regarded not the word of the Lord left his servants and his cattle in the field." These verses indicate that a number of people were taking Moses at his word, even though the majority still refused to believe the word of God through Moses.

This is a good lesson to us—when people see God working in us, they will begin to believe His Word. This is why the Lord Jesus Christ said, "Let your light so shine before men, that they may see your good works, and glorify your Father which is in heaven" (Matt. 5:16).

Exodus 9:29,30 records another incident of Moses' growing in boldness. He stated what he would ask God for, with complete confidence that it would take place as he said. Concerning the plague of the hailstorm, Moses told Pharaoh, "As soon as I am gone out of the city, I will spread abroad my hands unto the Lord; and the thunder shall cease, neither shall there be any more hail; that thou mayest know how that the earth is the Lord's. But as for thee and thy servants, I know that ye will not yet fear the Lord God." Moses' attitude toward prayer reminds us of Matthew 7:7: "Ask, and it shall be given you; seek, and ye shall find; knock, and it shall be opened unto you."

Was Moses' faith rewarded? The answer is found in Exodus 9:33: "And Moses went out of the city from Pharaoh, and spread abroad his hands unto the Lord: and the thunders and hail ceased, and the rain was not poured upon the earth."

Moses obeyed God to the letter even though he knew Pharaoh would have a negative response to everything he said. Moses had learned to believe God completely; he had learned that God has a program of progress. Moses and Aaron's obedience is again seen in Exodus 10:1-3: "And the Lord said unto Moses, Go in unto Pharaoh: for I have hardened his heart, and the heart of his servants, that I might shew these my signs before him: and that thou mayest tell in the ears of thy son, and of thy son's son, what things I have wrought in Egypt, and my signs which I have done among them; that ye may know how that I am the Lord. And Moses and Aaron came in unto Pharaoh, and said unto him, Thus saith the Lord God of the Hebrews, How long wilt thou refuse to humble thyself before me? Let my people go, that they may serve me."

Exodus 10:9,10 reveals that Pharaoh offered another compromise, but Moses boldly rejected it. In answer to Pharaoh's question concerning who would go into the wilderness to worship, Moses said, "We will go with our young and with our old, with our sons and with our daughters, with our flocks and with our herds will we go; for we must hold a feast unto the Lord" (v. 9). Then Pharaoh replied, "Let the Lord be so with you, as I will let you go, and your little ones: look to it; for evil is before you" (v. 10). Moses insisted on doing precisely what the Lord had instructed him to do. He would not leave anyone behind as they went into the wilderness to worship.

Verse 24 reveals another of Pharaoh's offers—he urged Moses to let the flocks and herds remain in Egypt while the people went into the wilderness to worship. Again, Moses steadfastly refused to compromise.

Pharaoh finally became so angered at Moses that he said to him, "Get thee from me, take heed to thyself, see my face no more; for in that day thou seest my face thou shalt die"

(v. 28). Moses solemnly responded, "Thou hast spoken well, I will see thy face again no more" (v. 29). In spite of the fact that Moses was driven from Pharaoh's presence, he became bolder in his faith and seemed to realize that God was about through with Pharaoh. As indicated previously, it seems that Pharaoh had weakened some along the way, but he still bitterly opposed God. Pharaoh was unaware at this time that his own life was hanging in the balance.

The Greatness of Moses

Although Moses was God's instrument in bringing plagues on Egypt, the Egyptians gained more and more respect for Moses and the Israelites. The Bible says, "The Lord gave the people favour in the sight of the Egyptians. Moreover the man Moses was very great in the land of Egypt, in the sight of Pharaoh's servants, and in the sight of the people" (Ex. 11:3). So although Moses did not gain favor before Pharaoh, he did before Pharaoh's people.

The greatness of Moses is indicated in that the Bible refers to him at least 826 times. Thus, we see that his faith and obedience won him a significant place in God's hall of fame.

Although Pharaoh was so angry at Moses that he threatened to kill him if he saw him again, Moses gave a final pronouncement from God before leaving: "Thus saith the Lord, About midnight will I go out into the midst of Egypt: and all the firstborn in the land of Egypt shall die, from the firstborn of Pharaoh that sitteth upon his throne, even unto the firstborn of the maidservant that is behind the mill; and all the firstborn of beasts. And there shall be a great cry throughout all the land of Egypt, such as there was none like it, nor shall be like it any more" (vv. 4-6).

Moses was fearless because he spoke for God. Proverbs 16:7 says, "When a man's ways please the Lord, he maketh even his enemies to be at peace with him." Because Moses was in the center of God's will, Pharaoh was unable to harm him. This reminds us of Elijah, who fearlessly stood before wicked Ahab and later killed the prophets of Baal. No one was able to touch Elijah's life because God was protecting him. And during the future Tribulation two witnesses will

appear whom the Antichrist will hate, but he will not be able
to do anything to them until God permits it.

So we see how Moses was strengthened to the extent that
he could fearlessly proclaim this great judgment on all of
Egypt. But notice how God evidenced His blessing on the
Israelites. Moses said, "But against any of the sons of Israel a
dog shall not even bark, whether against man or beast, that
you may understand how the Lord makes a distinction
between Egypt and Israel" (Ex. 11:7, NASB). What a bold
prophecy this was! The Israelites numbered about three
million at this time, and one can imagine all the commotion
they would cause in making final preparations to flee Egypt.
They would have to quickly gather all of their possessions,
and their animals would have to be herded together, yet no
dog would even bark at them! God shut their mouths as He
shut the lions' mouths for Daniel.

Notice especially the reason that God prevented the dogs
from barking at the Israelites—it was to be a sign to the
Egyptians: "That ye may know how that the Lord doth put a
difference between the Egyptians and Israel." Verse 8 says,
"And all these thy servants shall come down unto me, and
bow down themselves unto me, saying, Get thee out, and all
the people that follow thee: and after that I will go out. And
he went out from Pharaoh in a great anger."

Moses had a genuine faith in God's purpose and program,
and this produced a holy indignation against those who dared
try to thwart God. Moses' early timidity contrasts greatly
with the boldness he evidenced at this time. Earlier, he was
sure he was not the man for God to send, but later he stood
before Pharaoh and fearlessly pronounced God's judgment,
even though Pharaoh had threatened his life.

What made all this difference? Moses knew he was in the
will of God, so he had no fear of man. Concerning this matter
Psalm 56 is of much encouragement to us. The psalmist said,
"In God I will praise his word, in God I have put my trust; I
will not fear what flesh can do unto me. . . . In God have I
put my trust: I will not be afraid what man can do unto me"
(vv. 4,11).

A key to Moses' boldness is also found in Hebrews 11:27:
"By faith he forsook Egypt, not fearing the wrath of the
king: for he endured, as seeing him who is invisible." That is

it! Because Moses saw Him who is invisible—God—he did not fear Pharaoh. Moses knew that God's honor was at stake, so he refused to cower before Pharaoh.

Moses evidenced holy indignation because of Pharaoh's persistent arrogance, deceit, cruelty and impiety against God. Having left the presence of Pharaoh, the Lord told Moses and Aaron, "This month shall be unto you the beginning of months: it shall be the first month of the year to you" (Ex. 12:2). This chapter records God's instituting of the Passover. Nothing like it had ever happened before. But even though they had no previous experience, Moses and the Israelites faithfully carried out God's instructions to the last detail. Hebrews 11:28 says of Moses, "Through faith he kept the passover, and the sprinkling of blood, lest he that destroyed the firstborn should touch them."

Moses had the complete respect of his people at this point. All three million of them were ready to follow him. They did not really know where they were going, but they had confidence that Moses knew. He gained their complete confidence because he demonstrated complete faith and obedience.

Beginning the Journey

The response of the Israelites to the explicit instructions concerning the Passover is seen in Exodus 12:27,28: "The people bowed the head and worshipped. And the children of Israel went away, and did as the Lord had commanded Moses and Aaron, so did they." This was another indication of the confidence the Israelites had in Moses—a confidence so great they were willing to follow him even though they did not know what lay ahead.

But the first real test for them came after they had barely started on their way—they were going a different direction than they had expected! The shortest route from northern Egypt, where they were living, to the land of Canaan was only about a three-day journey, but they were going in another direction. They were going south toward the Red Sea. God had a reason for this, however.

Exodus 13:17,18 says, "It came to pass, when Pharaoh had let the people go, that God led them not through the way of the land of the Philistines, although that was near; for God said, Lest peradventure the people repent when they see war, and they return to Egypt: but God led the people about, through the way of the wilderness of the Red sea: and the children of Israel went up harnessed out of the land of Egypt." Even though the way seemed wrong to the people and may have seemed strange to Moses, God was working to accomplish His will. He was working on the heart of Pharaoh, on the hearts of the Israelites and in the heart of Moses. As far as Israel was concerned, God was working all things together for good—they were experiencing the truth stated later in Romans 8:28.

Moses had increased in faith to the extent that he did not question God about this detour. But as the Israelites went further, they came to an impasse; they were completely hemmed in. The pursuing Egyptians were behind them, mountains and marshes were on either side of them, and the Red Sea was ahead of them.

Exodus 14:10 says, "And when Pharaoh drew nigh, the children of Israel lifted up their eyes, and, behold, the Egyptians marched after them; and they were sore afraid: and the children of Israel cried out unto the Lord." They were gripped with fear at this point because they could not see any possibility of deliverance. In their despair they said to Moses, "Because there were no graves in Egypt, hast thou taken us away to die in the wilderness? Wherefore hast thou dealt thus with us, to carry us forth out of Egypt? Is not this the word that we did tell thee in Egypt, saying, Let us alone, that we may serve the Egyptians? For it had been better for us to serve the Egyptians, than that we should die in the wilderness" (vv. 11,12). Death seemed imminent to the Israelites, and in the face of it they expressed bitter feelings toward Moses.

Although Moses had not received any new orders from God, his faith was unshaken. Moses did not falter at this point even though he obviously could not humanly see any way out. We now realize why God took so much time and exercised so much patience in training His man. Moses had complete confidence that God knew what He was doing. Moses realized it was God's business to lead, and it was his business to believe and obey.

So Moses told the people, "Fear ye not, stand still, and see the salvation of the Lord, which he will shew to you to day: for the Egyptians whom ye have seen to day, ye shall see them again no more for ever. The Lord shall fight for you, and ye shall hold your peace" (vv. 13,14).

Imagine making a statement like that without any direct orders from God! Moses did not know precisely where they were going or what they would do, but his faith in God was unshakable. He did not falter, even when the people turned against him again. Their faith was weak, but his was strong because of the training he had received from God.

Notice how God responded to Moses after such a demonstration of faith: "Wherefore criest thou unto me? Speak unto the children of Israel, that they go forward" (v. 15). What orders! Remember, they were hemmed in on all sides, yet God commanded them to go forward. But Moses had such faith in God that when God said to go forward, Moses went forward. But what about the Red Sea?

God told Moses, "Lift thou up thy rod, and stretch out thine hand over the sea, and divide it: and the children of Israel shall go on dry ground through the midst of the sea" (v. 16). These were the detailed instructions concerning how they were to go forward, but there first had to be the willingness to go forward simply because God had commanded it. Moses was willing to go forward with God, so God then gave him the detailed instructions. If we are not willing to move forward with God, we need not expect that He will give us instructions.

God went on to explain to Moses, "And I, behold, I will harden the hearts of the Egyptians, and they shall follow them: and I will get me honour upon Pharaoh, and upon all his host, upon his chariots, and upon his horsemen. And the Egyptians shall know that I am the Lord" (vv. 17,18).

Moses trusted God, and God did not let him down. Forty years earlier, relying on mere human strength, Moses had killed one Egyptian, but by faith he was now about to destroy all of Egypt.

Think of the lesson we can learn from this. Through the death of the Lord Jesus Christ, He not only procured our salvation, but He also destroyed the power that Satan has over us (Heb. 2:14). Because the power has been broken, we may now resist Satan in the power of Christ (I Pet. 5:6-9; James 4:7). That the Lord Jesus Christ has overcome the power of the world is seen in His words: "In the world ye shall have tribulation: but be of good cheer; I have overcome the world" (John 16:33).

Moses' Obedience; Israel's Escape

So Moses did what God told him to do—he stretched out his hand over the Red Sea, and the Lord caused the water to divide so the Israelites could walk through (Ex. 14:21). God delivered His people as Moses had faith to take Him at His word!

Notice the response of the Israelites after they had been delivered: "Thus the Lord saved Israel that day from the hand of the Egyptians. ... And when Israel saw the great power which the Lord had used against the Egyptians, the people feared the Lord, and they believed in the Lord and in His servant Moses" (vv. 30,31, NASB). This is exactly what God wanted them to do. Israel was saved that day as it was united, or identified, with Moses.

This fact is emphasized in the New Testament. The Apostle Paul said, "Moreover, brethren, I would not that ye should be ignorant, how that all our fathers were under the cloud, and all passed through the sea; and were all baptized unto Moses in the cloud and in the sea" (I Cor. 10:1,2). Here we see that the word "baptized" does not always involve water, for these Israelites did not even get wet! The basic element involved in baptism is identification. Only as the Israelites were identified with Moses could they expect deliverance by God. In the New Testament water baptism shows one's identification with Jesus Christ as personal Saviour.

Then came the song of victory for the Israelites. It surely must have been prepared earlier because they were able to sing it as soon as they saw the judgment of God on the Egyptians and realized the great deliverance they had experienced. I personally think that Moses must have previously written this song, which is recorded in Exodus 15. At this point, Israel's faith looked beyond the Red Sea and Egypt all the way to Canaan.

Consider the spiritual growth Moses had experienced. His first 40 years were spent primarily in the courts of Egypt learning the basics. The next 40 years were spent in the desert learning to know God intimately. Then the experiences of the next year perfected his faith in God as he faced Pharaoh and led the Israelites out of Egypt. This proves that it takes time to know God. The longer Moses walked with the Lord, the more he increased in faith.

Chapter 16

God's Strategy for Deliverance

At this point, let us reconsider some of the plagues, emphasizing how God outlined His stategy of delivering Israel from Egypt.

It was immediately apparent that the king would greatly resist letting the Israelites go. The purpose of the plagues was stated in Exodus 3. God told Moses, "I am sure that the king of Egypt will not let you go, no, not by a mighty hand. And I will stretch out my hand, and smite Egypt with all my wonders which I will do in the midst thereof: and after that he will let you go" (vv. 19,20).

For many years the Egyptians had oppressed Israel, and God had allowed it, but the time had come for Him to act in behalf of His chosen people. God was going to take vengeance on those who had made slaves of the Israelites. But before He exercised vengeance, God displayed mercy. Thus, God outlined His strategy of a series of ten plagues.

The Egyptians were acquainted with many unpleasant natural phenomena, but they were to see a tremendous, supernatural demonstration in the announced series of afflictions. In fact, almost all—if not every one—of the plagues were aimed directly at one of their gods. Each plague came with an intensity they had never experienced before. The first three plagues affected both Israel and Egypt, but the last seven were geographically located so that the Israelites, who lived in northern Egypt, were not affected.

Moses not only predicted each plague, but each plague came to an end only when he used his God-given power to remove it. Such predictions have never been duplicated even with our modern weather satellites and electronic computers.

Moses was 100 percent accurate because he was announcing what God told him.

And besides this, Moses even announced that God would protect His own people in Goshen, thus showing the superior power of the God of Israel over the gods of Egypt. The Egyptians thought their gods were the greatest, but they soon realized that their gods were nothing before the eternal God.

The Purpose of the Plagues

The plagues served at least five distinct purposes. First, they gave a public demonstration of the mighty power of the Lord God. Even the magicians, who were Pharaoh's wise men, acknowledged this fact. When they were unable to produce lice as Moses and Aaron did, the magicians said to Pharaoh, "This is the finger of God" (Ex. 8:19). They admitted that it was a miracle far above anything they could perform.

Second, the plagues were the divine visitation of wrath; that is, they were a punishment of Pharaoh and his people for their cruel treatment of Israel. When the horrible plague of locusts came on Egypt, Pharaoh admitted his shameful treatment of Israel when he said to Moses, "I have sinned against the Lord your God, and against you. Now therefore forgive, I pray thee, my sin only this once, and intreat the Lord your God, that he may take away from me this death only" (10:16,17).

Third, the plagues were a judgment of God on the gods of Egypt. The gods of Egypt were really demons. Concerning the tenth and most severe plague, God said, "For I will pass through the land of Egypt this night, and will smite all the firstborn in the land of Egypt, both man and beast; and against all the gods of Egypt I will execute judgment: I am the Lord" (12:12).

Fourth, the plagues were a solemn warning to other nations that God would curse those who cursed Israel. When God first called Abraham and promised to make a nation of him, God told him, "I will bless them that bless thee, and curse him that curseth thee: and in thee shall all families of the earth be blessed" (Gen. 12:3).

After the Israelites had been delivered from Egypt and were finally ready to enter the land of Canaan, they sent spies into Jericho. There the spies met Rahab, the harlot, who told them, "I know that the Lord hath given you the land, and that your terror is fallen upon us, and that all the inhabitants of the land faint because of you. For we have heard how the Lord dried up the water of the Red sea for you, when ye came out of Egypt; and what ye did unto the two kings of the Amorites, that were on the other side Jordan, Sihon and Og, whom ye utterly destroyed. And as soon as we had heard these things, our hearts did melt, neither did there remain any more courage in any man, because of you: for the Lord your God, he is God in heaven above, and in earth beneath" (Josh. 2:9-11).

The Philistines had also heard about the plagues God brought on Egypt, as indicated by I Samuel 4:7,8: "The Philistines were afraid, for they said, God is come into the camp. And they said, Woe unto us! For there hath not been such a thing heretofore. Woe unto us! Who shall deliver us out of the hand of these mighty Gods? These are the Gods that smote the Egyptians with all the plagues in the wilderness."

Fifth, the plagues on Egypt also served as a series of testings for Israel while the nation was in Egypt. This fact is indicated by what Moses later asked the people: "Did ever people hear the voice of God speaking out of the midst of the fire, as thou hast heard, and live? Or hath God assayed to go and take him a nation from the midst of another nation, by temptations, by signs, and by wonders, and by war, and by a mighty hand, and by a stretched out arm, and by great terrors, according to all that the Lord your God did for you in Egypt before your eyes? Unto thee it was shewed, that thou mightest know that the Lord he is God; there is none else beside him" (Deut. 4:33-35).

Although the trials and burdens they experienced in Egypt were difficult for Israel to bear, when they had been delivered through the Red Sea, they were able to admit, "Who is like unto thee, O Lord, among the gods? Who is like thee, glorious in holiness, fearful in praises, doing wonders?" (Ex. 15:11).

The Arrangement of the Plagues

The arrangement of the plagues refers to the way they are grouped together—nine of the ten plagues are arranged in three groups of three plagues each. The severity of the divine judgment increased in intensity with each group of plagues.

The first group of three plagues interfered primarily with the comfort of Egypt. Israel also experienced these discomforts in the land of Goshen. The first plague affected the water by turning it into blood, leaving no water to drink. The second was an invasion of frogs that got into everything. The third was an invasion of lice. What a discomfort!

The second group of three plagues was primarily directed against the possessions of the Egyptians. The Israelites were exempted from these plagues (Ex. 8:22,23). There were swarms of insects that afflicted men and animals. Next, there was an epidemic disease that killed many cattle. The third plague in this group produced boils on men and animals.

The third group of three plagues was far more severe and brought desolation and death. There was hail and thunder, and fire was running along the earth, destroying everything in its course. There were locusts that consumed everything that was left. And there was darkness that could be felt—possibly a black dust storm.

The tenth plague, although last in order, was announced first when God gave Moses instructions about going before Pharaoh (4:23). This last plague had special significance to the Israelites, because it related to their redemption.

Plagues Establish the Faith of Israel

For 400 years the Israelites had been in a strange land of strange gods. These gods were revealed through the magicians, who were able to perform satanic deeds. The supernatural power of the magicians came from the demons who energized them. But most of the plagues that Moses and Aaron brought about could not be imitated by the magicians. So, in a sense, the plagues were instrumental in establishing the Israelites in a true knowledge of Almighty God in this land of strange gods. The true God revealed Himself in power so Israel would recognize not only His existence but also His omnipotence.

The Scriptures indicate that the Israelites had backslidden while in Egypt and that some were even worshiping the gods of the Egyptians. They still had this tendency even after they were delivered from Egypt, because later they made and worshiped a golden calf (Ex. 32:1-6). No doubt the calf was even related to their experience in Egypt because the Egyptians worshiped cattle.

But as the Israelites were in Egypt, they saw—by means of the plagues—the impotency of the false gods of Egypt and the omnipotence of the Lord God of Israel. Although the Israelites were affected by the first three plagues, they were delivered from the other ones. Inasmuch as God delivered them from the remaining plagues, He revealed Himself to Israel as God Almighty—He was able to do all things. He also revealed Himself to them as the Lord God—the ever-present God to help.

God revealed to the Israelites that the gods of the Egyptians could not stand before Him. This was seen especially in the first miracle performed before Pharaoh. Aaron threw down his staff, and it became a serpent (7:10). Pharaoh then called his wise men, and they threw down their staffs, and they became serpents. But the power of the true God over the false gods was demonstrated when Aaron's staff-turned-serpent swallowed up the staffs-turned-serpents of Pharaoh's wise men (v. 12).

Just as the power of the true God was seen to be much greater than that of the false gods of Egypt, so today we need to recognize that the power of God is much greater than that of Satan. In fact, Satan is actually a defeated foe. When the Lord Jesus Christ died on the cross, He broke the power of Satan, just as God broke the power of Egypt over the Israelites.

However, just as the nation of Egypt still existed even though it did not have such power, so Satan still exists even though his power has been broken. Satan attempts to gain power over the Christian, but no believer needs to yield to Satan's enticements. James 4:7 instructs: "Submit yourselves therefore to God. Resist the devil, and he will flee from you." The order is significant in this verse: first, "submit yourselves therefore to God"; second, "resist the devil, and he will flee from you." Since Satan is actually a defeated foe, we need to take a definite stand against anything he attempts to do in our lives.

As Aaron and Moses performed miracles before Pharaoh, the magicians of Egypt were allowed to demonstrate their powers on three different occasions. First, as we have seen, they threw down their staffs, and they turned into serpents just as Aaron's did (Ex. 7:10-13). Second, the magicians of Egypt were able to turn water into blood even as Aaron did (vv. 20-22). Third, the magicians of Egypt were able to bring forth frogs as Aaron did (8:1-7). Just as the frogs were not clean, so this reminds us that Satan's work is unclean.

Let us not overestimate Satan; he is able to perform the unusual, but his power cannot compare with the power of Almighty God. The most basic thing to realize about Satan is that he is an imitator. He desires to imitate God and God's power. This is demonstrated by the three miracles which the magicians of Egypt imitated by the power of Satan. Just as in the biblical parable where Satan sows tares among the wheat (Matt. 13:24,25), so Pharaoh sought to nullify the miracles of the true God by having his wise men imitate Aaron's miracles.

Satan is still at work today, imitating miracles with subtle methods and wiles of deceit. The Bible tells us, "Your adversary the devil, as a roaring lion, walketh about, seeking whom he may devour" (I Pet. 5:8). The Bible also tells us that Satan appears as "an angel of light" (II Cor. 11:14). We must remember that what seems right on the surface may simply be a tactic of Satan to draw us off the course of pleasing God in all that we do.

Because Satan's desire is to imitate the genuine work of God, we need much discernment. Thus, those who teach false doctrine and thereby are followers of Satan are those who have a form of godliness but deny the power of true godliness (II Tim. 3:5). Such people also are "ever learning, and never able to come to the knowledge of the truth" (v. 7).

The plagues brought on the Egyptians by God furnish a striking prophetic forecast of God's judgment during the coming Tribulation. Revelation 8—16 tells of these judgments. As God and Moses were vindicated in Egypt, so the Lord Jesus Christ will be vindicated in the end time (see Rev. 19:11,15,16).

Chapter 17

The Progressive Hardening
of Pharaoh's Heart

Four verses on the subject of the hardening of Pharaoh's heart are especially significant. As God was instructing Moses about going before Pharaoh, He told Moses, "I am sure that the king of Egypt will not let you go, no, not by a mighty hand" (Ex. 3:19). We observe from this verse that the omniscient God already knew the outcome.

Verse 20 reveals how God planned to counteract Pharaoh's refusal: "I will stretch out my hand, and smite Egypt with all my wonders which I will do in the midst thereof: and after that he will let you go." So while God told Moses that Pharaoh would not let the people go, He also explained how He planned to deal with Pharaoh.

God's announcement to Moses that He would harden Pharaoh's heart was first recorded in Exodus 4:21: "When thou goest to return into Egypt, see that thou do all those wonders before Pharaoh, which I have put in thine hand: but I will harden his heart, that he shall not let the people go." What a statement! These strong words have generated much discussion among Bible students. As we examine this subject, let us remember that this statement was made in the same context in which God told Moses what to say to Pharaoh: "I say unto thee, Let my son go, that he may serve me: and if thou refuse to let him go, behold, I will slay thy son, even thy firstborn" (v. 23). Thus, we see that the hardening of Pharaoh's heart was mentioned in connection with Pharaoh's absolute refusal to let Israel go, and this refusal brought the final plague.

196

God's Will and God's Nature

The question arises: Does God use His sovereignty and omnipotence to destroy anything that comes in His way? In answering this question, we must first consider God's will concerning the salvation of mankind. First Timothy 2:4 says of God, "Who will have all men to be saved, and to come unto the knowledge of the truth." So what does God want? He wants everyone to be saved.

This same truth is seen in II Peter 3:9: "The Lord is not slack concerning his promise, as some men count slackness; but is longsuffering to us-ward, not willing that any should perish, but that all should come to repentance." Here again we see that it is God's will that people be saved, and we can count on the fact that God will not do anything contrary to His own will.

Another important question is, What is God like? That is, What is His nature? His nature is to love, and John 3:16 highlights this aspect of His nature. Although God could use His sovereignty to punish and to destroy, He chooses rather to use His sovereignty to win others to Himself through exercising much longsuffering and mercy. But if His love is refused, God will exercise His sovereignty to eternally punish those who reject Him.

The Hardened Heart

As we consider the hardening of Pharaoh's heart, we must also consider what was meant by the individual Hebrew words that are translated "harden" or "hardening" in the King James Version. Three different Hebrew words were used, but they are similar in meaning. They basically mean "to be or become strong," "to strengthen or harden," "to make heavy or hard" and "to make sharp or hard."

Various translations render these words differently—"to render obstinate," "to make stubborn" or "to make strong." From these words and the translations of them we see that Pharaoh's feelings and attitudes were to become firm—they would not change. "To make strong" seems to be a primary meaning of the words involved. Pharaoh became strong in his feelings and attitudes against God. Foolhardiness is also implied by these words in that a strong-willed or strong-minded person often does things that are contrary to reason. Pharaoh was insensitive to any possible judgment that would result from the strong position he took.

Having considered this matter carefully, I believe that Pharaoh hardened his own heart, and then God hardened it further. Pharaoh first made his own heart hard, and then God confirmed, or further hardened, him in the position he had taken against God. It was as if the Lord were saying, "I will make Pharaoh's heart firm so that it will not move; his feelings and attitude toward Me and Israel will not change."

The hardening of Pharaoh's heart is ascribed to God ten times in the Book of Exodus. The verses indicate that God not only foreknew and foretold the hardening of Pharaoh's heart, but He also caused or effected it. On the other hand, it is stated just as often that Pharaoh hardened his own heart; that is, he made it strong, or firm. So we see that the hardening of Pharaoh's heart was just as much his own act as that of God's decree.

The progressive hardening of Pharaoh's heart needs to be traced from his first meeting with Moses and Aaron to the overthrowing of his army at the Red Sea. We have already referred to Exodus 3:19,20 and 4:21,23. In these verses we have seen that the Lord announced to Moses what he could expect when he went before Pharaoh. The key to understanding the hardening of Pharaoh's heart is found in Exodus 5:2: "Pharaoh said, Who is the Lord, that I should obey his voice to let Israel go? I know not the Lord, neither will I let Israel go." With these words Pharaoh exposed his rebellious attitude toward God. It is nowhere indicated that God had hardened Pharaoh's heart before this time. The Lord had told Moses, "I will harden his heart" (4:21), but this refers to a future time, and I believe it was after Pharaoh took his strong position as recorded in 5:2.

Through Moses, God had addressed Pharaoh when He gave the mandate, "Let my people go, that they may hold a feast unto me in the wilderness" (5:1). God gave Pharaoh an opportunity to obey; He addressed him in grace and did not at that time announce his judgments or bring them on the haughty king and his subjects.

Before God deals in wrath, He acts in mercy. This has always been God's way, and it is still the way of God today. There are many biblical illustrations of this. Before the world flood of Noah's time, God gave mankind 120 years of warning. Also, before the Israelites went into capitivity, God sent prophets who warned again and again that His judgment would fall if the people did not depart from their sin. God's compassion is especially seen in the words of the Lord Jesus Christ as He wept over Jerusalem: "O Jerusalem, Jerusalem, thou that killest the prophets, and stonest them which are sent unto thee, how often would I have gathered thy children together, even as a hen gathereth her chickens under her wings, and ye would not!" (Matt. 23:37).

How thankful we should be for the mercy of the Lord! Lamentations 3:22,23 expresses it in these words: "It is of the Lord's mercies that we are not consumed, because his compassions fail not. They are new every morning: great is thy faithfulness."

God's Judgment

Because Pharaoh determinedly resisted the sovereign will of God, God eventually had to turn him over to what might be called "judicial blindness." Proverbs 29:1 is applicable to a person such as Pharaoh: "He, that being often reproved hardeneth his neck, shall suddenly be destroyed, and that without remedy." God is absolutely fair in all of His dealings, and He gives sufficient opportunity for a person to repent, but He will not withhold the judgment of sin forever.

The New Testament tells of the judgment which the Lord Jesus Christ will bring on those who reject Him as Saviour. Referring to the judgment He will administer when He returns to earth, II Thessalonians 1:8,9 says, "In flaming fire taking vengeance on them that know not God, and that obey not the gospel of our Lord Jesus Christ: who shall be punished with everlasting destruction from the presence of the Lord, and from the glory of his power." How awful it is to reject God's grace!

Pharaoh was not able to escape judgment when he rejected God's grace, and neither is any other person able to do so. Be aware of the results of rejecting God. To resist the light results in increased darkness. To turn from the truth is to come more and more under the power of the archliar, Satan himself. Pharaoh was so dominated by the archliar that he not only rejected God's command, but he also referred to the command as "vain words" (Ex. 5:9).

Romans 1 sets forth the principle that the one who rejects the grace of God will eventually himself be rejected by God. "Because that which is known about God is evident within them; for God made it evident to them. For since the creation of the world His invisible attributes, His eternal power and divine nature, have been clearly seen, being understood through what has been made, so that they are without excuse. For even though they knew God, they did not honor Him as God, or give thanks; but they became futile in their speculations, and their foolish heart was darkened. Professing to be wise, they became fools, and exchanged the glory of the incorruptible God for an image in the form of corruptible man and of birds and four-footed animals and crawling creatures. Therefore God gave them over in the lusts of their hearts to impurity, that their bodies might be dishonored among them" (vv. 19-24, NASB). Notice also verse 26: "For this reason God gave them over to degrading passions" (NASB). It is a solemn matter to set one's will against Almighty God.

Pharaoh's Progressive Resistance

The verses that refer to the hardening of Pharaoh's heart indicate a progressive hardening. These verses also reveal when and how God intervened.

As we have indicated, the key to the hardening of Pharaoh's heart is found in Exodus 5:2, which records his response to the command to let the people go: "Pharaoh said, Who is the Lord, that I should obey his voice to let Israel go? I know not the Lord, neither will I let Israel go."

Then, notice especially what the Lord told Moses in Exodus 6:1: "Now you shall see what I will do to Pharaoh; for under compulsion he shall let them go, and under compulsion he shall drive them out of his land" (NASB).

God announced to Moses that He would harden Pharaoh's heart and perform signs and wonders in order to persuade Pharaoh and Egypt that God was who He said He was. God told Moses, "But I will harden Pharaoh's heart that I may multiply My signs and My wonders in the land of Egypt. When Pharaoh will not listen to you, then I will lay My hand on Egypt, and bring out My hosts, My people the sons of Israel, from the land of Egypt by great judgments. And the Egyptians shall know that I am the Lord, when I stretch out My hand on Egypt and bring out the sons of Israel from their midst" (7:3-5, NASB).

When would God harden Pharaoh's heart? Not until Pharaoh had hardened his own heart and absolutely refused to listen to Moses, God's representative. Aaron's first miracle before Pharaoh was the throwing down of his rod, which became a serpent. However, when Pharaoh called his wise men and they were able to perform a similar miracle, this caused Pharaoh's heart to be hardened and his mind to become more stubborn. When his magicians were able to duplicate the miracle, he apparently thought, "That shows that my god is just as strong and powerful as your God, so I'm not going to listen to you." It seemed to make no difference to Pharaoh that Aaron's rod-turned-serpent swallowed up those of the magicians. The Bible says, "Yet Pharaoh's heart was hardened, and he did not listen to them, as the Lord had said. Then the Lord said to Moses, 'Pharaoh's heart is stubborn; he refuses to let the people go' " (7:13,14, NASB).

Then followed several judgments, or plagues. After each one of these judgments, the hardening of Pharaoh's heart is emphasized. The obstinacy of his mind is seen in what the Bible has to say about him. After Aaron caused the water to turn into blood, the Bible says, "The magicians of Egypt did the same with their secret arts; and Pharaoh's heart was hardened, and he did not listen to them, as the Lord had said" (v. 22, NASB).

But even later when the magicians could not duplicate the miracles of Moses and Aaron, Pharaoh still refused to heed God's command; his mind was rigidly set. This is evident from Exodus 8:19: "Then the magicians said to Pharaoh, 'This is the finger of God.' But Pharaoh's heart was hardened, and he did not listen to them, as the Lord had said" (NASB).

Even when Pharaoh realized that the judgments were falling only on the Egyptians and not on the Israelites, his heart still remained firmly fixed against God. Exodus 8 concludes by saying, "Pharaoh hardened his heart at this time also, neither would he let the people go" (v. 32). Even after these awful plagues, Pharaoh's heart was hardened—it was firmly fixed, insensitive to the voice of God and unaffected by the miracles that were performed before him.

Even though God had told Moses that He would harden Pharaoh's heart, the first mention of God actually doing this is in Exodus 9:12: "The Lord hardened the heart of Pharaoh, and he hearkened not unto them; as the Lord had spoken unto Moses." As to the time this took place, the account involved indicates that it was during the sixth judgment God brought on Pharaoh and the Egyptians. The words "the Lord hardened the heart of Pharaoh" could be literally translated, "Jehovah made the heart of Pharaoh firm." God simply confirmed that which was already hardened.

Pharaoh's Insincere Confessions

Moses had warned Pharaoh not to persist in his hardness. Earlier, during the fourth plague, Moses had told Pharaoh, "Behold, I go out from thee, and I will intreat the Lord that the swarms of flies may depart from Pharaoh, from his servants, and from his people, to morrow: but let not Pharaoh deal deceitfully any more in not letting the people go to sacrifice to the Lord" (Ex. 8:29).

Note also what the Lord told Moses to say to Pharaoh: "Thus speaks the Lord God of the Hebrews, Let My people go, so they may serve Me; for if you refuse to let them go and persist in detaining them, beware! The Lord's hand will be on your livestock out in the field, on the horses, the donkeys, the camels, the herds and the flocks with a dreadful plague. The Lord will draw distinction between Israel's livestock and that of Egypt. Nothing that belongs to the Israelites shall die" (9:1-4, Berkeley).

Exodus 9:16 is a key statement revealing God's purpose for hardening Pharaoh's heart and for keeping him alive rather than destroying him: "But for this very purpose have I let you live, that I might show you My power, and that My name may be declared throughout all the earth" (Amplified). This same thought is expressed in Romans 9:17: "For the scripture saith unto Pharaoh, Even for this same purpose have I raised thee up, that I might shew my power in thee, and that my name might be declared throughout all the earth."

God puts rulers on the throne, and He removes them from the throne. This is the responsibility and prerogative of the sovereign God. God was, in effect, saying to Pharaoh, "Pharaoh, I have allowed you to come to the throne, and I have allowed you to live so I can prove to Egypt and to My people that I am God Almighty—that I have all power."

As the result of the plagues which followed, Pharaoh began to weaken. He even confessed that he had sinned, although he said this only in an attempt to get Moses and Aaron to stop the plague. Pharaoh said, "I have sinned this time; the Lord is the righteous one, and I and my people are the wicked ones. Make supplication to the Lord, for there has been enough of God's thunder and hail; and I will let you go, and you shall stay no longer" (Ex. 9:27,28, NASB).

Moses agreed to pray that God would stop the plague, but he was not deceived by Pharaoh's false confession. Moses said, "But as for you and your servants, I know that you do not yet fear the Lord God" (v. 30, NASB). That God had given Moses correct insight into Pharaoh's heart is seen from verses 34 and 35: "But when Pharaoh saw that the rain and the hail and the thunder had ceased, he sinned again and hardened his heart, he and his servants. And Pharaoh's heart was hardened, and he did not let the sons of Israel go, just as the Lord had spoken through Moses" (NASB). It is obvious from this incident that Pharaoh himself, not God, hardened Pharaoh's heart.

The hardening of Pharaoh's heart is also mentioned in Exodus 10. The Lord told Moses, "Go to Pharaoh, for I have hardened his heart and the heart of his servants, that I may perform these signs of Mine among them, and that you may tell in the hearing of your son, and of your grandson, how I made a mockery of the Egyptians, and how I performed My signs among them; that you may know that I am the Lord" (vv. 1,2, NASB). Pharaoh attempted to mock God, but God made a mockery of Pharaoh and the Egyptians.

Pharaoh continued to resist God, but the Egyptians feared that the nation would be ruined by the plagues brought on them by Moses. "Pharaoh's servants said unto him, How long shall this man be a snare unto us? Let the men go, that they may serve the Lord their God: knowest thou not yet that Egypt is destroyed?" (v. 7).

But Pharaoh would not give in to the suggestions of his people, nor would he submit to God. A plague of locusts followed, and again Pharaoh feigned confession of sin in order to be relieved of the plague. "Pharaoh hurriedly called for Moses and Aaron, and he said, 'I have sinned against the Lord your God and against you. Now therefore, please forgive my sin only this once, and make supplication to the Lord your God, that He would only remove this death from me' " (vv. 16,17, NASB).

God Hardens Pharaoh's Heart

But Pharaoh was not sincere, and the Lord was not through with him: "The Lord hardened Pharaoh's heart, and he did not let the sons of Israel go" (v. 20, NASB). Verse 27 emphasizes the same truth: "But the Lord hardened Pharaoh's heart, and he was not willing to let them go" (NASB).

By this time, Pharaoh was really angry. He said to Moses, "Get away from me! Beware, do not see my face again, for in the day you see my face you shall die!" (v. 28, NASB). Upon hearing Pharaoh's words, Moses solemnly said to him, "You are right; I shall never see your face again!" (v. 29, NASB). But before Moses left Pharaoh's presence, Moses told him of the coming judgment on the firstborn of Egypt, and then he "went out from Pharaoh in hot anger" (11:8, NASB).

Then the Lord told Moses, "Pharaoh will not listen to you, that My wonders and miracles may be multiplied in the land of Egypt. Moses and Aaron did all these wonders and miracles before Pharaoh; and the Lord hardened Pharaoh's stubborn heart, and he did not let the Israelites go out of his land" (vv. 9,10, Amplified). Notice from these verses that God hardened Pharaoh's already stubborn heart.

After the firstborn of Egypt had been destroyed and the Israelites had fled, God told Moses, "I will harden Pharaoh's heart, that he shall follow after them; and I will be honoured upon Pharaoh, and upon all his host; that the Egyptians may know that I am the Lord. And they did so" (14:4). This was the final hardening of Pharaoh's heart. Verse 8 says, "The Lord hardened the heart of Pharaoh king of Egypt, and he pursued after the children of Israel: and the children of Israel went out with an high hand."

God not only hardened the heart of Pharaoh, but He also hardened the hearts of the Egyptians so that they pursued the Israelites to the Red Sea (vv. 17,18). But the Lord drowned the Egyptians in the Red Sea after the Israelites had crossed over on dry ground. "Thus the Lord saved Israel that day out of the hand of the Egyptians; and Israel saw the Egyptians dead upon the sea shore. And Israel saw that great work which the Lord did upon the Egyptians: and the people feared the Lord, and believed the Lord, and his servant Moses" (vv. 30,31). What a climax!

Remember that the hardening of Pharaoh's heart is ascribed both to Pharaoh and to God. It is not necessary or right to make God the author of Pharaoh's stubbornness. And God did not arbitrarily or directly force on Pharaoh an obstinate and stubborn resistance to Himself. God can never be blamed for evil.

From the Book of James we learn that God does not solicit or cause a person to do evil. When a person does evil, it is because of his own depraved nature. James said, "Let no man say when he is tempted, I am tempted of God: for God cannot be tempted with evil, neither tempteth he any man: but every man is tempted, when he is drawn away of his own lust, and enticed. Then when lust hath conceived, it bringeth forth sin: and sin, when it is finished, bringeth forth death. Do not err, my beloved brethren" (1:13-16).

As we have seen, God told Moses about the hardening of Pharaoh's heart even before the plagues began. Although man looks on the outer appearance, God looks on the heart—He is a heart specialist!

During the first five plagues Pharaoh hardened his own heart. It was only after the sixth plague that God finally confirmed Pharaoh in his hardness. The extent to which

Pharaoh had hardened his own heart is seen in Exodus 5:2—he refused to acknowledge God or to do what He said.

During the last five plagues Pharaoh not only hardened his own heart, but God also confirmed Pharaoh in that hardness. Even after the magicians of Egypt were unable to duplicate the miracles of Moses and Aaron and admitted that the miracles were from God (8:19), Pharaoh still refused to submit to God.

Important Lessons for Today

It is dangerous for a person to know the truth and to deliberately sin against that knowledge. Pharaoh would not bend his will to the will of God, regardless of the power manifested by God.

From the hardening of Pharaoh's heart, we can learn some important lessons. First, God never allows any person to continue to scoff at Him. The Bible emphasizes this truth in Galatians 6:7: "Be not deceived; God is not mocked: for whatsoever a man soweth, that shall he also reap."

Second, God not only permits man to harden himself, but—after being patient and longsuffering—He also produces a stubbornly resistant and unyielding heart attitude in that person.

Third, for a time God withholds, or postpones, judgment on the person who hardens his heart against Him. These three facts are seen throughout the account of Exodus, and they are important principles for us to keep in mind.

The curse of sin makes the heart hardened toward God. At first God permits this stubbornness to be manifested toward Him, but eventually He confirms a person in that hardness and thus deliberately hardens the person's heart. The sinner's heart can become so stubbornly unyielding that it is no longer capable of turning from its fixed position against God. Thus, the sinner is brought into the judgment of damnation.

Perhaps someone reading these lines has resisted God just as Pharaoh did. If so, do you realize that your heart can become so hard that you may never again have a desire to turn to God?

Although God gave him opportunity again and again to repent, Pharaoh was so hardened in his ways that he refused to change his mind concerning God and his own need of salvation. After his heart was firmly fixed in its hardness, God then confirmed it so that Pharaoh never again had a desire to turn to God. As we have seen, Pharaoh's admission of being a sinner was not sincere at all but was only an attempt to stop whatever plague he was experiencing.

After the seventh plague Pharaoh's heart was so hard that judgment was the only course left to God. And with the judgment of God upon him, Pharaoh's heart was completely hardened by God. As a result, Pharaoh and his army pursued the Israelites and were overtaken by God's final stroke of judgment in the Red Sea. God's hardening of Pharaoh's heart only completed what Pharaoh had already done to his own heart.

This should remove every reason for questioning what God did. We are compelled to see that God left Pharaoh's heart in its natural state; that is, obstinate, inflexible and full of iniquity. God had a perfect right to allow Pharaoh to continue in a disobedient, God-defying attitude. Pharaoh had refused to obey God or to acknowledge Him in any way. In God's infinite wisdom and knowledge, He read with unerring accuracy what was in Pharaoh's heart, and He was completely justified in confirming Pharaoh in his hardness.

God knows your heart too. He knows whether or not you are full of stubbornness. God may allow you to go your own way until He finally has to bring some type of judgment on you. If you have trusted Jesus Christ as your personal Saviour, God's judgment will not be eternal damnation, but He could severely chasten you to bring you back into fellowship with Himself. But when death comes, there is no other opportunity for those who refuse to trust Jesus Christ as Saviour to be saved. The Bible says, "It is appointed unto men once to die, but after this the judgment" (Heb. 9:27).

New Testament Commentary

In considering what God has said about the hardening of Pharaoh's heart, we should give attention to a key New Testament passage on this subject. Romans 9 is frequently cited in explaining what was involved in the hardening of Pharaoh's heart. Yet even Romans 9 has been interpreted in different ways. We want to examine this passage, for it is the New Testament commentary on this Old Testament event.

"For the scripture saith unto Pharaoh, Even for this same purpose have I raised thee up, that I might shew my power in thee, and that my name might be declared throughout all the earth. . . . What if God, willing to shew his wrath, and to make his power known, endured with much longsuffering the vessels of wrath fitted to destruction: and that he might make known the riches of his glory on the vessels of mercy, which he had afore prepared unto glory" (vv. 17,22,23).

God resolved to use Pharaoh as an example of His sovereignty because Pharaoh was incorrigible—he was incapable of being corrected, for he was unalterably depraved. God simply used Pharaoh as He found him to demonstrate His power to the human race, an act of perfect justice to Pharaoh because all of God's demands were just.

The words "for this same purpose have I raised thee up" (v. 17) have caused many to stumble in their interpretation. These words do not mean that God created Pharaoh for the purpose of using him as a demonstration of damnation. Rather, they refer to God allowing Pharaoh to appear, or to be brought forward on the stage of events. God had a purpose to fulfill, and Pharaoh was the right person to be on the throne at that time in order for God to fulfill His purpose. That God is even in control of earthly powers is seen in Daniel 4:17: "This matter is by the decree of the watchers, and the demand by the word of the holy ones: to the intent that the living may know that the most High ruleth in the kingdom of men, and giveth it to whomsoever he will, and setteth up over it the basest of men." God has the right to place on the throne the person of His choice.

The significance of Romans 9:17 is that God allowed Pharaoh to be on the throne so that He could demonstrate His power.

Romans 9:22 is the first part of a long question in which Paul asked, "What if God, willing to shew his wrath, and to make his power known, endured with much longsuffering the vessels of wrath fitted to destruction?" Please note that God "endured with much longsuffering" and also that the vessels under discussion were those "fitted to destruction." Although God's righteous nature eventually led Him to demonstrate His wrath against evil, He withheld His wrath and endured patiently for a long time.

So we see that God had every right to destroy Pharaoh and all of Egypt much earlier than He did. When Pharaoh refused to obey or to even recognize Him (Ex. 5:2) and called God's words vain babblings (v. 9), God would have been completely justified in destroying Pharaoh and his people with a bolt of fire from heaven. But God held back—He endured with longsuffering, and in so doing He gave the entire world a demonstration of how He could be merciful, even to a blasphemer such as Pharaoh. But God's power and wrath were also revealed to the world when God accomplished His will through Pharaoh and finally brought judgment on him. God had every right to allow Pharaoh to continue in his disobedient, God-defying attitude and also to bring judgment on him at once.

Notice particularly the last words of Romans 9:22: "The vessels of wrath fitted to destruction." These are significant words. God did not fit the vessels for wrath nor were they fitted by God for destruction. The word "fitted" is not equivalent to "foreordained" or "foreknown." Rather, these vessels were fitted in the sense that they were ready, or ripe, for destruction. It was evident from what Pharaoh said and did that he was fully ready for judgment.

In our study of the first five plagues that God brought on Pharaoh and the Egyptians, we have seen that God did not touch Pharaoh himself; God allowed him to go on in his own destructive way. Even though Pharaoh said he did not know God and made it clear that he did not intend to listen to God, he was still spared from destruction in the first five plagues. This reveals that Pharaoh hardened his heart in spite of the fact that God was longsuffering and merciful to him. God sent a plague, and then through Moses He took it away, thereby giving Pharaoh every opportunity to repent. But he absolutely refused. Because of his rejection of God's grace in the first five plagues, God then further hardened, or confirmed, Pharaoh's hardened heart in the sixth plague.

It is not always the judgment of God that brings people to repentance. God was showing His mercy to Pharaoh, and this was in line with the principle stated in Romans 2:4-6: "Or do you think lightly of the riches of His kindness and forbearance and patience, not knowing that the kindness of God leads you to repentance? But because of your stubbornness and unrepentant heart you are storing up wrath for yourself in the day of wrath and revelation of the righteous judgment of God; who will render to every man according to his deeds" (NASB).

Notice also the significant statement made in II Peter 3:15: "And account that the longsuffering of our Lord is salvaticn."

Although God gave Pharaoh and the Egyptians every opportunity to repent and to turn to Him for salvation, they refused to do so. In refusing the mercy and longsuffering of God, they became vessels fitted to, or ready for, destruction.

God's Mercy and God's Judgment

God's dealings with Pharaoh and the Egyptians teach a valuable lesson to everyone today. God also expresses His mercy and longsuffering to sinners now, but He will not withhold His judgment forever. So one should not delay in trusting Christ as Saviour. As II Corinthians 6:2 says, "Behold, now is 'the acceptable time,' behold, now is 'the day of salvation' " (NASB).

There are many indications that God is withholding His wrath against sin today. He allows blasphemous people to go unhindered in what they are saying. There seems to be a drive to eliminate any reference to God in the classrooms of North America. At the same time, many are aggressively seeking to expose students to all kinds of filthy literature. In His longsuffering, God is allowing people to speak blasphemous words against Him, but He will not always withhold judgment. We must never forget that a day of judgment is coming.

God is withholding His wrath today so that He can reveal His mercy and glory to those who will accept His gift of salvation. We must remember that people are not lost because they are hardened; they are hardened because they are lost. And the reason for their lost condition is that all are born into this world with a sinful nature. "All have sinned, and come short of the glory of God" (Rom. 3:23).

So the hardening of Pharaoh's heart was the fruit of his sin. It was the result of his self-will, high-mindedness and pride, all of which result from sin. Pharaoh continued to abuse the freedom of the will which is present in every man and which makes it possible to remain obstinate and to resist the Word of God. When one continues to reject God's love, he will eventually experience God's judgment.

A sinner may resist the will of God as long as he lives, but such resistance plunges him into destruction and damnation at death. God never allows a person to scoff at Him without eventually experiencing judgment unless that person repents. Pharaoh scoffed at God, and God waited for some time without bringing destruction on him, but destruction finally came. After Pharaoh had hardened his heart against God, he was then used by God as a further demonstration of God's power.

The Bible alludes many times to the serious responsibility we have before God. To the Jews, Christ said, "Ye will not come to me, that ye might have life" (John 5:40). Stephen said to the same people, "Ye stiffnecked and uncircumcised in heart and ears, ye do always resist the Holy Ghost: as your fathers did, so do ye" (Acts 7:51). Solomon said, "He, that being often reproved hardeneth his neck, shall suddenly be destroyed, and that without remedy" (Prov. 29:1).

God's Desire for All Men

But Peter said, "The Lord is not slack concerning his promise, as some men count slackness; but is longsuffering to us-ward, not willing that any should perish, but that all should come to repentance" (II Pet. 3:9). God does not want to see people die in their sins; He "desires all men to be saved and to come to the knowledge of the truth" (I Tim. 2:4, NASB).

Through Ezekiel, God said, "I have no pleasure in the death of the wicked; but that the wicked turn from his way and live: turn ye, turn ye from your evil ways; for why will ye die, O house of Israel?" (Ezek. 33:11). The Book of Hebrews warns, "Wherefore (as the Holy Ghost saith, To day if ye will hear his voice, harden not your hearts, as in the provocation, in the day of temptation in the wilderness.) . . . Take heed, brethren, lest there be in any of you an evil heart of unbelief, in departing from the living God" (3:7,8,12).

Romans 2:4,5 says, "Or despisest thou the riches of his goodness and forbearance and longsuffering; not knowing that the goodness of God leadeth thee to repentance? But after thy hardness and impenitent heart treasurest up unto thyself wrath against the day of wrath and revelation of the righteous judgment of God." Thus, Galatians 6:7,8 warns, "Be not deceived; God is not mocked: for whatsoever a man soweth, that shall he also reap. For he that soweth to his flesh shall of the flesh reap corruption; but he that soweth to the Spirit shall of the Spirit reap life everlasting."

It is important that each person take these warnings from the Word of God seriously. But notice also the invitation that Christ extends to us: "Come unto me, all ye that labour and are heavy laden, and I will give you rest. Take my yoke upon you, and learn of me; for I am meek and lowly in heart: and ye shall find rest unto your souls. For my yoke is easy, and my burden is light" (Matt. 11:28-30). The Lord Jesus Christ also promised, "All that the Father giveth me shall come to me; and him that cometh to me I will in no wise cast out" (John 6:37). Have you trusted Jesus Christ as your personal Saviour? If not, do so today before it is eternally too late.

Chapter 18

The Progressive Intensity of the Plagues

There is an evident progression in the intensity of the ten plagues. Because the tenth plague—the killing of the firstborn—is worthy of special attention in itself, in this chapter we want to focus attention on the first nine. Only because Pharaoh refused to be influenced by the first nine plagues was the tenth severe judgment brought by God. However, God—in His omniscience—announced the tenth plague even at the beginning (Ex. 4:22,23).

As previously discussed, God had at least four purposes for bringing the plagues on Pharaoh and the Egyptians. First, they revealed God's mighty power, showing that He was greater than any of the gods of Egypt. The Egyptians were so entrenched in idol worship that the true God had to perform miracles to show who He was. Second, the plagues were to break Pharaoh's stubbornness so he would let the Israelites go. This was not accomplished, however, until the very end. Third, the plagues were to strengthen Moses' faith. He needed this strengthening as preparation for the years when he would be Israel's leader in the desert. Fourth, the plagues were meant to soften the hearts of the Israelites and cause them to want to leave Egypt. Even though life was difficult for the Israelites in Egypt, they were unwilling to leave at first. But the plagues made them willing to go.

Although skeptics often look at the account of the plagues and claim that they were only natural phenomena that had occurred periodically in a lighter form over Egypt, there are several reasons why this is not a valid view. God caused the people of that day to realize He was doing something on a special scale that was incomparable to

213

anything else. The plagues were brought on the country and then removed like clockwork, according to Moses' announcements. They came when he said they would come, and they stopped when he said they would stop.

The plagues revealed the protective power of God as He shielded His people. They also demonstrated the omnipotence of the true God and the impotence of the Egyptian gods. Although, under the power of Satan, the Egyptian magicians could imitate some of the miracles, they could not imitate all of them.

Then, too, the intensity of the plagues was something that had never been experienced before and will not be experienced again until God speaks during the coming Tribulation. If Pharaoh and the Egyptians were not convinced that the plagues were more than natural phenomena, they would never have allowed the Israelites to leave Egypt. But Pharaoh and the Egyptians were not only willing to let the Israelites go, they even drove them out of the country.

Before the plagues came on Egypt, God announced to Moses what He was about to do: "I am aware that the king of Egypt will not allow you to go except by a mighty hand, so I will stretch out My hand and strike Egypt with all the wonders I shall work there; after which he will send you away. And I will give this people such favor with the Egyptians that when you leave, you will not go empty-handed; but each woman shall request from her neighbor and from the lodger in her home silver and gold articles, and garments with which you will dress your sons and daughters. You shall strip the Egyptians" (Ex. 3:19-22, Berkeley).

We have discussed previously how Moses and Aaron obeyed God's instructions down to the last detail because they believed God. "Moses and Aaron did as the Lord ordered them, to the last syllable" (7:6, Berkeley). Thus faith and obedience were the keys to their success; Moses and Aaron did absolutely everything the Lord told them to do.

Moses and Aaron first went before Pharaoh and presented their credentials—Aaron's rod became a serpent right before Pharaoh's eyes! But then Pharaoh called his wise men and they "did the same by their secret formulas" (v. 11,

Berkeley). But Aaron's credentials were proven superior when his staff swallowed the others. Although Pharaoh did not accept the message of Moses and Aaron at this time, he had to deal with them as men of authority. The fact that Aaron's snake swallowed up the snakes of the Egyptian magicians revealed God's power over the gods of Egypt.

Moses' faith is seen throughout the process and progress of the plagues. Hebrews 11:27 gives credit to Moses in these words: "By faith he forsook Egypt, not fearing the wrath of the king: for he endured, as seeing him who is invisible." By faith he forsook Egypt and by faith he endured, because he saw the invisible God. Moses' faith grew; it was strengthened through the tests he faced and by the plagues on Egypt so that he saw and understood God more clearly.

Moses' faith was the means, or the instrument, by which God worked His mighty wonders on Egypt. Although God is almighty and, therefore, can do anything, He often chooses to express His power primarily through individuals. But God requires that the individuals have complete faith in Him. Thus, Moses' faith was the means by which God conducted great miracles on the earth.

Even though Moses and Aaron had miraculous credentials, Pharaoh refused to heed what they had to say. God then gave Moses and Aaron these instructions: "In the morning, when as usual he is going out to the water, stand by the river bank to meet him. Take in your hand the staff that became a snake and say to him, 'The Lord God of the Hebrews has sent me to you with the message: "Let My people go, so they may serve Me in the desert." But to date you have not listened' " (Ex. 7:15,16, Berkeley).

The First Plague

God then instructed Moses to tell Aaron to stretch his staff over the waters of Egypt "so they shall become blood in the whole country of Egypt, the contents of wooden and stone containers included" (v. 19, Berkeley).

The plague came about precisely as God had foretold. The rivers, especially the Nile, were affected along with all canals. All water was turned into blood. For seven full days this condition prevailed. Fish died and floated to the surface; the air reeked with corruption. There was no water to drink in the land, so the Egyptians had to dig near the riverbank for water (v. 24). Notice that the Egyptian wise men were able to imitate this same miracle by their secret formulas (v. 22).

The Egyptians worshiped the Nile, but the goddess of the Nile could do nothing about this plague. God Almighty was far greater than the sacred Nile. So this miracle struck directly at the gods of Egypt so that all would know the absolute power of the true God.

The Second Plague

Because Pharaoh refused to let the people go, a second plague was brought on him and the Egyptians.

"The Lord spake unto Moses, Go unto Pharaoh, and say unto him, Thus saith the Lord, Let my people go, that they may serve me" (Ex. 8:1).

God warned what the plague would be if Pharaoh refused: "If thou refuse to let them go, behold, I will smite all thy borders with frogs: and the river shall bring forth frogs abundantly, which shall go up and come into thine house, and into thy bedchamber, and upon thy bed, and into the house of thy servants, and upon thy people, and into thine ovens, and into thy kneading-troughs: and the frogs shall come up both on thee, and upon thy people, and upon all thy servants" (vv. 2-4).

Notice that God gave Pharaoh another chance to repent, inasmuch as He announced the plague in advance. The plague was to come on Pharaoh and the Egyptians only if Pharaoh refused to let the Israelites go. Because Pharaoh refused, "the Lord spake unto Moses, Say unto Aaron, Stretch forth thine hand with thy rod over the streams, over the rivers, and over the ponds, and cause frogs to come up upon the land of Egypt" (v. 5).

It is significant that this second plague involved frogs, because frogs were also an object of worship in Egypt. Again, the true God showed His superiority over the gods of Egypt. Because the frog was worshiped, it was sacrilegious for an Egyptian to attempt to destroy it. This fact made the plague especially horrible on the Egyptians.

But again, the magicians of Egypt were not to be outdone by Moses and Aaron. Verse 7 says that the magicians "did the same with their secret formulas; they brought up frogs on the Egyptian country" (Berkeley). How interesting—the Egyptians certainly did not need more frogs! Yet, while the magicians were able to imitate the miracle of producing frogs, they were unable to bring an end to this plague.

Pharaoh seemingly began to weaken, for he "called for Moses and Aaron, and said, Intreat the Lord, that he may take away the frogs from me, and from my people; and I will let the people go, that they may do sacrifice unto the Lord" (v. 8).

To make the supremacy and power of God more obvious, Moses said to him, "Glory over me: when shall I intreat for thee, and for thy servants, and for thy people, to destroy the frogs from thee and thy houses, that they may remain in the river only?" (v. 9). "Glory over me" implies "the honor is yours to tell me." All Pharaoh had to do was say the word to Moses and the plague would be stopped. In answer to Moses' question, Pharaoh replied, "To morrow" (v. 10). Moses agreed, for he said, "Be it according to thy word: that thou mayest know that there is none like unto the Lord our God" (v. 10). Notice again that the only one who could stop the plague was Moses, God's representative. The magicians of Egypt could not stop it. They, like Satan whom they served, could originate evil, but they could not stop its progress.

Faithful to his word, "Moses cried unto the Lord because of the frogs which he had brought against Pharaoh. And the Lord did according to the word of Moses; and the frogs died out of the houses, out of the villages, and out of the fields" (vv. 12,13). The ending of this plague was a miracle just as producing the frogs had been a miracle.

But think of what a mess all the dead frogs caused! "The people piled them in heaps till the land reeked" (v. 14, Berkeley). What was Pharaoh's response after the plague was ended? Verse 15 gives the answer: "But when Pharaoh noticed that relief had come, he stiffened his heart; he did not heed them, as the Lord had said" (Berkeley). Pharaoh hardened his heart again!

The Third Plague

Because of the further hardening of Pharaoh's heart, another plague was brought on him and the Egyptians. There is no indication that Pharaoh was forewarned of this third plague; the hardening of his heart after the second plague was reason enough for God to bring another judgment.

"The Lord said unto Moses, Say unto Aaron, Stretch out thy rod, and smite the dust of the land, that it may become lice throughout all the land of Egypt" (v. 16). Imagine what this terrible plague must have been like—millions of lice! But these judgments were coming on Pharaoh because he had refused to obey God or to even recognize Him (5:2).

The magicians of Egypt also attempted to imitate this third plague but were unable to do so (8:18). By imitating the plagues, the Egyptian magicians were attempting to show that the god they served (Satan) was as great as the God that Moses and Aaron served. However, they were able to do only what God allowed them to do. He had allowed them to imitate the previous miracles but not this one. This immediately brought consternation to the magicians, and they said to Pharaoh, "This is the finger of God" (v. 19). When God no longer permitted the magicians to duplicate miracles, the magicians were powerless, regardless of how hard they tried. This caused them to realize that the miracle Aaron had performed was truly of God.

The magicians were deriving their power from Satan, and from Job 1 and 2 we learn that Satan can only do what God allows him to do. Hebrews 2:14 tells how the Lord Jesus Christ broke the power of Satan: "Since then the children share in flesh and blood, He Himself likewise also partook of the same, that through death He might render powerless him who had the power of death, that is, the devil" (NASB). Satan's bounds are prescribed by God.

The plague of lice particularly vexed the Egyptians because they were scrupulously clean in their personal habits. This was especially true of the Egyptian priests. Although serving false gods, the Egyptian priests would repeatedly bathe and shave themselves in preparation for their sacred duties.

Also, since some of the animals were worshiped—such as the bulls and goats—they were kept very clean, but they also became infected with lice. No Egyptian man or animal was spared—there were lice on men and beasts (Ex. 8:17). Thus, God again executed judgment on the gods of Egypt so all would know that He was the true God.

Even though the Egyptian magicians told Pharaoh, "This is the finger of God" (v. 19), Pharaoh would not pay any attention to their words; his heart became all the harder. The magicians were convinced that this plague was the result of a much higher power than they knew about. However, there is no indication that the magicians voiced their opinion to Pharaoh more than once.

God exalted Himself above the gods of Egypt, and Philippians 2 tells us that Jesus Christ has been exalted above every name because He became obedient to death on the cross: "Wherefore God also hath highly exalted him, and given him a name which is above every name: that at the name of Jesus every knee should bow, of things in heaven, and things in earth, and things under the earth; and that every tongue should confess that Jesus Christ is Lord, to the glory of God the Father" (vv. 9-11). This passage is comparable to Isaiah 45:23: "I have sworn by myself, the word is gone out of my mouth in righteousness, and shall not return, That unto me every knee shall bow, every tongue shall swear."

These first three plagues which came on Pharaoh and the Egyptians were directed specifically at their comfort and cleanliness, and the Israelites as well as the Egyptians suffered from them. As Pharaoh became harder and harder, Israel was made to see that God was working in their behalf. This became more apparent later, as the plagues came only on the Egyptians, and the Israelites were spared. God allowed Satan to go just so far and no further as far as touching His own. The Israelites were subject to the basic influences of sin, but later, when God dealt out destruction on property and lives, the Israelites were spared.

The Fourth Plague

The first nine plagues can be grouped into three series, each consisting of three plagues. Therefore, the fourth plague began a new series. In the next three plagues God brought destruction on the property and lives of the Egyptians but spared Israel.

The fourth plague is recorded in Exodus 8:20-32. The magicians and their gods had been proven to be fakes, so they could not oppose the rest of the plagues. They had succumbed to the powers of the Almighty God. Satan and his demons were not able to imitate or withstand the plague God was about to bring on Pharaoh and the Egyptians.

The Lord told Moses, "Rise up early in the morning, and stand before Pharaoh; lo, he cometh forth to the water; and say unto him, Thus saith the Lord, Let my people go, that they may serve me. Else, if thou wilt not let my people go, behold, I will send swarms of flies upon thee, and upon thy servants, and upon thy people, and into thy houses: and the houses of the Egyptians shall be full of swarms of flies, and also the ground whereon they are" (vv. 20,21). Notice that God gave Pharaoh another opportunity to repent before He brought this plague. But, as happened previously, Pharaoh refused to repent and only further hardened his own heart against the Lord.

This plague involved "swarms of flies" (v. 21). In the King James Version the word "flies" is italicized, meaning there is no basis for the word in the original language but that it was added by the translators to assist the meaning. The original says only that there were swarms; what they were swarms of is not exactly specified. It may have been flies, as the King James translators indicated, but there are also other possibilities. The Berkeley Version says "gadflies," and the New American Standard Bible says "insects." It is probably best to understand these swarms as a mixture of all kinds of flies. Later, when the psalmist wrote of this plague, he referred to "divers sorts of flies" (Ps. 78:45).

Among these insects may well have been the particular beetle that was the emblem of the Egyptian sun god. If so, this plague was another demonstration of the power of the true God over the false gods of Egypt.

In announcing the fourth plague to Pharaoh, God said through Moses, "I will sever in that day the land of Goshen, in which my people dwell, that no swarms of flies shall be there; to the end thou mayest know that I am the Lord in the midst of the earth. And I will put a division between my people and thy people: to morrow shall this sign be" (Ex. 8:22,23).

The lice had previously brought much discomfort to the Egyptians, but that was nothing in comparison to the discomfort resulting from the swarms of insects because they actually fed on the flesh of the people. This is indicated by Psalm 78:45: "He sent divers sorts of flies among them, which devoured them." Thus, the swarms of insects directly affected human flesh as well as vegetation.

Consider the great contrast between the Israelites and the Egyptians. The Israelites were only slaves of the Egyptians, but the God of the slaves completely overcame the gods of their masters. The God of Israel brought judgment on the Egyptians, yet the Israelites were completely protected. What a God!

All of this was too much for Pharaoh, and again he weakened under the tremendous pressure. He finally granted permission for the Israelites to leave, but his permission included restrictions that tested Moses' willingness to compromise. The Bible says, "Then Pharaoh called for Moses and Aaron and said, 'You go and sacrifice to your God within our boundaries' " (Ex. 8:25, Berkeley). Pharaoh was not yet willing to let the Israelites completely leave the land of Egypt.

But notice Moses' response: "It would not be right to do that; for we would offer the Lord our God something offensive to the Egyptians. You see, if we offer something the Egyptians abominate right before their eyes, might they not stone us? We want to go three days' travel into the desert to sacrifice to the Lord our God the way He directs us" (vv. 26,27, Berkeley).

Moses took a firm stand against the offer of Pharaoh. In particular, he pointed out that the Israelites' sacrifices would be considered an abomination by the Egyptians. Moses probably referred not only to the method of sacrificing but also to the animals sacrificed. The Egyptians considered various animals to be sacred, and they would be outraged if they saw the Israelites sacrificing these animals.

Pharaoh yielded to Moses' reasoning on this matter and then offered a second compromise: "I will let you go, that ye may sacrifice to the Lord your God in the wilderness; only ye shall not go very far away: intreat for me" (v. 28). Pharaoh was asking Moses to pray for him, while at the same time laying down restrictions about the Israelites' leaving Egypt.

Moses responded, "Behold, I go out from thee, and I will intreat the Lord that the swarms of flies may depart from Pharaoh, from his servants, and from his people, to morrow: but let not Pharaoh deal deceitfully any more in not letting the people go to sacrifice to the Lord" (v. 29). Moses boldly warned Pharaoh not to change his mind as he had done previously. But in spite of Moses' warning, after the swarms of insects were removed from Pharaoh and his people, "Pharaoh hardened his heart at this time also, neither would he let the people go" (v. 32). The Berkeley Version says, "Pharaoh set his mind stubbornly; he did not let the people go."

The Fifth Plague

Pharaoh's belligerent attitude resulted in the fifth plague, which is referred to in Exodus 9:1-7. The Lord told Moses, "Call on Pharaoh and tell him, 'Thus speaks the Lord God of the Hebrews, Let My people go, so they may serve Me; for if you refuse to let them go and persist in detaining them, beware! The Lord's hand will be on your livestock out in the field, on the horses, the donkeys, the camels, the herds and the flocks with a dreadful plague. The Lord will draw distinction between Israel's livestock and that of Egypt. Nothing that belongs to the Israelites shall die' " (vv. 1-4, Berkeley).

God again gave Pharaoh fair warning with an opportunity to obey, but again Pharaoh only further hardened his heart. This plague struck at the possessions of Pharaoh and the Egyptians, and next to health, this is what man values the most. But while this plague came on the livestock of Egypt, the livestock of Israel were unharmed.

By announcing that the plague would not begin until the next day, God gave Pharaoh 24 hours to repent. But since Pharaoh did not repent, God brought the plague precisely as He had announced.

Imagine the effect that the serious disease had on the Egyptian's animals. Egypt's sacred cows would have been dying everywhere, but in Israel the cattle would have been totally unaffected. Among the Egyptians there would have been death of livestock among the wealthy as well as among the poor. The horses of the rich died; donkeys of the poor died; camels that carried their merchandise to foreign countries died; oxen that plowed the fields died; sheep that constituted the great portion of Egyptian wealth died. The land was everywhere filled with death. Many are going bankrupt today, and unemployment is high, but imagine what it was like in that day due to the tremendous losses suffered by the Egyptians.

As this plague became so awful among the Egyptians, Pharaoh had an investigation made to see whether or not the Israelites in Goshen were affected. Exodus 9:7 says, "Pharaoh sent to investigate and found that not one of the Israelites' animals was dead; yet Pharaoh's mind was set; he did not let the people go" (Berkeley). This reveals how hard Pharaoh's heart really was; even after proof that this was obviously of God, he refused to humble himself before God. This was deliberate sinning against better knowledge. Again and again God had given him opportunity to repent, but Pharaoh only became more rebellious toward God.

Pharaoh was now ready for God's final judgment, but true to His character, God still extended mercy to Pharaoh. This especially reminds us of Romans 9:22: "What if God, willing to shew his wrath, and to make his power known, endured with much longsuffering the vessels of wrath fitted to destruction."

The Sixth Plague

Because of the hardness of Pharaoh's heart, another plague was brought on him and the Egyptians. Since Pharaoh's heart was incurably hardened, the Bible speaks from this point on of God's hardening Pharaoh's heart.

God told Moses and Aaron, "Both of you fill your hands with ashes from the furnace and, with Pharaoh looking on, let Moses toss it up to the sky. It will turn to fine dust all over the land of Egypt, that settles upon man and beast and causes boils that break out in open sores" (Ex. 9:8,9, Berkeley).

They did precisely as the Lord instructed, and all people and animals in Egypt were affected. Verse 11 says, "The scribes could not stand before Moses because of the sores: for the scribes as well as the rest of the Egyptians were covered with sores" (Berkeley). We then read this significant statement: "And the Lord hardened the heart of Pharaoh, and he hearkened not unto them; as the Lord had spoken unto Moses" (v. 12). Because Pharaoh had hardened his own heart against God so many times, he became one of the "vessels of wrath fitted to destruction" (Rom. 9:22); God hardened his heart.

God instructed Moses, "Rise up early in the morning, and stand before Pharaoh, and say unto him, Thus saith the Lord God of the Hebrews, Let my people go, that they may serve me. For I will at this time send all my plagues upon thine heart, and upon thy servants, and upon thy people; that thou mayest know that there is none like me in all the earth. For now I will stretch out my hand, that I may smite thee and thy people with pestilence; and thou shalt be cut off from the earth. And in very deed for this cause have I raised thee up, for to shew in thee my power; and that my name may be declared throughout all the earth" (Ex. 9:13-16).

The King James Version gives the impression that God created Pharaoh just to show His power and majesty. However, notice how the same verses are translated in another version: "Then the Lord said to Moses, Rise up early in the morning and stand before Pharaoh and say to him, Thus says the Lord, the God of the Hebrews, Let My people go, that they may serve Me. For this time I will send all My plagues upon your heart, and upon your servants and your people, that you may recognize and know that there is none like Me in all the earth.

"For by now I could have put forth My hand and have struck you and your people with pestilence, and you would have been cut off from the earth. But for this very purpose have I let you live, that I might show you My power, and that My name may be declared throughout all the earth" (Amplified).

Although Pharaoh was a vessel fitted for destruction, God exercised much longsuffering and patience in his behalf. God saw in Pharaoh a person who was obstinate to the point of rebelling against God Himself, yet God let him live so that the whole world would know that God was truly God. But we must remember that the longsuffering and mercy of God cannot continue to be scoffed at without suffering the consequences.

Pharaoh continued to oppose God and all that He stood for. Through Moses, God asked Pharaoh, "As yet exaltest thou thyself against my people, that thou wilt not let them go?" (v. 17). Because of Pharaoh's obstinacy, God brought another plague on him and the Egyptians.

The Seventh Plague

Because Pharaoh had refused to heed God in any way, God told Pharaoh through Moses, "Behold, to morrow about this time I will cause it to rain a very grievous hail, such as hath not been in Egypt since the foundation thereof even until now. Send therefore now, and gather thy cattle, and all that thou hast in the field; for upon every man and beast which shall be found in the field, and shall not be brought home, the hail shall come down upon them, and they shall die" (Ex. 9:18,19).

Notice that the Egyptians were acquainted with hailstorms, but this was to be a plague of hail such as the land had never experienced before. God said He would send the hail the next day, which gave Pharaoh another day of grace to submit to God and allow the Israelites to leave.

Although one day may seem to be a short time to consider this, remember that Pharaoh had already had days, weeks and months to consider the matter. So another entire day really was an abundant extension of God's grace. Pharaoh had deliberately hardened his own heart so many times that even this added day of grace made no impact on him. God's announcement of coming judgment fell on ears that refused to hear; Pharaoh's heart had become like clay hardened by the sun.

Notice, however, that some Egyptians responded to God's message of coming judgment: "He that feared the word of the Lord among the servants of Pharaoh made his servants and his cattle flee into the houses: and he that regarded not the word of the Lord left his servants and his cattle in the field" (vv. 20,21). These two verses reveal that a person's actions demonstrate whether or not he really believes God. Though some believed what God said, many others did not think that such a hailstorm would really come.

In accordance with God's instructions, "Moses stretched forth his rod toward heaven: and the Lord sent thunder and hail, and the fire ran along upon the ground; and the Lord rained hail upon the land of Egypt. So there was hail, and fire mingled with the hail, very grievous, such as there was none like it in all the land of Egypt since it became a nation. And the hail smote throughout all the land of Egypt all that was in the field, both man and beast; and the hail smote every herb of the field, and brake every tree of the field" (vv. 23-25).

But against the backdrop of this awful judgment is a verse that reveals God's protection of His own: "Only in the land of Goshen, where the children of Israel were, was there no hail" (v. 26). Goshen was part of Egypt, but God controlled the circumstances so that the Israelites were untouched by the judgment that Egypt experienced.

Notice what Pharaoh's response was to this awful judgment: "Pharaoh sent, and called for Moses and Aaron, and said unto them, I have sinned this time: the Lord is righteous, and I and my people are wicked. Intreat the Lord (for it is enough) that there be no more mighty thunderings and hail; and I will let you go, and ye shall stay no longer" (vv. 27,28). Although Pharaoh seemed to be conscious of his wickedness before God, it was only a feigned confession made in order to escape judgment.

Moses told Pharaoh, "As soon as I am gone out of the city, I will spread abroad my hands unto the Lord; and the thunder shall cease, neither shall there be any more hail; that thou mayest know how that the earth is the Lord's. But as for thee and thy servants, I know that ye will not yet fear the Lord God" (vv. 29,30).

Moses was not fooled by Pharaoh's false confession. God had given Moses insight so he knew what was in Pharaoh's heart and was not fooled in any way. This reveals how hardened Pharaoh really was; it did not bother him even to fake a confession of sin to God. But God knows what is in each person's heart, and He was not deceived for one minute. Chapter 9 concludes with these words: "And the heart of Pharaoh was hardened, neither would he let the children of Israel go; as the Lord had spoken by Moses" (v. 35).

God had showered His mercies on Pharaoh, but Pharaoh had refused to respond positively in any way. So in the remaining plagues God further hardened Pharaoh's heart so as to fulfill His plan of total revelation of Himself as absolutely sovereign.

The Eighth Plague

God next told Moses, "Go in unto Pharaoh: for I have hardened his heart, and the heart of his servants, that I might shew these my signs before him" (Ex. 10:1). This statement about the Lord's hardening Pharaoh's heart is also repeated in verse 20: "But the Lord hardened Pharaoh's heart, so that he would not let the children of Israel go." But as we have seen, it was only because Pharaoh had hardened his own heart that God further hardened it.

The eighth plague was one of locusts. The Bible says, "And Moses and Aaron went to Pharaoh and said to him, 'Thus says the Lord, the God of the Hebrews, "How long will you refuse to humble yourself before Me? Let My people go, that they may serve Me. For if you refuse to let My people go, behold, tomorrow I will bring locusts into your territory. And they shall cover the surface of the land, so that no one shall be able to see the land. They shall also eat the rest of what has escaped—what is left to you from the hail—and they shall eat every tree which sprouts for you out of the field.

"Then your houses shall be filled, and the houses of all your servants and the houses of all the Egyptians, something which neither your fathers nor your grandfathers have seen, from the day that they came upon the earth until this day." ' And he turned and went out from Pharaoh" (vv. 3-6, NASB).

Up to this time Moses had been content to repeat God's demand for Israel's release. However, Pharaoh's failure to keep his royal word had caused Moses to lose all respect for him in his position as king. Pharaoh's promises had been false, and his confessions of sin had produced no change in his life or attitude. Pharaoh was no longer ignorant of Jehovah, but he was willfully obstinate and defiant toward Him.

All of this caused Moses to completely alter his tone—no longer did Moses treat Pharaoh as a sovereign king but as the sinner he really was. After Moses had delivered God's pronouncement of judgment, he turned and left Pharaoh's presence, apparently without even giving him an opportunity to respond. Moses saw no further need of reasoning with Pharaoh about these matters, because Pharaoh had set his heart against God.

After Moses had left, "Pharaoh's servants said to him, 'How long will this man be a snare to us? Let the men go, that they may serve the Lord their God. Do you not realize that Egypt is destroyed?' " (v. 7, NASB). This indicates that Pharaoh's servants were more than willing to let Israel go because their country was being ruined by the plagues. But Pharaoh's heart was obstinate, and he refused to let Israel go. The battle between the king of Egypt and the God of Israel was in full force. Pharaoh was soon to find that he was no match for his opponent in this battle.

After Pharaoh's servants urged him to let the Israelites go, Pharaoh called Moses and Aaron back into his presence and offered a third proposal to them. Pharaoh said, "Go, serve the Lord your God: but who are they that shall go?" (v. 8). When Moses responded that all Israelites—young and old—with their possessions were to go (v. 9), Pharaoh charged him with having an evil plot and said, "Not so: go now ye that are men, and serve the Lord; for that ye did desire. And they were driven out from Pharaoh's presence" (v. 11). Probably no one in the Egyptian court had heard anyone stand up before the king as Moses and Aaron did.

Although Pharaoh drove Moses and Aaron from his presence, he was not rid of them or their God by any means, for next we read that the Lord told Moses, "Stretch out thine hand over the land of Egypt for the locusts, that they may come up upon the land of Egypt, and eat every herb of the land, even all that the hail hath left" (v. 12).

Moses did as the Lord instructed, "and the locusts went up over all the land of Egypt, and rested in all the coasts of

Egypt: very grievous were they; before them there were no such locusts as they, neither after them shall be such. For they covered the face of the whole earth, so that the land was darkened; and they did eat every herb of the land, and all the fruit of the trees which the hail had left: and there remained not any green thing in the trees, or in the herbs of the field, through all the land of Egypt" (vv. 14,15).

Locusts were one of the greatest terrors of the Middle East. They consumed all vegetation wherever they went. These locusts came at the bidding of God, and they would depart only at the bidding of God. They were an evident sign to Pharaoh and to the Egyptians that God was truly God. These creatures were fulfilling the secret counsels of their Creator.

During the coming time of judgment known as the Tribulation, there will also be a plague of locusts. Those who have not trusted Christ as Saviour and, therefore, are left on earth after the Rapture of the Church, will experience this judgment during the Tribulation.

This coming judgment is recorded in Revelation 9:1-6: "And the fifth angel sounded, and I saw a star from heaven which had fallen to the earth; and the key of the bottomless pit was given to him. And he opened the bottomless pit; and smoke went up out of the pit, like the smoke of a great furnace; and the sun and the air were darkened by the smoke of the pit. And out of the smoke came forth locusts upon the earth; and power was given them, as the scorpions of the earth have power.

"And they were told that they should not hurt the grass of the earth, nor any green thing, nor any tree, but only the men who do not have the seal of God on their foreheads. And they were not permitted to kill anyone, but to torment for five months; and their torment was like the torment of a scorpion when it stings a man. And in those days men will seek death and will not find it; and they will long to die and death flees from them" (NASB). We must learn that we cannot scoff at God's grace and forever escape His judgment.

After the plague of locusts on Egypt, there was nothing else Pharaoh could expect but death. That was about all that was left—everything else had been destroyed. Because of the devastation of the locusts, "Pharaoh hurriedly called for

Moses and Aaron, and he said, 'I have sinned against the Lord your God and against you. Now therefore, please forgive my sin only this once, and make supplication to the Lord your God, that He would only remove this death from me' " (Ex. 10:16,17, NASB).

Pharaoh admitted that he had sinned against both God and Moses and Aaron, and he begged them to entreat God for him just once more. How gracious and longsuffering did Pharaoh expect Moses and God to be?

But the longsuffering of God and Moses is seen in that Moses "went out from Pharaoh, and intreated the Lord. And the Lord turned a mighty strong west wind, which took away the locusts, and cast them into the Red sea; there remained not one locust in all the coasts of Egypt" (vv. 18,19). However, the following verse solemnly states, "But the Lord hardened Pharaoh's heart, so that he would not let the children of Israel go" (v. 20).

By this time, Pharaoh had sinned away his opportunity to experience God's grace. He had so hardened himself that he was no longer sensitive to God's voice. He could not expect any more mercy from God and, therefore, he was used by God to make Egypt and Israel—and all the world—see the power and majesty of God. All would gain a greater knowledge of God because of Pharaoh's hardening his heart against God.

The Ninth Plague

The ninth plague affected the sun, which was also worshiped by the Egyptians. God told Moses, "Stretch out your hand toward the heavens, that there may be darkness over the land of Egypt, a darkness which may be felt" (Ex. 10:21, Amplified).

This plague affecting the sun also revealed the power of the God of Israel over the gods of Egypt. The sun was sacred to the Egyptians, and even the name "Pharaoh" was related to a word meaning "sun."

Moses did as the Lord instructed. "And there was a thick darkness in all the land of Egypt three days" (v. 22). When the light and heat of the sun was obscured from Egypt, it meant that Egypt's most powerful god had suddenly become powerless. If the Egyptians had only realized that there was One mightier than the sun—the Creator of the sun—and that He was dealing with them in judgment!

Different explanations have been given concerning how the sun was darkened to such an extent. A sandstorm has been suggested, since the East has experienced sandstorms of such intensity that one could not see his hand in front of his face. Whatever the means, there was a darkness over Egypt of such intensity that "they saw not one another, neither rose any from his place for three days: but all the children of Israel had light in their dwellings" (v. 23).

All activity in Egypt was paralyzed, except in Goshen where God's people were unaffected. What a judgment this was on the Egyptians! Their greatest deity had deserted them, for he was powerless before the true God. No doubt many of the Egyptians wondered if they would ever see light again. What a fitting climax this plague was for the other plagues. God is light (I John 1:5), and darkness is the absence of light. Thus, this plague gave sobering evidence that Egypt was being abandoned by God and that nothing but death could possibly be expected.

The three days of darkness that Egypt experienced is a reminder of the three hours of darkness that the world experienced when Jesus Christ died on the cross to pay the penalty for sin (Matt. 27:45). When He died on the cross, the Lord Jesus Christ had all of our sin on Him. "For he hath made him to be sin for us, who knew no sin; that we might be made the righteousness of God in him" (II Cor. 5:21).

The most reasonable explanation for why the world became darkened at the time of the crucifixion was that God could not look on His Son because He had our sins on Him. Habakkuk 1:13 says of God, "Thou art of purer eyes than to behold evil, and canst not look on iniquity." While the Lord Jesus Christ had our sins on Him, the Heavenly Father covered the world with darkness so as not to look on Him. This explains why Jesus called out to the Father, "My God, my God, why hast thou forsaken me?" (Matt. 27:46). The Lord Jesus Christ was willing to go through all of this so we might have forgiveness of sin and eternal life by believing on Him as our personal Saviour.

While the Egyptians were experiencing a darkness so great that it could be felt, the Israelites were experiencing the brightness of God's blessing. The Bible does not explain how there could be darkness on the Egyptians and light on the Israelites at the same time, but the all-powerful God would not have difficulty in accomplishing this task. While the Egyptians were living in a darkness which could not be lighted, the Israelites had a light which could not be darkened.

Although this was true physically of the Egyptians and the Israelites, it is also true spiritually of those who reject God and those who believe God. Since God is light, those who trust Jesus Christ as personal Saviour are children of light. But those who do not trust Jesus Christ as Saviour are children of darkness.

John 3:18,19 says, "He that believeth on him is not condemned: but he that believeth not is condemned already, because he hath not believed in the name of the only begotten Son of God. And this is the condemnation, that light is come into the world, and men loved darkness rather than light, because their deeds were evil."

There is light in the presence of the Lord, but separation from Him brings darkness. The Bible explains what the Lord Jesus Christ will do when He returns to earth to establish His kingdom: "In flaming fire taking vengeance on them that know not God, and that obey not the gospel of our Lord Jesus Christ: who shall be punished with everlasting destruction from the presence of the Lord, and from the glory of his power" (II Thess. 1:8,9). No wonder Hebrews 10:31 says, "It is a fearful thing to fall into the hands of the living God."

But the good news is that Jesus Christ has paid for our sin, and if we trust Him as Saviour we will be delivered from condemnation and darkness. Colossians 1:13 says that God "hath delivered us from the power of darkness, and hath translated us into the kingdom of his dear Son." So as we consider the matter of light and darkness, let us not forget how the subject relates to the Person of God. "This then is the message which we have heard of him, and declare unto you, that God is light, and in him is no darkness at all" (I John 1:5).

When the judgment of darkness came on Egypt, Pharaoh called for Moses and told him, "Go, serve the Lord; only let your flocks and your herds be detained. Even your little ones may go with you" (Ex. 10:24, NASB). This was Pharaoh's fourth and final compromise offer. Pharaoh wasn't dumb; he realized that people are attached to their property and that if the Egyptians could keep the property of the Israelites, then they could be assured that the Israelites would return. But Moses was not about to accept a compromise offer. He said, "Not a hoof will be left behind" (v. 26, NASB).

Pharaoh was now past feeling, and the omniscient God also knew that he was unchangeable. Thus, the Bible says again, "But the Lord made Pharaoh's heart stronger and more stubborn, and he would not let them go" (v. 27, Amplified).

Then the proud king, unchanged by all of these judgments, said to Moses, "Get away from me! See that you never enter my presence again, for the day you see my face again you shall die!" (v. 28, Amplified). Moses answered Pharaoh, "Thou hast spoken well, I will see thy face again no more" (v. 29).

Although Moses was normally a tranquil person, at that point he expressed himself strongly and emphatically to Pharaoh. Moses then delivered the announcement of the tenth plague that was to come on Pharaoh. Then "he went out from Pharaoh in a great anger" (11:8). Because Moses had his eyes fixed on God, he did not fear the wrath of the king (see Heb. 11:27).

The announcement that Moses gave Pharaoh concerning the final plague was a revelation that God had given Moses when He called him at the burning bush. God knew this plague would be necessary, and the time had finally come. The Lord told Moses, "Yet will I bring one plague more upon Pharaoh, and upon Egypt; afterwards he will let you go hence; when he shall let you go, he shall surely thrust you out hence altogether" (Ex. 11:1).

I can just see Moses as he raised himself to his full height and poured an overwhelming torrent of denunciation and warning on Pharaoh and announced his and Egypt's doom. Moses said, " 'Thus says the Lord, "About midnight I am going out into the midst of Egypt, and all the first-born in the land of Egypt shall die, from the first-born of the

Pharaoh who sits on his throne, even to the first-born of the slave girl who is behind the millstones; all the first-born of the cattle as well.

"Moreover, there shall be a great cry in all the land of Egypt, such as there has not been before and such as shall never be again. But against any of the sons of Israel a dog shall not even bark, whether against man or beast, that you may understand how the Lord makes a distinction between Egypt and Israel." And all of these your servants will come down to me and bow themselves before me, saying, "Go out, you and all the people who follow you," and after that I will go out.' And he went out from Pharaoh in hot anger" (vv. 4-8, NASB).

We have previously considered the significance of the statement that not even a dog would bark at the Israelites as they prepared to leave Egypt. This was a miracle in itself. It showed again the great distinction that God made between His people and the Egyptians.

The last time that Moses saw Pharaoh's face was when he announced this judgment. Moses had been faithful to the work God had called him to do; he had delivered instructions to Pharaoh precisely as God gave them. Thus, Exodus 11:3 says, "Moreover the man Moses was very great in the land of Egypt, in the sight of Pharaoh's servants, and in the sight of the people."

But in spite of the announcement that the firstborn of those who did not believe God and act on the basis of their belief would be killed, the Lord told Moses, "Pharaoh shall not hearken unto you; that my wonders may be multiplied in the land of Egypt" (v. 9). After the tenth plague came on Pharaoh and the Egyptians, they begged the Israelites to leave their country.

These nine plagues had accomplished the purposes of God. The Egyptian gods were proven to be fraudulent, the Lord God was proven true and all powerful, Pharaoh was proven to be one of the "vessels of wrath fitted to destruction" (Rom. 9:22), and Moses was proven to be a great and powerful servant of God.

Chapter 19

The Progressive Compromises of Pharaoh

Having considered the increasing intensity of the plagues, we want to now examine the compromises offered by Pharaoh as these plagues were brought on him and the Egyptians.

As frequently pointed out, when Moses and Aaron first came to Pharaoh, he would not obey the Lord or even give Him recognition. Pharaoh said, "Who is the Lord, that I should obey his voice to let Israel go? I know not the Lord, neither will I let Israel go" (Ex. 5:2). Pharaoh also referred to the words of God spoken through Moses and Aaron as vain, or idle, words (see v. 9).

Even though Moses received this strong reaction from Pharaoh, he knew what God had already said concerning the judgments He would bring on Pharaoh and the Egyptians. It must have been apparent to Moses even at this time that he would have to exercise patience in waiting on Pharaoh, yet he knew there was no need to compromise God's requirements since God would perform His will in spite of Pharaoh.

We must learn this important lesson also. We do not have to compromise with Satan, for we have the promise of God that He will give us victory in the end as we allow Him to work in our lives. As we are faced with adverse circumstances, we can know that God is accomplishing in our lives what is for our best and for His glory.

Romans 8:28,29 reminds us of this: "And we know that all things work together for good to them that love God, to them who are the called according to his purpose. For whom he did foreknow, he also did predestinate to be conformed to the image of his Son." Thus, God allows difficult things to come into our lives so that He can make us more like Jesus Christ.

For the Christian, there is victory. This is why the Apostle Paul said in the same chapter of Romans, "What shall we then say to these things? If God be for us, who can be against us? He that spared not his own Son, but delivered him up for us all, how shall he not with him also freely give us all things? Who shall lay anything to the charge of God's elect? It is God that justifieth. Who is he that condemneth? It is Christ that died, yea rather, that is risen again, who is even at the right hand of God, who also maketh intercession for us" (vv. 31-34).

The believer has no reason whatever to give in to any of Satan's compromises. The Lord Jesus Christ provides everything we need to live a godly life and to resist the advances of Satan.

We can count on the Lord Jesus Christ to do His work in our lives. Philippians 1:6 says, "Being confident of this very thing, that he which hath begun a good work in you will perform it until the day of Jesus Christ." When is the "day of Jesus Christ"? It will be the day when He returns to take His own to heaven to be with Himself. But until then, He will continue to perform the work He has begun in us.

The Bible emphasizes that Jesus Christ is all that we need. This truth is especially seen in I Corinthians 1:30: "But of him are ye in Christ Jesus, who of God is made unto us wisdom, and righteousness, and sanctification, and redemption." Since Christ is all we need, we can say with the Apostle Paul, "Thanks be to God, which giveth us the victory through our Lord Jesus Christ. Therefore, my beloved brethren, be ye stedfast, unmoveable, always abounding in the work of the Lord, forasmuch as ye know that your labour is not in vain in the Lord" (15:57,58)

There is always triumph in Jesus Christ. Why? Because of what He accomplished when He died on the cross for us. Hebrews 2:14,15 reveals that Christ broke the power of Satan over us, enabling us to experience victory in Christ. That is why James 4:7 says, "Submit yourselves therefore to God. Resist the devil, and he will flee from you." We should take this firm stand; we do not need to accept any compromises that Satan offers us.

Because Pharaoh would not obey God or even recognize Him, he and the land of Egypt began to experience plagues. The purpose of these plagues was to cause Pharaoh to see the need of recognizing and obeying God. But not until after the progressive severity of the first four plagues was Pharaoh even willing to discuss the possibility of the Israelites' leaving Egypt.

First Compromise Offer

After the fourth judgment, which was the plague of swarms of insects on the entire land of Egypt, Pharaoh called for Moses and Aaron and told them, "Go ye, sacrifice to your God in the land" (Ex. 8:25). The key word to notice is "in." Pharaoh did not want them to leave the land but to sacrifice within the boundaries of Egypt. He saw no reason why the Israelites could not make sacrifices to their God in the land where they were living.

Pharaoh's offer to Moses also contains a lesson for us. The counterpart to the suggestion he was making is heard today and is expressed something like this: "You can be as religious as you want, but don't become so narrow that you make a complete break with the world." In other words, be a Christian if you have to be, but keep on living like the world lives. To follow such a philosophy is to be conformed to the world and to its way of thinking.

Pharaoh did not insist that Israel bow down to his gods, so in a sense he did make them a "reasonable" offer. Surely, he reasoned, they can carry on their religion here as well as anyplace else; there's room for everyone, so why demand a complete separation?

If Moses had accepted Pharaoh's compromise offer, Israel would have been placed on the same level with Egypt and the God of Israel on the same level as the gods of Egypt. The Egyptians could then have said, "We see no difference between us—you have your worship, and we have our worship—it's all alike." And this is what many are thinking today; they fail to see the distinction between Christianity and religion because so many believers have not really separated themselves from the world.

As a result, some say, "It doesn't matter what you believe, just as long as you are sincere. We are all going to the same place, so why be so separated?" But what does the Bible say? John 14:6 records the words of Christ: "I am the way, the truth, and the life: no man cometh unto the Father, but by me." Acts 4:12 says, "Neither is there salvation in any other: for there is none other name under heaven given among men, whereby we must be saved." So there is a sharp distinction between Christianity and religion; Christianity is a right relationship with a person—the Lord Jesus Christ.

Throughout the Scriptures, Egypt represents the world. The Israelites were frequently warned not to go down to Egypt because this was, in effect, relying on the arm of flesh rather than relying on God. The "world" refers to people or a way of thinking that ignores God. Galatians 1:4 says that Christ "gave himself for our sins, that he might deliver us from this present evil world."

Although Christians are *in* the world, they are not *of* the world. Jesus told His followers, "If ye were of the world, the world would love his own: but because ye are not of the world, but I have chosen you out of the world, therefore the world hateth you" (John 15:19). Notice the strong words of James 4:4: "Ye adulterers and adulteresses, know ye not that the friendship of the world is enmity with God? Whosoever therefore will be a friend of the world is the enemy of God."

Although we do not wish to be disliked by anyone, we must obey the injunction to "go forth therefore unto him without the camp, bearing his reproach" (Heb. 13:13). If we are going to please God in our daily walk, it is necessary for us to be separate from the world. This is why the Bible says, "Wherefore come out from among them, and be ye separate, saith the Lord, and touch not the unclean thing; and I will receive you, and will be a Father unto you, and ye shall be my sons and daughters, saith the Lord Almighty" (II Cor. 6:17,18).

When Pharaoh made his first compromise offer, Moses firmly replied, "It is not right to do so, for we shall sacrifice to the Lord our God what is an abomination to the Egyptians. If we sacrifice what is an abomination to the Egyptians before their eyes, will they not then stone us? We must go a three days' journey into the wilderness and sacrifice to the Lord our God as He commands us" (Ex. 8:26,27, NASB). Inasmuch as the Egyptians considered certain animals to be sacred, they would have been highly offended if the Israelites had killed those animals as an offering; it would have been considered a sacrilege. The worship of the Israelites was utter foolishness to them.

This reminds us of what Paul said in I Corinthians 1:18: "For the preaching of the cross is to them that perish foolishness; but unto us which are saved it is the power of God." Paul also said, "We preach Christ crucified, unto the Jews a stumblingblock, and unto the Greek foolishness; but unto them which are called, both Jews and Greeks, Christ the power of God, and the wisdom of God. Because the foolishness of God is wiser than men; and the weakness of God is stronger than men" (vv. 23-25).

First Corinthians 2:14 says, "But a natural man does not accept the things of the Spirit of God; for they are foolishness to him, and he cannot understand them, because they are spiritually appraised" (NASB). Spiritual truths can be discerned only by those who are in right relationship to Jesus Christ; an unbeliever is not able to evaluate spiritual truths.

A believer recognizes that all he has is due to what Christ has accomplished for him on the cross. This is what caused Paul to say, "But God forbid that I should glory, save in the cross of our Lord Jesus Christ, by whom the world is crucified unto me, and I unto the world" (Gal. 6:14). This verse reveals that if we have accepted Christ as Saviour, we have died to the world and are to take our place as dead to the world.

We cannot expect anything good to come from the world. This is why the Lord Jesus said, "If the world hate you, ye know that it hated me before it hated you. If ye were of the world, the world would love his own: but because ye are not of the world, but I have chosen you out of the world, therefore the world hateth you. Remember the word that I said unto you, The servant is not greater than his lord. If they have persecuted me, they will also persecute you; if they have kept my saying, they will keep your's also" (John 15:18-20).

Moses' refusal to accept Pharaoh's compromise offer revealed that Moses clearly understood the necessity of a complete separation between Israel and Egypt if Israel was to serve God as He desired. Far too many people try to serve God and cling to the things of the world at the same time. Far too few are able to identify with I John 3:1: "Behold, what manner of love the Father hath bestowed upon us, that we should be called the sons of God: therefore the world knoweth us not, because it knew him not." What a shame it is that so many believers want recognition from the world as well as recognition from God.

As he responded to Pharaoh, Moses clearly understood that he was under orders from God. Moses said they would sacrifice to God "as he shall command us" (Ex. 8:27). How wonderful it is when a believer has a clear comprehension of God's will for his life. This is something that Satan likes to confuse and neutralize—as he successfully did in the Garden of Eden.

When we know that God has spoken, that should settle the matter for us. But it did not settle it for Eve; she was completely deceived by Satan. And often the fact that God has spoken does not settle anything for a believer who is deceived by the temptations of the world. But God has clearly instructed that we are not to be a friend of the world. The world and the believer have nothing in common, and the believer who is a friend of the world is committing spiritual adultery.

The Book of Colossians tells believers that we are not only dead to the world, but we are alive to Christ. "If ye then be risen with Christ, seek those things which are above, where Christ sitteth on the right hand of God" (3:1). In other words, we are to apply, or fix, our minds on heavenly things. The passage goes on to say, "Set your affection on things above, not on things on the earth. For ye are dead, and your life is hid with Christ in God" (vv. 2,3). When a person trusts Jesus Christ as Saviour, he dies to the world and is made alive to Jesus Christ.

Second Compromise Offer

After his first compromise offer was declined, Pharaoh said to Moses, "I will let you go, that you may sacrifice to the Lord your God in the wilderness; only you shall not go very far away. Make supplication for me" (Ex. 8:28, NASB). This was really only a modification of the first compromise offer, and it was even more subtle than Pharaoh's first suggestion. The Enemy does not like the believer to be out of his sight. Keeping the Israelites close would have allowed Pharaoh and the Egyptians to control them. Pharaoh was not really yielding to God's demand that he let the Israelites go.

It is understandable that Pharaoh was not easily persuaded to let the Israelites go; they were his slaves, and he gained much by having them in his country. He was willing to lengthen their "chains" so they could go a little distance into the wilderness, but he did not want to lose control of them completely.

This reminds us of one of the greatest temptations a Christian faces—some are always urging him not to be fanatical in what he believes. It's all right with them if he wants to be religious, but they encourage him not to take his Christianity too seriously. The implication is that you should not let Christianity spoil your life. Some say, "I don't mix my religion with my business." This is a trick of the Devil that causes a person to attempt to hang on to the world while still endeavoring to live for Christ. The one who has genuinely trusted Christ as Saviour should recognize that he owes everything to Christ and nothing to the world.

Some think the believer will lose all joy if he becomes too serious about his Christianity. But those who are long faced and miserable are not the ones who have separated completely from the world; rather, they are those who have compromised with the world and have a troubled conscience. An individual's church attendance sometimes indicates that he is far more concerned about enjoying the pleasures of this world on weekends than he is about fellowshiping with other believers and hearing the teaching of the Word of God. So maintaining a border position suits the purpose of the Enemy very well. Satan is thus able to keep the person from being totally committed to either position.

Moses had been sent to Pharaoh for the single purpose of leading the children of Israel out of Egypt, and he was not about to compromise, no matter how small that compromise may have been. May we also learn the importance of carrying out God's clear commands without compromising with the

Enemy. When we know that we have done what the Lord wants us to do, we will experience a joy that is beyond comparison.

The Lord Jesus Christ came into this world so that He might lead us out of it. This does not mean that He is going to take us to heaven right away. Those of us who trust Him as Saviour are given a task to do, and that is why He leaves us on earth. If we had no task, it would be better for us to die the moment we trust Him as Saviour so we would be taken to heaven to be with Him.

The Lord Jesus leaves us here not only so that we can proclaim the message of salvation to others but also so that He can mature us in the Christian faith. And part of the maturing process is to realize that, as believers, we are to be separated from the world. We are not to be yoked together with unbelievers.

The Bible says, "Do not be bound together with unbelievers; for what partnership have righteousness and lawlessness, or what fellowship has light with darkness? Or what harmony has Christ with Belial, or what has a believer in common with an unbeliever? Or what agreement has the temple of God with idols? For we are the temple of the living God; just as God said, 'I will dwell in them and walk among them; and I will be their God, and they shall be My people. Therefore, come out from their midst and be separate, says the Lord' " (II Cor. 6:14-17, NASB). Although believers are in the world, they are not to be of the world.

Because Moses understood the principle of separation from the world, he did not even respond when Pharaoh made the compromise suggestion that the Israelites go into the wilderness but that they not "go very far away" (Ex. 8:28). In Moses' mind no compromise was possible because God had said He was going to lead them out and take them to Himself. This reveals that the promises of God give us strength to stand against compromising suggestions. We will not compromise our standards as long as we keep God's commands before us.

In the Scriptures separation involves two aspects. There is separation *from* whatever is contrary to the will of God, and there is separation *to* God Himself. Being separated from the world does not mean that we lose contact with it. Worldliness is not simply contact with the world; it is complying with or comforming to the world. When we are separated from the world and separated to God, the reward is incomparable communion and fellowship with God.

In His great prayer for His own, the Lord Jesus Christ said, "I do not ask Thee to take them out of the world, but to keep them from the evil one" (John 17:15, NASB).

Third Compromise Offer

Pharaoh's third compromise offer was made after the seventh plague, which was a plague of thunder, hail and fire. The offer was made after Moses had announced the coming plague of locusts. Pharaoh and the Egyptians had never experienced anything like what Moses predicted. Egypt was in ruins because of the previous plagues, and Pharaoh and the Egyptians could imagine what a plague of locusts would do to their country. Moses said that the locusts "shall fill thy houses, and the houses of all thy servants, and the houses of all the Egyptians; which neither thy fathers, nor thy fathers' fathers have seen, since the day that they were upon the earth unto this day" (Ex. 10:6).

Such a pronouncement of judgment caused Pharaoh's servants to say to him, "How long shall this man be a snare unto us? Let the men go, that they may serve the Lord their God: knowest thou not yet that Egypt is destroyed?" (v. 7). Pharaoh then called Moses and Aaron and said to them, "Go, serve the Lord your God; but who are to go?" (v. 8, Berkeley). Moses replied that young and old, sons and daughters, flocks and herds were going so that all could participate in a feast to the Lord (v. 9).

Pharaoh then presented his third compromise offer: "May the Lord be with you if I intend to let you and your little ones go! Look out! You are plotting mischief! No, indeed! You men go and serve the Lord, for that is what you wanted!" (vv. 10,11, Berkeley). Having said this to Moses and Aaron, Pharaoh then drove them out of his presence.

This amounted to a test concerning natural affection. Pharaoh approved of the men going but implied that they should not interfere with the worldly advancements of their families. This compromise demands our special attention because the test involved is common today.

Many think it is unreasonable for parents to expect their children to conform to their standards. The implication is that parents have outmoded standards and that it is unreasonable to expect the younger generation to live by them. But families cannot live by two different standards. This is as unreasonable as the Egyptians expecting the Israelite men to worship in the wilderness while their families remained in Egypt. Children are actually loaned to parents by God, and we parents are responsible for training them to live as they should. This is an awesome responsibility, for what we sow in their lives we will later reap. Galatians 6:7,8 states a timeless principle: "Do not be deceived, God is not mocked; for whatever a man sows, this he will also reap. For the one who sows to his own flesh shall from the flesh reap corruption, but the one who sows to the Spirit shall from the Spirit reap eternal life" (NASB).

Ephesians 6:4 admonishes, "Fathers, do not provoke your children to anger; but bring them up in the discipline and instruction of the Lord" (NASB). Perhaps the most familiar biblical text on child training is Proverbs 22:6: "Train up a child in the way he should go: and when he is old, he will not depart from it." These are God's words, not man's ideas.

Pharaoh was wise enough to know that if the Israelite men left their families in Egypt, they would return to the families, because their love would draw them back. Pharaoh took into account the strong bonds within the family. Regrettably, those bonds are growing weaker today. It seems that many parents could not care less about what happens to their children, particularly regarding spiritual training. No doubt this is because many Christian parents are still spiritually "in Egypt" and are occupied with the things of this world rather than with eternal matters. All believers ought to live with eternity's values in view.

It is wonderful that parents are concerned about providing materially for their children, but some parents see only the material needs of their children. However, things never truly satisfy. And often, in the end, the children resent their parents, who gave them things but did not give of themselves. Christian parents should not only be concerned about giving their time and attention to their children, but they should also help their children develop a proper relationship with the Lord.

The rearing of our children is our direct responsibility, and we must never think that we can shift that responsibility to someone else. Because of certain circumstances in our lives, we may have to rely on others for help, but we must always recognize that the responsibility is directly ours.

Unfortunately, family discipline has been relaxed today to the extent that there is hardly any discipline at all. The Scriptures are not given their proper place in the home. Children are allowed to choose their own companions, and many Christian parents seem to make no serious effort to bring their children out of spiritual Egypt. Perhaps the reason for this is that many of the parents themselves are still in spiritual Egypt.

The training of children is a solemn responsibility, and in these days of laxity and lawlessness, proper training of children is an ever-increasing problem. When Pharaoh suggested that the Israelites leave their families in Egypt, Moses probably thought of his own childhood training and remembered how thoroughly his own parents had done their job.

As we think of parental responsibility, we learn from Joshua about the leadership that a Christian parent should exercise in his family. Joshua said to the Israelites, "If it is disagreeable in your sight to serve the Lord, choose for yourselves today whom you will serve: whether the gods which your fathers served which were beyond the River, or the Gods of the Amorites in whose land you are living; but as for me and my house, we will serve the Lord" (Josh. 24:15, NASB).

In our own home Mrs. Epp and I trained our children in spiritual truths from the time they were able to understand. They were taught Bible verses and Bible stories, as well as hymns and gospel songs. We had a regular devotional time, and the children simply grew up in this atmosphere. Later, when they became teenagers and considered further schooling, it was a common understanding that they would go to Bible school first. They all did this, and some later went

on to further schooling. I say this only to point out that it is
necessary to begin a child's spiritual training at the earliest
age.

The Apostle Paul reminded Timothy, "From a child thou
hast known the holy scriptures, which are able to make thee
wise unto salvation through faith which is in Christ Jesus"
(II Tim. 3:15). Some parents do not come to know Christ as
Saviour until their children are older, but those parents who
know Christ when their children are young should start
spiritual training early. Although we have many wonderful
Sunday schools and even Christian child care centers, the
parents are directly responsible for the training of their
children.

The suggestion that the Israelites leave their families in
Egypt can be compared to present-day parents leaving their
children in spiritual Egypt. It would be the same as
permitting their children to have their own way, allowing
them to conform to the world, permitting them to grow up
without the fear of the Lord, neglecting their spiritual
training and simply ignoring God's command that parents
bring their children up "in the nurture and admonition of the
Lord" (Eph. 6:4).

We are not going to warp the personalities of our children
if we restrain them, nor are we going to warp their characters
by diligently teaching them truths concerning God at a very
early age. Within the heart of every individual is the desire to
learn about God. This fact is indicated in Ecclesiastes 3:11:
"He has made everything appropriate in its time. He has also
set eternity in their heart" (NASB). Within the heart of each
individual is a vacuum that only the knowledge of and proper
relationship to God can fill. It is important, therefore, that
parents not neglect the spiritual training of their children.

How refreshing it is to see a parent who is faithful in his
family responsibility. Each Christian parent should desire to
have said of him what God said of Abraham: "For I know
him, that he will command his children and his household
after him, and they shall keep the way of the Lord" (Gen.
18:19). Before the Israelites entered the land of Canaan, God
gave them these clear instructions: "These words, which I
command thee this day, shall be in thine heart: and thou
shalt teach them diligently unto thy children, and shalt talk

of them when thou sittest in thine house, and when thou walkest by the way, and when thou liest down, and when thou risest up" (Deut. 6:6,7).

So in response to Pharaoh's question concerning who planned to leave Egypt, Moses said everyone was to go, young and old alike. Moses had a firm answer because he knew God's will and wanted to be faithful to it.

Fourth Compromise Offer

Pharaoh's fourth offer was made to Moses during the ninth plague, which was a plague of terrible darkness. Pharaoh called for Moses and said, "You go and serve the Lord; only leave your flocks and herds behind, while you take your little ones along" (Ex. 10:24, Berkeley).

This last compromise offer by Pharaoh was an appeal to coveteousness. It was an attempt to get Moses to separate his relationship with the Lord from his business activity. Satan plants the same idea in the minds of believers today. It is not uncommon to hear of those who boast that they do not let their religious activities mix with their business activities. This reveals the perseverance with which Satan disputes our separation to God.

Since Pharaoh could not convince Moses and the Israelites to sacrifice in the land of Egypt, he tried to convince them to leave the land of Egypt without taking anything along to offer as sacrifices to God. Had they left Egypt without their livestock, they would have been unable to really worship the Lord as He intended.

In this compromise offer we see Satan's attempt to divide the loyalties of the heart so a person will try to serve two masters. The Bible contains many examples of those who had divided loyalties. The Apostle Paul wrote concerning a former companion, "Demas hath forsaken me, having loved this present world" (II Tim. 4:10).

But in contrast to such a person, note what Paul said concerning Timothy: "I hope in the Lord Jesus to send Timothy to you shortly, so that I also may be encouraged when I learn of your condition. For I have no one else of kindred spirit who will genuinely be concerned for your welfare. For they all seek after their own interests, not those

of Christ Jesus. But you know of his proven worth that he
served with me in the furtherance of the gospel like a child
serving his father" (Phil. 2:19-22, NASB).

Ananias and Sapphira had divided loyalties to the extent
that they even lied to God. Acts 5 tells how they sold
property and claimed to give the full price when they had
actually held back part of it. The sin was not keeping part of
the price of the land, for they were not required to give the
full price. Rather, the sin was lying about giving the full
price. This was the sin of pretense. But such sins happen
when a person's treasures are in spiritual Egypt, which also
causes his affections to remain there.

The important question really is, Does God have the title
to all that you possess? Some feel that only a tenth belongs
to the Lord, and the rest belongs to them. The right
perspective, however, is to realize that everything we have
comes from the Lord; therefore, everything belongs to Him.

Of course, as far as the government is concerned, we own
everything we possess. But the Christian realizes that
everything he has comes from the hand of God. God has said,
"For every beast of the forest is mine, and the cattle upon a
thousand hills. I know all the fowls of the mountains: and
the wild beasts of the field are mine. If I were hungry, I
would not tell thee: for the world is mine, and the fulness
thereof" (Ps. 50:10-12).

Deuteronomy 10:14 says, "Behold, the heaven and the
heaven of heavens is the Lord's thy God, the earth also, with
all that therein is." Along this same line, Psalm 24:1 declares,
"The earth is the Lord's, and the fulness thereof; the world
and they that dwell therein." The New Testament echoes this
same truth: "For the earth is the Lord's, and the fulness
thereof" (I Cor. 10:26).

Many Christians fail God in the area of their possessions
The emphasis of our materialistic age is, "Give yourself to
God if you must, but do not consecrate your possessions to
His service." This kind of thinking originates with Satan
himself. How tragic it is that some Christians have been
enabled by God to accumulate many possessions, and yet
they do not consecrate them to the Lord.

Although we are not now living under the Mosaic Law,
we need to remember the solemn charge that God gave to

Israel: "Will a man rob God? Yet you are robbing Me! But you say, 'How have we robbed Thee?' In tithes and contributions. You are cursed with a curse, for you are robbing Me, the whole nation of you!" (Mal. 3:8,9, NASB). We are not living under the Law, so the regulation of the tithe is not directly binding on us. However, the principle of giving back to God a portion of what He has given to us should still apply. If a tithe was required under the Law, surely we should be willing to do as much under grace! Are we holding back offerings that belong to God? If so, God will not bless our lives.

In answer to Pharaoh's suggestion that the Israelites leave their livestock in Egypt, Moses firmly declared, "Our livestock must therefore come with us; not a hoof shall be left behind, because from them we shall take to serve the Lord our God, and we do not know what to use for the Lord's service until we reach there" (Ex. 10:26, Berkeley). Moses took a firm stand on putting everything at God's disposal; he would not leave anything in Egypt.

Moses told Pharaoh that they did not know what they would use for the Lord's service until they reached their destination. This statement gives us insight into how Moses determined the will of God. He realized that the mind of God could not be discerned so long as they left anything in Egypt. Moses realized that he and the Israelites had to leave Egypt with all of their possessions. Then—and only then—would they know what the Lord's will for service really was.

It is a time-honored principle of God that we must be willing to obey before He will reveal His will to us. John 7:17 says, "If any man will do his will, he shall know of the doctrine, whether it be of God, or whether I speak of myself." This means that we must be willing to lay everything on the altar; we must present ourselves to God with no strings attached.

Paul said it in these words: "I urge you therefore, brethren, by the mercies of God, to present your bodies a living and holy sacrifice, acceptable to God, which is your spiritual service of worship. And do not be conformed to this world, but be transformed by the renewing of your mind, that you may prove what the will of God is, that which is good and acceptable and perfect" (Rom. 12:1,2, NASB).

Some Christians ask, "What does God want me to do?"
Some say, "Lord, I would present all my goods to You if I
only knew what You want me to do with them." But that's
not God's method. He does not reveal His will to us until we
put everything at His disposal—ourselves first of all.

Moses absolutely resisted any temptation to compromise
with Pharaoh by leaving any livestock behind. With clear
spiritual insight, Moses saw through every compromise offer
extended by Pharaoh, and his reply was clear and decisive in
each case. From all of this, we can see the necessity for
absolute obedience to God. The call of God is to separation—complete separation. We must devote to God everything He has given us and use it for His glory.

The world urges us to remain in the land and to be neigh-
borly, but we have only one obligation—to be separated to
God. We must always remember that "friendship of the
world is enmity with God" (James 4:4). Romans 8:7,8
emphasizes the same truth: "Because the mind set on the
flesh is hostile toward God; for it does not subject itself to
the Law of God, for it is not even able to do so; and those
who are in the flesh cannot please God" (NASB). One who
lives by the standards of the world, or his old nature, does
not please God in any way.

Although he lived long before these verses were ever
penned, Moses grasped this spiritual truth and totally refused
any compromise offer from Pharaoh. Moses boldly told Pharaoh that not even a hoof would be left behind (Ex. 10:26).

Such a response made Pharaoh angry. He said to Moses,
"Get away from me and see to it that you never come near
me again; for if I ever see you again, you die!" (v. 28,
Berkeley). But even these words did not frighten Moses.
" 'Correctly spoken,' Moses replied, 'you will not see me
again' " (v. 29, Berkeley).

Moses was able to face Pharaoh as he did only because he
was in right relationship to God and realized that no compromise would be acceptable to God. Moses had laid everything on the altar as far as his worship of and service to God
was concerned. Have you done the same? Or do you have
divided loyalties between the world and God? The believer
experiences deeply satisfying joy only when he is separated
from the world and is separated to God.

Chapter 20

The Final Judgment

After the ninth plague, Pharaoh was so angry with Moses that he told him to leave and stay away—and threatened that if he ever saw Moses again he would kill him (Ex. 10:28). Moses agreed with Pharaoh that he would never see him again (v. 29).

Before leaving Pharaoh, however, Moses announced God's final judgment on Pharaoh and the Egyptians. Although the nature of this judgment was news to Pharaoh, it was not new to Moses because God had told him about it before any of the plagues began. When God called Moses at the burning bush in the desert, He said to him, "When thou goest to return into Egypt, see that thou do all those wonders before Pharaoh, which I have put in thine hand: but I will harden his heart, that he shall not let the people go. And thou shalt say unto Pharaoh, Thus saith the Lord, Israel is my son, even my firstborn: and I say unto thee, Let my son go, that he may serve me: and if thou refuse to let him go, behold, I will slay thy son, even thy firstborn" (4:21-23).

But in spite of the fact that God, in His omniscience, knew that He would finally have to bring this judgment on Pharaoh, He still demonstrated much longsuffering and mercy to Pharaoh. God gave Pharaoh many opportunities to repent and turn to Him, but Pharaoh absolutely refused to do so. Because Pharaoh and Egypt had not heeded God's commands or responded to His mercy, God brought this final judgment on them.

This reminds us of how graciously God deals with lost sinners concerning salvation. It is also a reminder of how graciously He deals with believers concerning yielding totally

251

to Him. God is longsuffering and full of mercy, but if He is rejected, He must finally act in judgment or discipline, depending on whether the person is an unbeliever or a believer. Although we do not know when that time is, there apparently comes a day when God says, "I will wait no longer." And remember, "It is a fearful thing to fall into the hands of the living God" (Heb. 10:31).

The Bible reveals that judgment awaits those who refuse God's mercy and reject Christ as Saviour. Hebrews 9:27 says, "It is appointed unto men once to die, but after this the judgment." Proverbs 29:1 warns, "He, that being often reproved hardeneth his neck, shall suddenly be destroyed, and that without remedy." Second Thessalonians 1:8,9 tells how the unsaved will be destroyed when Christ returns to earth: "In flaming fire taking vengeance on them that know not God, and that obey not the gospel of our Lord Jesus Christ: who shall be punished with everlasting destruction from the presence of the Lord, and from the glory of his power."

The final judgment of all the unsaved will take place before the Great White Throne. Revelation 20:11-15 says, "And I saw a great white throne and Him who sat upon it, from whose presence earth and heaven fled away, and no place was found for them. And I saw the dead, the great and the small, standing before the throne, and books were opened; and another book was opened, which is the book of life; and the dead were judged from the things which were written in the books, according to their deeds.

"And the sea gave up the dead which were in it, and death and Hades gave up the dead which were in them; and they were judged, every one of them according to their deeds. And death and Hades were thrown into the lake of fire. This is the second death, the lake of fire. And if anyone's name was not found written in the book of life, he was thrown into the lake of fire" (NASB).

So it is tremendously important for each person to respond to God's longsuffering and mercy while there is still time. Hebrews 3:7-9 pleads, "Therefore, just as the Holy Spirit says, 'Today if you hear His voice, do not harden your hearts as when they provoked Me, as in the day of trial in the wilderness, where your fathers tried Me by testing Me, and saw My works for forty years' " (NASB).

Those who lift their hearts in pride against God, as did Pharaoh, will be brought low. All must someday give recognition to Jesus Christ whether they have trusted Him as Saviour or not. This truth is emphasized in Philippians 2:9-11: "Wherefore God also hath highly exalted him, and given him a name which is above every name: that at the name of Jesus every knee should bow, of things in heaven, and things in earth, and things under the earth; and that every tongue should confess that Jesus Christ is Lord, to the glory of God the Father."

The contest between Pharaoh and Jehovah was almost ended. There had been abundant opportunity for Pharaoh to repent of his haughty defiance, but he refused to do so. There had been warning after warning and plague after plague, but Pharaoh's heart was still hardened. Therefore, after God had again confirmed this hardness, He brought the final plague on Pharaoh and the Egyptians.

Announcement of the Final Plague

Moses' announcement of the final plague is recorded in Exodus 11. Verse 1 is the key to understanding its purpose: "The Lord said unto Moses, Yet will I bring one plague more upon Pharaoh, and upon Egypt; afterwards he will let you go hence; when he shall let you go, he shall surely thrust you out hence altogether." Not only would Pharaoh be willing to let the Israelites go, he would actually push them out of his country. This reveals the folly of fighting against God, because He finally brings a person to his knees. The creature is impotent before his omnipotent Creator.

Proverbs 19:21 says, "There are many devices in a man's heart; nevertheless the counsel of the Lord, that shall stand." Because God is omnipotent, He was able to accomplish with Pharaoh what He pleased. "The king's heart is in the hand of the Lord, as the rivers of water: he turneth it whithersoever he will" (Prov. 21:1). Isaiah 14:27 emphasizes this same truth: "For the Lord of hosts hath purposed, and who shall disannul it? And his hand is stretched out, and who shall turn it back?"

Even Pharaoh—the king of the most powerful empire in the world—was not able to successfully resist God. Pharaoh eventually had to recognize what King Nebuchadnezzar later recognized: "Those that walk in pride he [God] is able to abase" (Dan. 4:37).

But Pharaoh's heart was hardened against God because he refused from the beginning to obey God or to even give recognition to Him (Ex. 5:2). What Pharaoh did not realize was that God can grind to powder the hardest heart and completely humble the haughtiest spirit.

The Lord said to Moses, "Speak now in the hearing of the people, and let every man solicit and ask of his neighbor, and every woman of her neighbor, jewels of silver and jewels of gold. And the Lord gave the people favor in the sight of the Egyptians. Moreover the man Moses was exceedingly great in the land of Egypt, in the sight of Pharaoh's servants and of the people.

"And Moses said, Thus says the Lord, About midnight I will go out into the midst of Egypt; and all the first-born in the land [the pride, hope and joy] of Egypt shall die, from the first-born of Pharaoh who sits on his throne, even to the first-born of the maid-servant who is behind the hand mill; and all the first-born of beasts. There shall be a great cry in all the land of Egypt, such as has never been, nor ever shall be again" (11:2-6, Amplified).

God had waited and waited on Pharaoh, and Moses had been patient as he warned Pharaoh of coming judgment. But both God and Moses were to be vindicated. Moses, however, only announced this final judgment, which was entirely from God. The Passover lamb speaks of salvation, and salvation is only of God, although men are used to announce the message.

In the last days the Lord Jesus Christ will be vindicated when He returns to earth. He, in longsuffering, allows mankind now to go against His will, but there will come a time when His omnipotence will be recognized by all. Thus, Christ told the Apostle John, "I am he that liveth, and was dead; and, behold, I am alive for evermore, Amen; and have the keys of hell and of death" (Rev. 1:18).

Under the inspiration of the Holy Spirit, the Apostle John looked ahead to the Second Coming of Christ and wrote: "And out of his mouth goeth a sharp sword, that with it he should smite the nations: and he shall rule them with a rod of iron: and he treadeth the winepress of the fierceness and wrath of Almighty God. And he hath on his vesture and on his thigh a name written, King of Kings, and Lord of Lords" (19:15,16).

These verses refer to that time when the Lord Jesus Christ, with the angels and His saints, will return to earth to bring an end to Gentile world power, which will then be headed up by the Antichrist. After destroying Gentile rule, the Lord Jesus Christ will then establish the kingdom of God on earth.

When God speaks to mankind, it is important that His message not be refused. Hebrews 12:25 says, "See that ye refuse not him that speaketh. For if they escaped not who refused him that spake on earth, much more shall not we escape, if we turn away from him that speaketh from heaven." And verse 29 adds, "For our God is a consuming fire."

As Israel prepared to leave Egypt, God instructed, "Let every man borrow of his neighbour, and every woman of her neighbour, jewels of silver, and jewels of gold" (Ex. 11:2). The word "borrow" does not accurately convey the meaning of the Hebrew word from which it is translated. The Hebrew word is *shaal*, which basically means "to ask."

The Israelites were to ask the Egyptians for the back wages owed them. And because of the respect the Egyptians had learned to have for the Israelites, as well as their fear as a result of the last plague, they gave as they were asked (12:35,36). For many long years the Israelites had toiled as slaves, so what they asked was rightfully theirs. God gave the Israelites favor before the Egyptians, and even this greatly helped Israel to recognize the sovereignty of their God.

In Moses' last words to Pharaoh, he gave God's announcement of a coming plague that would destroy all the firstborn of Egypt (11:4,5). God warned, "There shall be a great cry throughout all the land of Egypt, such as there was none like it, nor shall be like it any more" (v. 6).

God further explained, "But against any of the Israelites either man or beast, not a dog shall bark—to show you how the Lord distinguishes between Egypt and Israel" (v. 7, Berkeley). This is striking proof that every creature is ultimately under the control of the Creator. Imagine the weeping and horror that would sweep across the land on that night, and yet with all of this commotion, a dog would not so much as bark against any of the Israelites.

God's purpose in controlling the dogs was clearly stated: "To show you how the Lord distinguishes between Egypt and Israel" (v. 7, Berkeley). The dogs' remaining quiet while about three million Israelites hustled here and there could only be explained, even by the Egyptians, as a miracle of God. This would cause them to see that God was truly at work.

The ability God had to control the dogs at this time is a reminder of how He later shut the mouths of the lions when Daniel was thrown into their den. Early the next morning, the king hurried to the den and found Daniel safe. The king asked, "O Daniel, servant of the living God, is thy God, whom thou servest continually, able to deliver thee from the lions?" (Dan. 6:20). Daniel replied, "My God hath sent his angel, and hath shut the lions' mouths, that they have not hurt me: forasmuch as before him innocency was found in me; and also before thee, O king, have I done no hurt" (v. 22).

What great power God has, and what a significant contrast there is between the believer and the unbeliever! It should be a tremendous encouragement to every believer to realize that nothing can happen to him unless God allows it.

Having announced the last plague to Pharaoh, Moses said, " 'All these nobles of yours shall come down to me and bow deeply to me, begging of me. Do go out; you and all your followers!' And after that I will go out" (Ex. 11:8, Berkeley). Having said this, Moses "went out from Pharaoh in a great anger" (v. 8).

Moses had endured all he could of Pharaoh's blaspheming God, even at times claiming to confess his sins but evidencing that he was not sincere. The longsuffering of Moses and of God was at an end; the stage was completely set for Israel's emancipation. The Lord told Moses, "Pharaoh will not listen to you, so that My mighty works may multiply in the land of Egypt" (v. 9, Berkeley). Exodus 11 concludes by saying, "Moses and Aaron did all these wonders in the presence of Pharaoh; but the Lord encouraged Pharaoh in his own way and he did not allow the Israelites to leave his country" (v. 10, Berkeley).

A New Beginning

Before detailed instructions were given to Moses concerning Israel's preparation for the Passover, God said to Moses and Aaron, "To you let this month be the first, the month with which your year begins" (Ex. 12:2, Berkeley). In a real sense, this was the beginning of Israel as a nation.

After giving the Israelites detailed instructions for preparing and eating the Passover lamb, God said, "You shall eat it thus: [as fully prepared for a journey] your loins girded, your shoes on your feet, and your staff in your hand; and you shall eat it in haste. It is the Lord's passover" (v. 11, Amplified). As we have said, this haste of the Israelites would have caused much commotion, but not even a dog barked at them.

God told the Israelites, "I will pass through the land of Egypt this night, and will smite all the first-born in the land of Egypt, both man and beast; and against all the gods of Egypt I will execute judgments [proving their helplessness]. I am the Lord" (v. 12, Amplified).

In contrast to the judgment He would bring on the Egyptians, God promised the Israelites, "The blood shall be for a token or sign to you upon [the doorposts of] the houses where you are, [that] when I see the blood, I will pass over you, and no plague shall be upon you to destroy you, when I smite the land of Egypt" (v. 13, Amplified). The blood was the provision for Israel's escape from God's final judgment on Egypt.

Referring to this time and to the leadership that Moses exercised, Hebrews 11:28 says, "Through faith he kept the passover, and the sprinkling of blood, lest he that destroyed the firstborn should touch them."

The significant element in protecting the Israelites was the blood. Some might wonder, Why blood? The Bible emphasizes the importance of blood when it says, "The life of the flesh is in the blood: and I have given it to you upon the altar to make an atonement for your souls: for it is the blood that maketh an atonement for the soul" (Lev. 17:11).

Hebrews 9:22 says, "And almost all things are by the law purged with blood; and without shedding of blood is no remission [forgiveness]." The only way of salvation has been purchased for us by the shed blood of the Lord Jesus Christ. Colossians 1:14 says, "In whom we have redemption through his blood, even the forgiveness of sins."

The Israelites were not able to escape the judgment of the slaying of the firstborn on their own merits but only on the merits of the blood which they applied to the doorposts. It would have been futile for any Israelite to have reasoned that some other action would be acceptable to God. No matter how reasonable some other method might have seemed, nothing was acceptable except the application of the shed blood. So, too, many today think there are several ways of salvation and that sincerity is all that is necessary. But no matter how reasonable this seems, no one will be saved from condemnation unless he applies the shed blood of Christ by believing in Him as personal Saviour.

Israel was not able to escape the Passover judgment just because the people had been chosen by God to be the nation through whom He wanted to specifically work. Although the nation as such was spared, the only way an individual could escape judgment was to exercise personal faith in what God said should be done and to act on that faith.

God's plan of salvation is the same for all people, and all the Old Testament sacrifices of Israel looked forward to the time when Christ would shed His blood for the sins of the whole world. The Bible says, "He is the propitiation for our sins; and not for our's only, but also for the sins of the whole world" (I John 2:2).

No one can buy his way to heaven, as explained in I Peter 1:18,19: "You were not redeemed with perishable things like silver or gold from your futile way of life inherited from your forefathers, but with precious blood, as of a lamb unblemished and spotless, the blood of Christ" (NASB). And as we have pointed out, Hebrews 9:22 reveals that forgiveness is impossible without the shedding of blood.

To those who place their faith in the shed blood of Christ to take away sin, John 6:37 promises, "Him that cometh to me I will in no wise cast out." John 3:18 says, "He that believeth on him is not condemned: but he that believeth not is condemned already, because he hath not believed in the name of the only begotten Son of God." But notice the wonderful promise of Christ recorded in John 5:24: "I say unto you, He that heareth my word, and believeth on him that sent me, hath everlasting life, and shall not come into condemnation; but is passed from death unto life."

After God had finished his instructions to the Israelites concerning the Passover, the Bible says, "The people bowed the head and worshipped. And the children of Israel went away, and did as the Lord had commanded Moses and Aaron, so did they" (Ex. 12:27,28).

The plague came precisely as God said it would: "At midnight the Lord slew every first-born in the land of Egypt, from the first-born of Pharaoh who sat on his throne to the first-born of the prisoner in the dungeon, and all the first-born of the livestock. Pharaoh rose up in the night, he, all his servants, and all the Egyptians; and there was a great cry in Egypt, for there was not a house where there was not one dead" (vv. 29,30, Amplified).

After some of the previous plagues Pharaoh had feigned repentance but had not been willing to let the Israelites leave Egypt. In this case, however, "he called for Moses and Aaron by night, and said, Rise up, get out from among my people, both you and the Israelites; and go, serve the Lord, as you said. Also take your flocks and your herds, as you have said, and be gone! And [ask your God to] bless me also" (vv. 31,32, Amplified).

This action by Pharaoh was a fulfillment of what God had told Moses earlier: "Now shalt thou see what I will do to Pharaoh: for with a strong hand shall he let them go, and with a strong hand shall he drive them out of his land" (6:1).

At his last meeting with Pharaoh, Moses told him, "All these thy servants shall come down unto me, and bow down themselves unto me, saying, Get thee out, and all the people that follow thee: and after that I will go out" (11:8). This verse was fulfilled precisely as Moses said, for after the firstborn of the Egyptians were killed, "the Egyptians were urgent with the people to depart, that they might send them out of the land in haste; for they said, We are all dead men" (12:33, Amplified).

Earlier, God had promised that the Israelites would not leave Egypt empty-handed. He had instructed the Israelites, "Let every man solicit and ask of his neighbor, and every woman of her neighbor, jewels of silver and jewels of gold" (11:2, Amplified). The people did exactly what they were told: "The Israelites did according to the word of Moses; and they [urgently] asked of the Egyptians jewels of silver and of gold, and clothing. The Lord gave the people favor in the sight of the Egyptians, so that they gave them what they asked. And they stripped the Egyptians [of those things]" (12:35,36, Amplified).

No doubt some of the silver and gold which the Israelites requested of the Egyptians was later used in constructing the tabernacle. Perhaps some was even kept and later became part of the temple. Clothing was certainly necessary because the Israelites were headed for the wilderness and did not know how their needs would be taken care of.

Referring to God's deliverance of Israel from Egypt, the psalmist later wrote: "He brought them forth also with silver and gold: and there was not one feeble person among their tribes. Egypt was glad when they departed: for the fear of them fell upon them" (Ps. 105:37,38).

Israel's Indirect Route

When Israel fled Egypt, they could have gone from northern Egypt, where they lived, directly to the land of Canaan. This direct route would have taken only a matter of days. But God knew it was not best for them to go that way because of the enemies they would encounter. The Bible says, "When Pharaoh had allowed the people to go, God did not lead them by way of the Philistines' land, although that was a shorter route; for God considered that, on tasting war, the people might feel regret and go back to Egypt. So God detoured the people toward the desert by the Red Sea. In martial order the Israelites went up from the land of Egypt" (Ex. 13:17,18, Berkeley).

God knew that the tests of faith that the Israelites would face on a direct route to Canaan would be too severe for them, so He led them another way. God also knows the amount of testing that we are able to endure, and I Corinthians 10:13 assures believers, "No temptation has overtaken you but such as is common to man; and God is faithful, who will not allow you to be tempted beyond what you are able; but with the temptation will provide the way of escape also, that you may be able to endure it" (NASB).

There was another reason, however, why God did not take the Israelites on a direct route to Canaan. This reason had to do with Pharaoh. In telling Moses where to camp, the Lord said, "For Pharaoh will say of the Israelites, They are entangled in the land; the wilderness has shut them in. I will harden (make stubborn, strong) Pharaoh's heart, that he will pursue them, and I will get Me honor and glory over Pharaoh and all his host, and the Egyptians shall know that I am the Lord" (Ex. 14:3,4, Amplified).

God impressed on the mind of every Israelite that their deliverance was totally His undertaking, not theirs. He gave the instructions, and He would protect them as they obeyed His instructions. God was fulfilling what He had promised Moses earlier in Exodus 6:6-8.

God had provided and would continue to provide everything needed by the Israelites to accomplish His will. This was especially seen as God led Israel in the path He had chosen and also protected them from the Egyptians by "the pillar of cloud by day and the pillar of fire by night" (13:22, Amplified). The fire at night enabled the Israelites to see where they were going, whereas the Egyptians could not, and the pillar of cloud by day kept the Israelites hidden from the Egyptians.

It is obvious from these events that when God says He will provide for us, He remains absolutely faithful to His word. This fact is especially seen in His plan of redemption for mankind. Throughout Old Testament times the sacrifices looked forward to the Lamb of God who would come to take away sin. God was faithful to His word, and when John the Baptist saw the Lord Jesus Christ, he said, "Behold, the Lamb of God who takes away the sin of the world!" (John 1:29, NASB). God has provided salvation for all mankind, but each individual must personally trust Christ as Saviour in order to have that salvation applied to his life.

A New Era of Leadership

Moses' reaction to all that took place was especially significant. His faith was being tested to the limit as he sought God's strategy for Israel because, humanly speaking, it involved insurmountable obstacles. The Lord said to Moses, "Tell the Israelites to turn back and encamp before Pihahiroth, between Migdol and the [Red] Sea, before Baal-zephon. You shall encamp opposite it by the sea. For Pharaoh will say of the Israelites, They are entangled in the land; the wilderness has shut them in" (Ex. 14:2,3, Amplified).

Here is the situation Moses faced: On the one side was the impassable mountain range of Baal-zephon; on the other side were vast sand dunes which a traveler could not survive; behind Israel was the pursuing Egyptian army; and in front was the Red Sea.

Humanly speaking, they were trapped and would surely be destroyed. But as Hudson Taylor used to emphasize, if the Devil hems you in on all four sides, you can always look up; you can always talk to God. Moses' previous training in God's school really paid off at this time. Although the Israelites could not accept their situation without murmuring and wavering, Moses was able to remain stable because of his faith in God.

Moses realized the truth stated in the New Testament: "Without me ye can do nothing" (John 15:5). Moses had the same concept that was later expressed by the Apostle Paul: "I can do all things through Him who strengthens me" (Phil. 4:13, NASB).

God knew how Pharaoh would reason after the Israelites were gone. Although Pharaoh refused to recognize Him, God knew what was in his heart and how he would think about a given situation. Knowing that Pharaoh's heart was hardened against Him, God told Moses, "I will harden (make stubborn, strong) Pharaoh's heart, that he will pursue them, and I will get Me honor and glory over Pharaoh and all his host, and the

Egyptians shall know that I am the Lord" (Ex. 14:4, Amplified).

Remember that Pharaoh had first hardened his own heart and that God had endured his rebellion with much longsuffering and mercy. But since Pharaoh refused to turn to God in any way, God further hardened his heart in the position he had taken. And Pharaoh demonstrated how hard his heart was. Although many things had occurred which could only be explained as a direct intervention of God, Pharaoh assumed that the Israelites would get entangled and lose their way in the land. He still failed to see that God was delivering the Israelites.

As the Israelites were hemmed in on all sides, their morale must have been at an all-time low. This was their first real test as a nation, and it had to be fully met in order to establish them for what they would face on their journey to Canaan. All they could see was impending death, *but God*—what significant words—*but God* was working in their behalf.

Israel's Spiritual Immaturity

God wanted to teach the Israelites some valuable lessons about trusting in Him, and their situation provided the key opportunity. They could not go in any direction; therefore, they were forced to look up to Him. As the Egyptians pursued them, the Israelites revealed their spiritual immaturity, for they complained to Moses, "Did you take us away to die in the desert because there are no graves in Egypt? Why did you treat us this way, to bring us out of Egypt? Did we not tell you in Egypt, 'Leave us alone; let us serve the Egyptians!' Better for us to work for the Egyptians than to die in the desert" (Ex. 14:11,12, Berkeley).

In their state of spiritual immaturity, the Israelites were able to see only what was around them; their attention was not focused on God. Even when they were not focusing attention on themselves, they were looking to man; they were watching to see what Moses would do. When he did not act as they thought he should, they became discouraged and began to complain and fear for their lives. So we see that the Israelites were still only babes in faith. They needed to exercise their faith before they could be considered spiritually mature.

The Israelites' reactions illustrate the principle that before one can progress with God, he must come to a complete end of himself. As long as the Israelites had reason to trust in themselves, they saw no need to depend on God. But when the circumstances seemed hopeless, thereby bringing them to the end of themselves, they were eventually forced to turn their eyes to God. Then progress was made in their spiritual lives.

This was a counterpart to the New Testament truth that we must die to self before we can live to God (John 12:24). We, too, must realize that we have no might or power against the Enemy; therefore, we need to depend on God. Sometimes God hems us in to teach us to fix our eyes completely on Him.

Although the Israelites were wavering in their faith, Moses' faith remained solid because it was in God, not in others or in himself. Moses had learned from past experience that God does not make mistakes. Even though Moses did not know how God was going to accomplish His will, he was confident that God had a solution to the problem. Previous experiences had taught him that God often has a plan of victory that is far different from any human plan. Although Moses could not see into the future, he moved forward on the basis of his faith in God.

With such confidence in God, Moses spoke to the people and endeavored to instill the same faith in them. Moses admonished them, "Do not fear! Stand by and see the salvation of the Lord which He will accomplish for you today; for the Egyptians whom you have seen today, you will never see them again forever. The Lord will fight for you while you keep silent" (Ex. 14:13,14, NASB). What a statement of faith! These are key verses concerning the unshakable faith that Moses had in God.

God's man had been well prepared, not only intellectually but also experientially. He knew God, and he appropriated the promises of God. Moses' confidence was completely settled in God so that he was full of faith and was able to make such a positive declaration. God's work in him was accomplished! After that God could use him to train others to exercise faith in God. And this is what happened when Moses encouraged the Israelites to take a stand for God.

Reflect on the contrasts we have seen in Moses' life. At age 40 when Pharaoh discovered that he had killed an Egyptian, Moses fled in fear because his eyes were not fixed on God. Even at age 80 when God called him at the burning bush, Moses still had many misgivings. But Moses finally came to the end of himself when he was rejected by his own people (5:21-23), and he learned to put his trust in God only. From this time onward, Moses' faith grew by leaps and bounds. God never moves ahead until He has all things, including His chosen men, well trained and ready to accomplish His will.

So by faith, Moses issued a statement that day which, to a weak and faithless Israel, seemed sheer fantasy. Exodus 14:13,14 records Moses' words which instructed the people to not fear, to stand still, and to see the salvation of the Lord (although God had not given Moses any direct orders of procedure). Let us consider these three commands in more detail.

The Three Commands

Fear not. Israel was completely hemmed in, and a vicious Egyptian army was on its way, and yet Moses said, "Fear ye not" (Ex. 14:13). This statement revealed that Moses was not trusting in human wisdom but in God's wisdom.

Consider some of the situations in which God's people were told not to fear. Abram (Abraham) won a great victory by rescuing his nephew Lot, but he was in serious danger because of the possibility of the defeated armies reorganizing and coming against him. However, God told him, "Fear not, Abram: I am thy shield, and thy exceeding great reward" (Gen. 15:1).

After Joshua had experienced an overwhelming victory at Jericho, he met failure and defeat at Ai. He was afraid that Israel would not be able to face its enemies again. But God told him how to put away the sin from among them and then said, "Fear not, neither be thou dismayed: take all the people of war with thee, and arise, go up to Ai: see, I have given into thy hand the king of Ai, and his people, and his city, and his land" (Josh. 8:1).

When the Lord appeared to Gideon, who later led a small army against great numbers, he was terrified and feared for his life. However, the Lord said to him, "Peace be unto thee; fear not: thou shalt not die" (Judg. 6:23).

When Solomon, the son of David, was anointed king, he faced awesome responsibilities, which included building the temple of God. God encouraged Solomon through the words of David: "Be strong and of good courage, and do it: fear not, nor be dismayed: for the Lord God, even my God, will be with thee; he will not fail thee, nor forsake thee, until thou hast finished all the work for the service of the house of the Lord" (I Chron. 28:20).

When the Lord Jesus Christ was on earth and His followers were discouraged, He told them, "Fear not, little flock; for it is your Father's good pleasure to give you the kingdom" (Luke 12:32).

Perhaps one of the most familiar and best-loved verses that has encouraged believers down through the ages is Psalm 23:4: "Yea, though I walk through the valley of the shadow of death, I will fear no evil: for thou art with me; thy rod and thy staff they comfort me."

Isaiah summed it up beautifully with these words: "Thou wilt keep him in perfect peace, whose mind is stayed on thee: because he trusteth in thee. Trust ye in the Lord for ever: for in the Lord Jehovah is everlasting strength" (Isa. 26:3,4).

Stand still. Even though the Israelites did not know what to do, it seemed totally unreasonable of Moses to expect them to "stand still" (Ex. 14:13). In essence, this was a military order and was equal to telling them to stand by until they received further orders. In many ways, one of the hardest things believers must do is to wait on God. We are impatient just as the Israelites were, and we want to act before God has revealed His plan and purpose to us.

But there comes a time when all activities must stop and we must simply wait on God for His orders. It is part of our human nature to be restless and fidgety; we think we have to be doing something. We often hear the statement, "Don't just stand there; do something!" Faith, however, raises the attention of the believer to the very throne of God, far above the difficulty involved. Such a believer is able to stand still and wait on the Lord.

Earlier, when Moses had come to the end of himself, God said to him, "Now shalt thou see what I will do to Pharaoh" (6:1). But it was not until Moses stood still and waited on the Lord that God acted in his behalf. Following the account of this time of waiting on the Lord, we read God's promise to accomplish Israel's deliverance by Himself (vv. 6-8).

See the salvation of the Lord. Moses exhorted the Israelites to trust God in the face of impending death and to see Him work in their behalf (14:13). Nothing is gained by restless and anxious efforts. The Israelites could not go anywhere or do anything to help themselves. What an opportunity this was for God to teach them great spiritual lessons! This should remind us of Philippians 4:6,7: "Be anxious for nothing, but in everything by prayer and supplication with thanksgiving let your requests be made known to God. And the peace of God, which surpasses all comprehension, shall guard your hearts and your minds in Christ Jesus" (NASB).

Think of how helpless the Israelites were. Could they dry up the Red Sea? Could they level the mountains? Could they bridge the impassable sand? Could they annihilate the armies of Egypt? All of these things were impossible for them to do, but nothing is impossible with God.

It was not necessarily "great" faith that was needed but simply faith in God. When the disciples of Jesus were not able to cast out a demon, they came to Him and asked why. He answered them, "Because of the littleness of your faith; for truly I say unto you, if you have faith as a mustard seed, you shall say to this mountain, 'Move from here to there,' and it shall move; and nothing shall be impossible to you" (Matt. 17:20, NASB).

Moses had passed the test of handling a seemingly impossible situation with flying colors! He was gloriously vindicated in his faith because God at once intervened with a mighty hand and gave him the direction he needed.

The Lord said to Moses, "Why do you call to Me? Tell the Israelites to move forward. Raise your staff and stretch out your hand over the sea; divide it, so that the Israelites may go right through the sea on dry ground" (Ex. 14:15,16, Berkeley).

Notice that Moses did not have to wait for God's orders. When God told him to move forward, He explained how he should go about it. But what an unusual miracle was about to take place! Never had such a miracle occurred before, and it took faith in God to believe that it could occur at this point. Moses had told the people to stand still and see the salvation of the Lord, and God's instructions were a fulfillment of Moses' challenge. They saw salvation which only the Lord could provide.

The Lord delights in shutting His people in to Himself and then displaying His grace and power in achieving the impossible. Just as God did this for the Israelites, He also wants to do it for us. God works in us and through circumstances to accomplish His distinctive will. We all have our trials, and often they seem to present impossibilities as great as the Israelites faced. But even though the Devil can hem us in on all sides, he cannot prevent us from looking to God and depending on Him to deliver us. We can talk to God about our problem and wait on Him to show us the way of deliverance. The Lord's message to us is that we not fear but that we stand still and see His salvation. As we hold our peace, the Lord fights for us.

Throughout the testings and trials of Israel and through the ten plagues God brought on the Egyptians, we see how He fought for His own people all along. He had worked in their behalf before, and He did not fail them at the Red Sea. What a wonderful God we have!

God's Protection

Having instructed Moses to use his staff to divide the Red Sea, God told him, "And I, behold, I will harden the hearts of the Egyptians, and they shall follow them: and I will get me honour upon Pharaoh, and upon all his host, upon his chariots, and upon his horsemen" (Ex. 14:17). Verse 8 records how the Lord hardened Pharaoh's heart so that he pursued the children of Israel, and verse 17 reveals that He hardened the Egyptians' hearts, causing them to follow the Israelites into the Red Sea.

The hearts of the Egyptians were also hardened because they had refused to turn to God, even though they, too, had been given many opportunities for repentance. Pharaoh and the Egyptians revealed that they were truly "vessels of wrath fitted to destruction" (Rom. 9:22). They were "fitted to destruction" because they continuously rebelled against God and refused to obey or even to recognize Him. They had mocked God by refusing His longsuffering and mercy, and God brought an end to their defiance and constant rebellion.

Although judgment was about to come on the Egyptians, God's protecting hand was on the Israelites. The Bible says, "Then the Angel of God, who had been moving ahead of Israel's camp, withdrew and went behind them—the column of cloud withdrew from the front and stood behind them—and came between the camp of Egypt and the camp of Israel; it was cloud and darkness; it also lit up the night; so they did not get close to each other at night" (Ex. 14:19,20, Berkeley).

The cloud protected the Israelites because it was a cloud of darkness to the Egyptians. At night the pillar of fire made it possible for the Israelites to travel, whereas the Egyptians were unable to do so. Thus, we see God's wonderful mercy in protecting His people.

Moses then did as God instructed him: "Moses then stretched out his hand over the sea and the Lord moved the sea all night by a mighty east wind turning the sea into dry land. The waters were divided and the Israelites went into the midst of the sea on dry ground. To their right and to their left the waters formed a wall for them" (vv. 21,22, Berkeley). What marvelous deliverance the Lord provided for His own! They passed through the place of death and were delivered to life.

This reminds us of Romans 6, which tells how the believer is baptized with Jesus Christ into His death and is raised to newness of life (vv. 3,4). Just as the Israelites had life by passing through the place of death, so the believer is made alive to the Lord after trusting Him as Saviour and being identified with Him in His death (Rom. 6:5; Gal. 2:20).

The Lord had said that He would harden the hearts of Pharaoh and the Egyptians so they would pursue the Israelites, and this is precisely what happened. "In hot pursuit the Egyptians followed them, all the horses, the chariots and the horsemen of Pharaoh into the midst of the sea'' (Ex. 14:23, Berkeley). How presumptuous and rebellious can people be? The dividing of the Red Sea was such an obvious miracle of God, yet this fact did not even slow down the Egyptians. All they could think about was capturing the Israelites, so they followed them through the divided waters of the Red Sea.

But notice how God protected His own people by hindering the Egyptians: "Around 6:00 in the morning the Lord looked upon the Egyptian army from the column of fire and cloud and brought on panic among the Egyptian host; He clogged their chariot wheels and made them move so heavily that the Egyptians said, 'Let us get away from the Israelites, for the Lord is fighting for them against the Egyptians'" (vv. 24,25, Berkeley). What an acknowledgment! The Egyptians realized that the Lord was fighting for the Israelites against them. Moses had told the Israelites, "The Lord shall fight for you, and ye shall hold your peace" (v. 14).

God was completely vindicated; He said that all people would know that He was truly God. Not only did these two nations understand this fact, but all the world was caused to realize it, as evidenced by the song of praise that followed.

As we consider how the Lord acts in behalf of His own, Psalm 118:5-9 is a significant passage: "I called upon the Lord in distress: the Lord answered me, and set me in a large place. The Lord is on my side; I will not fear: what can man do unto me? The Lord taketh my part with them that help me: therefore shall I see my desire upon them that hate me. It is better to trust in the Lord than to put confidence in man. It is better to trust in the Lord than to put confidence in princes." This is God's Holy Word.

We need also to remember the promise of the Lord recorded in Hebrews 13:5,6: "I will never leave thee, nor forsake thee. So that we may boldly say, The Lord is my helper, and I will not fear what man shall do unto me." When we are on God's side, we have nothing to fear because He will fight the battle for us.

When Israel had safely arrived at the east bank of the Red Sea with the Egyptians pursuing them, God said to Moses,

"Stretch out your hand over the sea and let the waters flow back upon the Egyptians, over their chariots and their horsemen. So Moses stretched out his hand over the sea and at break of day the sea returned to its usual flow, with the Egyptians fleeing against it. The Lord tumbled the Egyptians into the middle of the sea. The waves rolled back and submerged the chariots and their drivers together with the whole army of Pharaoh that had followed them into the sea; not even one of them was left" (Ex. 14:26-28, Berkeley). This was God's stroke of death on the enemies of God and Israel.

This is a reminder of how the power of God will be exercised on unbelievers in the end time when the Lord Jesus Christ returns to earth, as recorded in Revelation 19. At that time the Lord Jesus Christ will be vindicated as He brings justice on His enemies.

Some endeavor to explain away the miracles of the Bible. Those who subscribe to liberal theology have even said that it can be proven that the water in the Red Sea at the place where Israel crossed was only about six inches deep at that time of year. But as is often the case, it takes greater faith to believe what liberal theologians say than to believe what the Bible says. What a miracle it would have been if the entire Egyptian army had drowned in only six inches of water!

Complete Deliverance

The deliverance of Israel was finished. It was a complete deliverance, not just a partial one. God had told the Israelites, "I will bring you out from under the burdens of the Egyptians, and I will rid you out of their bondage, and I will redeem you with a stretched out arm, and with great judgments" (Ex. 6:6). When the waters covered the Egyptian army, the Lord had fulfilled His word to Israel—He completely broke the power of Egypt. Egypt still exists as a nation, but it has never been the world power that it was at the time of Moses.

God's breaking the power of Egypt is an illustration of how Christ broke the power of Satan. Hebrews 2:14,15 says, "Since then the children share in flesh and blood, He Himself likewise also partook of the same, that through death He might render powerless him who had the power of death, that is, the devil; and might deliver those who through fear of death were subject to slavery all their lives" (NASB). Just as Egypt still existed after its power was broken, Satan exists now, even though his power has been broken. Believers need not submit to the temptations of Satan; rather, they are to submit to God and resist Satan (James 4:7).

The Egyptian army was drowned in the Red Sea, "but the Israelites had walked on dry ground in the middle of the sea with the waters for their wall to the right and to the left. So did the Lord save Israel that day from Egypt's dominance, and Israel saw the Egyptians dead on the seashore" (Ex. 14:29,30, Berkeley). At first the Red Sea was an impossible wall, or barrier, to the Israelites, but when it was opened up by God, it became a wall of protection on both sides. What a principle this is for us to recognize! Some of the impossibilities we face are actually what God wants to use in our lives to eventually make us what He wants us to be.

The concluding verse of Exodus 14 says, "When Israel looked upon the mighty work which the Lord had wrought upon Egypt, the people revered the Lord and came to believe in the Lord and in His servant Moses" (v. 31, Berkeley). At last Moses was completely vindicated! God was proven true and all powerful. Israel, as well as Moses, was established in faith. All the Egyptian gods were proven completely impotent and even nonexistent.

Exodus 15 records the song of victory which Moses and the Israelites sang to the Lord. This song may have been written prior to this occasion as Moses, by faith, looked ahead to Israel's complete deliverance.

The first 13 verses express the victory that the Israelites had just experienced and relate so well to God's promised deliverance in Exodus 6:6. The next three verses looked ahead to the future victories that Israel would experience as God continued to fight for them. The news of God's deliverance of Israel spread rapidly to other nations, as indicated by Joshua 2:9-11.

Thus concludes this moving account of scripture revealing how God strengthened His man Moses and used him to deliver Israel from Egypt.